MOVIES AND THE REAGAN PRESIDENCY

MOVIES AND THE REAGAN PRESIDENCY

Success and Ethics

Chris Jordan

Westport, Connecticut
London

Library of Congress Cataloging-in-Publication Data

Jordan, Chris, 1960–
    Movies and the Reagan presidency : success and ethics / Chris Jordan.
        p. cm.
    Includes bibliographical references and index.
    ISBN 0–275–97967–9 (alk. paper)
    1. Motion pictures—Social aspects—United States. I. Title.
PN1995.9.S6J67 2003
302.23'43'097309048—dc21   2002190868

British Library Cataloguing in Publication Data is available.

Library of Congress Catalog Card Number: 2002190868
ISBN: 0–275–97967–9

First published in 2003

Praeger Publishers, 88 Post Road West, Westport, CT 06881
An imprint of Greenwood Publishing Group, Inc.
www.praeger.com

Printed in the United States of America

∞™

The paper used in this book complies with the
Permanent Paper Standard issued by the National
Information Standards Organization (Z39.48–1984).

10 9 8 7 6 5 4 3 2 1

For my Father and Mother, who, by example,
taught me the satisfactions of learning.

Contents

Acknowledgments

My deepest thanks to the following people for helping bring this book to fruition: my father, Bryce Jordan, my mother, Jonelle Jordan, Ron Bettig, Jeanne Hall, Tom Schatz, Janice Ascolese, Jane Caputi, Gary Scharnhorst, Peter White, Gabriel Meléndez, Eric Levy, Alana Laurence Inugai, and the staff at Impressions Book and Journal Services.

Chapter 1

Defining Reagan-Era Hollywood

In 1993, Sylvester Stallone reflected on the confluence between movie fantasy and political reality that occurred during President Ronald Reagan's two terms in office from 1981 to 1988. "I ended up becoming very defensive. Remember when Reagan bombed Quaddafi? He said 'After seeing Rambo, I know what to do.' And then Saddam used it in his bunker. He said 'This is not Rambo.' Can you imagine? It became synonymous with a mindset. I became a ... symbol. I was always worried when I traveled abroad. There were always a lot of threats. When I went to Cannes they said I'd be dead. When I would go to third world countries, it was not so pretty."[1]

Stallone's amazement stemmed from how a character he invented while working in the dream factory of Hollywood—avenging Vietnam veteran John Rambo—became a worldwide symbol of the Reagan administration's hawkish military initiatives in Afghanistan, the Middle East, and Central America. Like the character of Rambo, Reagan-era cinema is a product of intersecting changes in presidential policymaking, Hollywood movie form and content, and American culture, which cannot be solely attributed to one man's influence.

Nonetheless, Ronald Reagan's election to the presidency in 1980 made him a causal agent of an intersection between government policy, changes in Hollywood's patterns of ownership and structure, the movies' construction of the success ethic, and prevailing trends in American economic and cultural relations. While the exploration of the Protestant success ethic is a hallmark of American cinema, the movies' inflection of this theme has not always coincided with prevailing economic and ideological trends in the filmed entertainment industry's patterns of ownership and mode of production. Nor has Hollywood's construction of the success ethic in conservative fashion always been in synchronization with political, economic, and social trends in American culture. However, Reagan's construction of the Protestant success ethic forged an intersection between these elements of American culture.

The origins of the success myth lie in a tension between economic individualism and collectivism. Wealth historically has been constructed by the Protestant success ethic as a symbol of God's beneficence, and the fruitful use of riches, rather than the mere possession of them, was deemed most important in judging a person's spiritual worth. This "Christian casuistry of economics" struck a balance between social stewardship and competitive laissez-faire economics.[2]

Richard Slotkin defines the 1980s as an era during which Reagan drew upon this mythology by enthusiastically proclaiming that the rogue entrepreneur would create new wealth that would benefit all if government merely retreated from regulating the marketplace. While the origins of this idea lie in Adam Smith's belief that a so-called invisible hand governs marketplace relations, it became with the rise of industrialism a mythology of economic destiny that attributed American industry's rapid growth over the post–Civil War era to the availability of cheap and plentiful frontier land and the rough-and-ready westerner's transformation of it from hostile wilderness to a Garden of Eden through his violent subjugation of Native American savages. Andrew Jackson equated Indian-fighting, with its Protestant connotation of regeneration through violence, as the means of establishing a republican order in a savage wilderness.[3] The Protestant success ethic encapsulated this frontier spirit in its insistence on the importance of white values of civilization and moral self-discipline in transforming America from a wilderness to a society of self-governing, middle-class citizens. With the maturation of American industry over the first half of the twentieth century, rapid increases in manufacturing productivity rather than limitless frontier resources became the mythological engine driving economic growth and facilitating middle-class prosperity.[4] Business literature of the 1920s lauded American industrialism as a continuation of the frontier process.

In the wake of World War II, Reagan, along with other Cold War ideologues, invoked this frontier mythology by establishing a zero-sum relationship between communism and capitalism. Implicitly equating so-called Godless Communists with the threat of otherness, Reagan argued that the very existence of the Soviet Union threatened an American way of life, predicated on an ever-rising average standard of living made possible by American industry's freedom from government regulation. As the economy stalled during the 1970s under stagflation (a combination of stagnant economic growth and inflation) and high unemployment, Reagan argued that the "flabby patriotism" (to quote John Wayne) of big government was to blame for promoting a counterculture of economic and moral complacency.[5]

Upon being elected president, Reagan pitched his program of tax cuts and deregulation as a means of making industry, rather than government, the engine of economic prosperity. Hollywood's metamorphosis into a vertically and horizontally integrated cluster of tightly diversified entertainment conglomerates under Reaganomics and deregulation provides an instructive example of how the former movie actor used this success mythology to garner support for programs that enabled an international investment class to consolidate its ownership over Hollywood. The assimilation of Hollywood's major studios into an increasingly global entertainment cartel was accompanied by a return to principles of bottom-line conservatism in movie production practices and record-setting profits for the filmed entertainment industry. While the industry's vertical and horizontal reintegration under Reaganomics and deregulation was responsible for its record profits, Hollywood's return to economic health over the 1980s was also traceable to its production of movies that resonated within the culture of conservative backlash promoted by Reagan.

Biracial buddy movies such as *Rocky III* (1981) and *Die Hard* (1988) sought to attract crossover audiences of blacks and whites by celebrating a success ethic of racial integration predicated on the integration of different races into families. *Rocky III*, for example, draws clear-cut lines between blacks who are assimilable into a middle-class white world of suburban family life and hostile racial and ethnic others who threaten the ideal of interracial harmony. The biracial buddy movie's dramatization of this Reagan-era theme is exemplified across a variety of movies ranging from *An Officer and a Gentleman* (1982) to *Trading Places* (1983). Music-video movies like *Flashdance* (1983) and *Dirty Dancing* (1987) targeted a teenage audience by making the film musical over into a synergistic promotion for movies, music, and fashion. Designed to conflate participation in an adolescent world of style with romantic fulfillment, the music-video movie celebrates rites of heterosexual courtship, familial coupling, and conformity to biologically circumscribed labor roles that Reagan praised as integral for the restoration of American economic and moral health.

The yuppie movie genre, inaugurated by *Kramer vs. Kramer* (1979), represented an attempt to focus on the concerns of the upwardly mobile white suburbanites that Hollywood targeted amid its cultivation of mall multiplexes, cable television, and videocassette as integrated avenues of movie distribution and exhibition. Movies about yuppies celebrated the professional middle class as an exemplar of a Reagan-era success ethic that distinguished itself from the idle elite above and the immoral poor below on the basis of moral merit and self-made status.

To try to bracket Reagan-era cinema as a freestanding period in Hollywood history is impossible because the institutional, marketplace, and cultural forces that shaped it emerged from conditions that preceded the president's two terms in office. Nonetheless, the Reagan era is definable as a watershed period in Hollywood history during which the president's mobilization of the success ethic initiated trends in the industry and its movies that continue today.

FREE-MARKET ECONOMICS
AND REAGAN-ERA CINEMA

Ronald Reagan actively defined his presidency by using the Carter administration as its antithesis. If Jimmy Carter encouraged Americans to accept a more modest standard of living as a way of coping with seemingly intractable unemployment and double-digit inflation, Reagan declared that the key to restoring the nation's economic health was to run government like a business and make individuals accountable for their economic destinies.

Complementing this belief was Reagan's assertion that individual economic freedom was threatened by mounting Cold War tensions. At stake, he argued, was the future of capitalism itself unless the United States halted Soviet aggression through investment in military buildup. *Business Week* noted in 1981 that Presidential candidate Ronald Reagan's campaign platform of free-market economics, tax cuts, and aggressive military expenditure offered a "sharp contrast with [President] Carter's economics."[6]

Reagan's program of conservative economic reform proved a tonic for the ailing filmed entertainment industry. After teetering on bankruptcy during the late 1960s, Hollywood was poised for a return to financial solvency in the late 1970s in the wake of *Jaws'* (1975; $260 million) successful reinvention of movies as multimedia texts with worldwide appeal.[7] Praising conservative economic reform as the key to restoring American industry's stability and growth, Reagan implemented free-market economic and deregulatory reforms that promoted the assimilation of Hollywood's major studios into multinational conglomerates.

The orchestration of huge deals involving corporate mergers and acquisitions became a source of fascination within Reagan-era culture, reflecting a perception of the businessman entrepreneur as a brazen upstart renewing an American dream of prosperity. Cable magnate Ted Turner, News Corporation owner Rupert Murdoch, Viacom owner Sumner Redstone, and others burst onto *Forbes* magazine's annual listing of the 400 richest individuals in the United States, accompanying other media entrepreneurs whose ranks so swelled over the 1980s that approximately 25 percent of the magazine's 1992 list consisted of individuals who owed all or part of their wealth to media ownership.[8] Media moguls such as Turner were touted as brash, self-made men whose dogged pursuit of economic opportunity benefited society as a whole, illustrating how American business has always sought to exploit associations with frontier individualism, moral merit, and wealth. In an article entitled "Rebel with a Cause,"

Broadcasting praised Turner in 1980 in terms that could have been scripted by Sylvester Stallone, describing the forty-one-year-old millionaire as "a professional underdog, continually setting himself up against long odds, and beating them." Federal Communications Commission (FCC) Chairman Charles Ferris proclaimed that Turner "demonstrates great American spirit and great faith in the free-enterprise system. He's willing to take risks, willing to tread in areas not touched before. He has the courage of a pioneer."[9]

In actuality, this construction of Turner as a log cabin-to-the-boardroom success hero giving the entrenched networks their comeuppance obscured concentrations of ownership in the communications industry made possible by Reagan and the FCC. Tax reforms that Reagan argued would promote new opportunities in the communications industry actually enabled international investors to generate the capital necessary to consolidate their ownership over filmed entertainment production, distribution, and exhibition. The 1981 Economic Recovery Tax Act, passed by a surprisingly cooperative Congress, promoted greater short-term banking investment in the entertainment industry by lowering corporate tax rates. The measure initiated a flurry of mergers and acquisitions that accelerated Hollywood's transformation into a cluster of huge vertically and horizontally integrated communications conglomerates.[10]

Reagan's free-market orientation was forged in postwar Hollywood, where he evolved from a New Deal liberal into a fierce supporter of Cold War success values who argued that Communism posed an imminent threat to the movie industry as well as American culture at large. Denouncing Hollywood labor unions as a safe haven for Communist sympathizers, Reagan testified as a friendly witness before the House Un-American Activities Committee (HUAC) during the early 1950s and aligned himself with studio executives anxious to rein in a workforce no longer under their direct control. It was also during Reagan's presidency of the Screen Actors Guild (SAG) that the organization approved a waiver for Music Corporation of America (MCA) that allowed the company to integrate its talent agency with its movie and television production operations. The deal shaped the future of Hollywood by establishing agents as "packagers" of deals between studios and talent agencies.[11]

As president, Reagan advanced a longstanding agenda of returning Hollywood to a studio system of filmed entertainment production, distribution, and exhibition by implementing policies that further raised barriers of entry to the filmed entertainment industry and curtailed the ideological diversity of Hollywood's movies over the 1980s. With the exception of Radio-Keith-Orpheum (RKO), which ceased movie production in 1948, four of the so-called big five studios (Warner Bros., Paramount, Metro-Goldwyn-Mayer (MGM), Twentieth Century Fox) and all of the so-called little three studios (Universal, Columbia, and United Artists) that historically have controlled filmed entertainment production and distribution were assimilated over the 1980s into tightly diversified multinational conglomerates with interlocking interests in multiplex theaters, cable television, videocassette distribution, and network television.

Gulf & Western (owner of Paramount) sold off all but its media holdings over the 1980s and renamed itself Paramount Communications. Warner Communications downsized during the early 1980s only to expand through a marriage with Time in 1989 that created Time Warner, a model of tight diversification with holdings in movies, TV production, cable, records, and book and magazine publishing. News Corporation owner Rupert Murdoch purchased Twentieth Century Fox in 1985, integrating his newspaper and magazine holdings with the venerable movie studio's film library, its ongoing movie and television productions, and a nationwide chain of independent television stations. With his acquisition of the Metromedia chain of independent television stations, Murdoch became a media industry giant virtually overnight by vertically integrating a "fourth" national TV network, a major studio's film library and production operations, and a magazine and newspaper empire. Having been involved since the 1960s in the television and leisure park industries, Disney buttressed its theme park operations and expanded into retailing by aggressively merchandising its animated characters and movie titles. Disney also expanded its motion picture output, focused on a youth audience, and controlled costs by employing out-of-work actors whose services could be inexpensively secured.[12]

Other studios underwent less successful mergers in the 1980s. After the flop of several big-budget releases, including *Heaven's Gate* (1980; $3 million), United Artists collapsed and merged with Metro-Goldwyn-Mayer in 1981. Coca-Cola purchased Columbia Pictures in 1982 and formed Tri-Star Pictures in partnership with CBS and Home Box Office (HBO). What began as an integrated theatrical, pay-TV, and network television distribution company fed by Columbia productions ended as a troubled venture when Coca-Cola sold Tri-Star and Columbia to Sony Corporation in 1989. Universal, purchased by MCA in 1962, remained a subsidiary of the company throughout the 1980s as MCA attempted to compensate for its decreasing share of the box office by buying into toy manufacturing, music publishing, television broadcasting, and a theater chain. Of all its investments, MCA's development of Universal Studios in Orlando, near Disney World, showed the most promise. International investment in Hollywood increased with Pathe Communications' purchase of MGM in 1985 and Matsushita's acquisition of MCA in 1990.

This resurrection of the studio system under successive waves of mergers and acquisitions resulted in a return to the practice of signing exclusive, multi-picture deals with bankable stars, producers, and directors. As a writer, director, and star, Sylvester Stallone gained tremendous influence as a turnkey talent package. Creative Artists Agency (CAA), which represented Stallone for almost twenty years, wielded great influence over its clients' negotiations with studios on the basis of its roster of stars. Founded by alumni of the William Morris Agency's TV department, CAA had a roster of talent including Steven Spielberg, Kevin Costner, Tom Cruise, and Michael Douglas.

Thomas Schatz is correct in noting that the New Hollywood's adoption of this system of movie packaging freed Steven Spielberg to develop a directorial style of narrative structure, camera movement, and editing in *Jaws* that was replicated industry wide as filmmakers and audiences alike became familiar with it.[13] This high-concept mode of production, summarized by Spielberg's observation that the best movie ideas are those that "you can hold in your hand," proved the perfect complement for an emerging era of blockbuster moviemaking in which escalating budgets required movies to have immediate appeal to the largest possible audience. Coined by ABC programming executive Barry Diller during the early 1970s, the term "high-concept" refers to a mode of movie production that favors projects that can be summarized in a thirty-second television spot and sold in a single sentence. The condensability and immediate familiarity of the high-concept movie's premise appealed to studio executives and the public because it provided a "misunderstanding-proof" strategy of movie production and marketing.[14]

Jaws provided a template for this highly adaptable style of storytelling by integrating the premise of Peter Benchley's best-selling novel into a remake of *Creature from the Black Lagoon* (1954) that combined horror, the buddy movie, and the family melodrama into a suspense-filled spectacle of dazzling visual complexity. Producers Don Simpson and Jerry Bruckheimer parlayed this high-concept style into a hit-making mode of production that provided Paramount studios with some of the most profitable movies in Hollywood history, including *Flashdance* ($95 million), *Beverly Hills Cop* (1984; $234 million), *Top Gun* (1986; $176 million), *Beverly Hills Cop 2* (1987; $153 million), and *Days of Thunder* (1990; $82 million).

The astronomical salaries demanded by Spielberg, Bruckheimer and Simpson, and other Hollywood talent with proven track records of commercial popularity contributed to the drastic increases in moviemaking costs that accompanied the industry's adoption of a blockbuster mode of production. Paramount justified Eddie Murphy's six-picture, $25 million contract by observing in 1988 that virtually all of its recent $100 million blockbusters (*Top Gun, Fatal Attraction* [1987], *Coming to America* [1988]) involved exclusive or semi-exclusive ties with stars, directors, and producers.[15] A self-described "bottom fisherman," Disney's Jeffrey Katzenberg signed down-on-their-luck actors Bette Midler and Richard Dreyfuss and revived their careers in *Down and Out in Beverly Hills* (1986).[16]

Lax antitrust law enforcement encouraged the reintegration of the major movie studios' production and distribution activities with movie exhibition. Douglas Gomery writes that the Justice Department challenged only 0.7 percent of the mergers between 1982 and 1986 in which the parties were required to file for antitrust approval. The Carter administration maintained a 2.5 percent rate of challenge.[17] With their purchase of first-run exhibition chains in large urban areas, the major studios reconnected the profitable link between filmed entertainment production, distribution, and exhibition severed by the studios' forced sale of their exhibition sites under the 1948 Paramount decree. As the mall multiplex replaced older downtown auditoriums, Hollywood focused on movies with presold, crossover appeal to suburban audiences. Incumbent in this agenda was Hollywood's focus on movie genres with appeal to multiple audience segments.

This reliance on crossover audiences became imperative amid the major studios' strategy of basing their annual revenues on the runaway success of a few costly blockbusters. The *New York Times* observed in 1987 that the cost of a movie made by a major studio rose from $2.3 million in 1975, to $8 million in 1980, to $17.5 million in 1986, with marketing expenses averaging $7.5 million. Under these conditions, the average movie didn't turn a profit until it earned $30 million in theatrical film rentals.[18]

Cost control became a studio mantra as risk escalated. Each expenditure that led to the $31 million final cost of *Beverly Hills Cop* was approved in advance by Paramount Chairman Frank Mancuso. The studio also maintained day-to-day control over the production by shooting in Los Angeles and conducting a weekly recap of how the movie was faring in terms of shooting days and budget. A second unit director traveled to Detroit to film background shots while the principal actors stayed on the studio lot and other locations within forty-five minutes.[19]

The amount spent on a handful of annual releases ultimately proved to be a highly effective means of generating even greater box-office receipts. The *Washington Post* noted in 1991 that for the first time nine movies had made more than $100 million during a twelve-month period the previous year. Not surprisingly, the old record of seven movies topping the $100 million tally was only a year old. Prior to that, no more than five films had ever earned that much during a single year.[20] Several blockbusters of the 1980s anticipated this record-setting trend. *Top Gun* cost $17.5 million to produce and market, but became the blockbuster hit of 1986, grossing $270 million in revenue, including $50 million in videocassette sales. *Beverly Hills Cop 2* grossed $33 million over the four-day Memorial Day weekend after its release in 2,326 theaters.[21] Shrewd marketing tactics designed to sell movies to huge audiences proved integral in generating revenues of this magnitude.

Incumbent in the biracial buddy movie's pairing of a white lead and a black costar was an attempt to appeal to multiple races of moviegoers by casting a handful of black stars in roles with proven appeal to white audiences. A dramatic change occurs between *Rocky* (1976) and *Rocky III* as Apollo Creed (Carl Weathers) evolves from a race-baiting black boxing champion modeled on Muhammad Ali to a docile sidekick who manages Rocky in his preparation for a title defense against Clubber Lang (Mr. T).

The transformation of movies into loosely structured narrative forms that could be reiterated across a variety of shopping experiences abstracted the dividing line between moviegoing and other forms of leisure-time consumption. Music-video movies based on the form and style of the classical Hollywood musical lent themselves to cross-marketing campaigns designed to integrate fashion, television, and music. With the exception of *The Graduate* (1967) and *Easy Rider* (1969), Hollywood did not significantly cross-market rock music and movies until producer Robert Stigwood transformed the Broadway hit *Jesus Christ Superstar* (1973) into an event movie that boosted soundtrack album sales and ticket sales for the theatrical stage production. Between its soundtrack recording, touring stage production, and film, *Jesus Christ Superstar* earned approximately $125 million for Stigwood and MCA.[22] Stigwood subsequently acquired the film rights to The Who's 1969 landmark rock opera *Tommy*, adapted it into a 1975 motion picture with backing from Columbia Pictures, and rerecorded it as a soundtrack album featuring popular artists such as Eric Clapton and Tina Turner. While the film and soundtrack album were commercially successful, *Rolling Stone* observed that *Tommy*'s real significance was its marketing-driven integration of rock music and film.[23]

Stigwood's release of *Saturday Night Fever* (1977) as an album soundtrack and a movie on the basis of a carefully coordinated rollout strategy represented a further step forward in Hollywood's adoption of sophisticated cross-marketing techniques. Based on a *New York* magazine story on the underground disco culture of the 1970s, *Saturday Night Fever* ($139.4 million) demonstrated that a film musical could be successfully marketed as an event movie on the basis of a twenty-five-word premise reducible to a single, striking image.

However, the advent of Music Television Videos (MTV) proved an effective means of creating marketplace synergies between movies, fashion styles, and music soundtracks and mobilizing suburban adolescent audiences. Shaped by the classical Hollywood musical while also departing from it, *Flashdance* (1983), *Footloose* (1984), and *Dirty Dancing* (1987) combined the American film musical's style of direct address and performance spectacle with a postclassical high-concept visual style that facilitated the extraction of song-and-dance scenes for re-presentation on MTV and in nightclubs.

Yuppie movies such as *Kramer vs. Kramer* (1979) and *The Big Chill* (1983) reflected Hollywood's attempt to reach an audience of baby boomer adults that attended movies less often as they entered parenthood. In many ways, yuppie movies capitalized on the media's construction of the upwardly mobile young professional as a lifestyle trend, universalizing a narrow slice of class experience. The yuppie movie's definition of middle-class life in terms of earned suburban affluence implicitly echoed the mall's circumscription of public space in terms of shared class habits of consumption. Furthermore, the construction of the yuppie as a self-made success hero was rooted in a perception of wealth as an index of moral merit.

DEREGULATION, "SHAREABILITY," AND REAGAN-ERA CINEMA

Reagan's belief that tax cuts for business and individuals would enable business leaders to create new jobs was complemented by his conviction that government regulation of industry imposed unnecessary restrictions on business efficiency. Freeing business of cumbersome restrictions on cross-industry forms of ownership would provide consumers with greater choice by promoting the cultivation of new communications technologies, including videocassette, cable television, and satellite, promised Federal Communications Commission (FCC) Chairman Mark Fowler. Describing television as a toaster with pictures rather than a mass medium with a responsibility to promote constructive cultural dialogue, Fowler undermined broadcasters' traditional fiduciary responsibility over the public airwaves by implementing policies that made market forces rather than government the overseer of broadcast content. Ted Turner portrayed himself as a populist David battling the Goliaths of network television, proclaiming that Congress and the FCC would "go for the people and cable, because they're for more voices. They're not for the monopolies."[24]

Implicit in this association of deregulation with giving the people what they want and pioneering a new horizon of programming choice on American television was an avoidance of its actual effects on the communications industry. While tax cuts provided the capital for large conglomerates to expand their control over the communications industry through vertical integration, the Reagan administration's relaxation of restrictions on patterns of ownership within the broadcast industry facilitated these companies' horizontal colonization of new media such as cable television and existing television networks. In 1984, for example, the FCC raised the number of television stations a single company could own and shortened the length of time an owner had to retain a station before selling it.[25] These measures enabled the major conglomerates to complement their ownership of first-run theaters with cable and broadcast television outlets. Recognizing the synergies to be gained through cooperation, the cable and filmed entertainment industries fostered cross-ownerships through movie studio investment in basic cable services and negotiated contracts that provided cable with exclusive access to Hollywood's latest hits.[26]

The FCC's refusal to repeal the Financial Interest and Syndication Rules in 1980 enabled the major studios to retain the profits generated by the televised exhibition of their movies and television shows over their own networks. The so-called fin-syn rules were introduced during the early 1970s and halted the network practice of retaining financial interest in and/or distribution rights over independently produced programs aired by them. The Prime Time Access Rule (PTAR) also forced the networks to open up one hour of prime time programming each evening for their affiliates to fill with their choice of programs. The rule increased the demand for syndicated series and movies and provided an additional incentive for studios to focus their efforts on television production.[27]

As a former producer and host of the TV show *General Electric Theater*, Reagan had long advocated Hollywood's transformation of television into an ancillary source of revenue for the studios. In a letter he wrote as Governor of California to Lou Greenspan, executive director of the Producers Guild of America, Reagan contended "Hollywood should be allowed, like a candy store, to make the pictures in the backroom and sell them in the front. The selling can be a form of pay television where the theatre becomes the living room—something it has already become, but for bargain-basement entertainment."[28]

As president of the Screen Actors Guild in the mid-1950s, Reagan helped arrange a special waiver for MCA that enabled the company's talent agency to cast its own talent in television shows produced by its Revue, Inc. production company. The deal paved the way for a system of independent production in which studios sought to control costs by buying packages of film and television talent assembled by huge agencies.

Reagan's deregulatory agenda facilitated this integration of movies and TV by promoting partnerships and cross-ownerships between the major studios and national cable franchises, which enabled the producer-distributors to minimize risk and push films into secondary markets such as cable television and videocassette. While remakes and series were a staple of studio-era Hollywood designed to capitalize on audience loyalties, for the first time the success of franchises such as *Beverly Hills Cop* resulted in the eclipse of box-office revenues in 1986 ($1.67 billion) by prerecorded videocassette revenues ($2.16 billion) in the United States and Canada.[29] This trend accelerated during the 1980s and 1990s.

While directors have migrated between television and movies since the 1950s, the Paramount decree of 1948 forbade the major studios from owning television networks by outlawing monopolistic forms of media ownership. The most the movie companies could do was to buy stock in local television stations while refraining from participation in management of them.[30] Under Reagan-era deregulation policies, however, the big three broadcast networks were integrated into multinational conglomerates. In 1986, Capital Cities (owner of a chain of metropolitan newspapers) purchased ABC and General Electric (owner of RCA) purchased NBC. In 1987, real estate investor Laurence Tisch acquired CBS.

Upsizing television actors into movie stars and reincarnating weekly prime time shows as movies became common practice as TV-trained directors began directing movies and the small screen became a stepping stone for actors seeking big-screen marketability. Hollywood elevated presold television stars Tom Hanks, Eddie Murphy, Michael J. Fox, and Bruce Willis to A-list and blockbuster movie stars with low risk, and it downsized movies with built-in audience appeal like *Fame* (1980) and *Dirty Dancing* (1987) into television dramas. Paramount signed African-American comedian Arsenio Hall to an exclusive film and TV contract and created *The Arsenio Hall Show* as a showcase for him after his costarring role in the hit *Coming to America* with Eddie Murphy.[31]

Hollywood's focus on maximizing shareability between movies and television and aggressively targeting youth audiences further motivated the industry's institutionalization of high concept as a mode of production. The familiarity of the high-concept premise stems from a youth audience's endless exposure to movies on television. As a shorthand form of storytelling, high-concept movies can evoke a narrative premise without fully developing it, merge, mix, and match narrative traditions, and play them against each other as hybrid forms of entertainment emerge. Viewer attention shifts to other levels of the film presentation, such as glossy color schemes, rapid-fire editing, and dizzying camera movements that challenge comprehension and intensify emotional engagement.[32]

An Officer and a Gentleman, 48 Hrs. (1982), *Trading Places, Staying Alive, Flashdance* (1983), *Footloose,* and *Beverly Hills Cop* (1984) exemplify how Paramount became Hollywood's most successful studio during the 1980s by reiterating a high-concept "fish out of water" premise across the romantic melodrama, the screwball comedy, the musical, and the police buddy movie. *Beverly Hills Cop* is representative of the studio's high-concept integration of this theme with an action-adventure police buddy movie, a striking visual style, a hit music soundtrack, and an aggressive marketing strategy that traded on star Eddie Murphy's presold appeal to television audiences.[33] Paramount cast Murphy as Axel Foley, a working-class black detective who travels to Beverly Hills to apprehend the murderer of his childhood friend, thus using the movie's premise to reiterate the comedian's role as a convict on temporary release in *48 Hrs.* and a panhandler-turned-Wall Street investor in *Trading Places* and trading upon his familiarity to audiences as the only black cast member of *Saturday Night Live.*

As a police buddy movie, *Beverly Hills Cop* incorporates Murphy's assimilation into an all-white workplace family with his eradication of forces identified by Reagan as threats to domestic race and class relations, including international political terrorism, drug trafficking, and foreign government corruption. Director Martin Brest codes these themes into the movie's striking construction of visual space, crowding the mise-en-scène with reflective mirror surfaces and high-priced abstract art that both evoke the look of high-fashion magazine advertising and define Beverly Hills as a closed society of class privilege and material decadence.

Beverly Hills Cop's reiteration as a music video designed to promote The Pointer Sisters' "Neutron Dance" and Glen Frey's "The Heat is On" reveals the role of television advertising in shaping its high-concept style. Conceived as advertisements, music videos ape a vignette-based visual style adopted by television advertising during the late 1970s in order to fit ads into shorter time slots amid rising network prices. Dispensing with product information and concrete reason-why persuasion, this style of advertising seduces viewers with a montage of lifestyle images, carefully timed with music, which sells feeling and emotion rather than direct appeals to logic.[34] Crowded with interludes of visual excess such as violent shoot-outs, car chases, and brief comedy routines, *Beverly Hills Cop* has a modular structure that allowed it to be reiterated as a theatrical trailer, a music video, a fifteen-second television advertising spot, and a print advertising campaign. Paramount carefully coordinated an ad campaign months before the movie's release across theaters, television, and print media.

The narrative structure of *Flashdance* illustrates how director Adrian Lyne grafted this music-video style of storytelling onto the film musical. Incumbent in this mode of production was an overriding emphasis on using lifestyle to define character and narrative. To extend Janet Maslin's observation that *Footloose* "overexplains" Ren McCormick's (Kevin Bacon) status as an outsider, one might note that he is defined as such largely on the basis of his New Wave–inspired clothing rather than the sense of brooding sexuality or existential teenage angst that defined earlier screen rebels such as James Dean and Marlon Brando.[35]

MTV's agenda of targeting white suburban adolescents shaped its systematic avoidance of artists with appeal to black and ethnic audiences, while high concept's marketplace-driven integration of style and aesthetics resulted in the characterization of alternatives to a bourgeois norm of white suburban identity in terms of countercultural otherness.[36] While *Flashdance*'s heroine derives artistic inspiration from the urban culture in which she lives, the streets also prove to be a breeding ground for forces of corruption that threaten her integration into a middle-class culture of marriage and family. Shaped by Hollywood's agenda of targeting a mallgoing audience of suburbanites, *Risky Business* also characterizes an urban culture of pimps and prostitutes as a threat to the white, middle-class world of a well-heeled North Chicago high school student. High-concept moviemaking's dichotomous distinction between a consumer culture of respectable values and a countercultural world of otherness made it the perfect vehicle for dramatizing the ideological concerns of the Reagan era.

GENRE MOVIES AND MYTHS

While industrial changes within Hollywood and a focus on carefully gauging and responding to marketplace trends shaped the biracial buddy movie, the MTV music-video movie, and the yuppie movie, Reagan's construction of the Protestant success ethic molded these genres as well. Reagan's philosophy of a self-regulating marketplace was predicated on the notions that capitalism is a social contract between government and people and that the individual's freedom to pursue his or her own economic welfare is a hallmark of democracy. In proposing this ideology as the basis for America's economic recovery in the wake of New Deal liberalism, Reagan offered a bridge to the past as the key to America's future.

Proposed by seventeenth-century English philosopher John Locke, the ideology of government by contract presupposes that the state should be governed by the law of nature that the individual's pursuit of happiness, when conducted rationally, promotes cooperation and, in the long run, the coexistence of private happiness and general welfare. This philosophy of limited government and economic autonomy shaped Thomas Jefferson's conviction that America's future as a society of self-governing "natural aristocrats" depended on the recognition of talent rather than birthright as the basis for class mobility.[37] Benjamin Franklin argued that individuals could effect their own salvation through self-improvement, but that they needed to be free in order to accept this responsibility. The poor, in particular, could be transformed into productive citizens by being given the opportunity to work for wealth instead of receiving handouts. The mythology of the American frontier further edified this conviction by promising respite from the overcrowding of the industrial centers of the East on the basis of seemingly inexhaustible land and natural resources.

Drawing upon this mythology during his two-term tenure from 1967 to 1975, Governor Reagan framed California's regressive real estate tax Proposition 13 in terms of this frontier ideology of individual control over discretionary income and private property, dovetailing it when he ran for president with an entrepreneurial spirit that fit neatly with a rightward attitude shift among baby boom–age voters. Supply-side economic theory sold the concept of economic bounty rather than shrinking opportunity during an era in which the service industry's displacement of a manufacturing economy nonetheless generated growing disparities in race, gender, and class mobility. According to a U.S. Federal Reserve study cited by the *New York Times* in 1992, the share of wealth held by the richest 1 percent of U.S. households increased from 31 percent in 1983 to 37 percent in 1989 during the Reagan and Bush presidencies.[38]

Movie genres historically have evolved in order to address and symbolically resolve contradictions within American culture between competing race, gender, and class constructions of the success ethic. Cultural studies scholars since the 1960s have recognized race, gender, and class as principal points of intersecting ideological tensions in studio-era genres such as the western, the screwball comedy, and the family melodrama. Robin Wood maintains that all film genres can be examined in terms of ideological oppositions between white and other, man and woman, and individual and community that order the definition of ideals like capitalism, the work ethic, marriage, and success and wealth.[39] Schatz similarly contends that genre films maintain a sense of continuity between the cultural past and present and portray American culture as intransigently rooted in this set of fundamental tenets.[40]

A genre's sustained success depends on the significance of the conflicts it addresses and its flexibility in adjusting to the audience's and the filmmakers' evolving attitudes toward those conflicts. The sustained popularity of a genre over time indicates the irreconcilable nature of ideological oppositions that can only be temporarily resolved on the basis of a so-called happy ending that implies through its built-in sense of ambiguity the complexity of the conflicts addressed in the genre film.[41]

Wood maintains that the self-conscious treatment of ideological tensions in movies like *McCabe and Mrs. Miller* (1971), *Taxi Driver* (1976), and *Looking for Mr. Goodbar* (1976) stretched the parameters of generic form to near disintegration, revealing a crisis of faith in genres as symbolic mediators of the success ethic. By the late 1970s and during the 1980s, however, the success of filmmakers such as George Lucas and Steven Spielberg had ushered in an age of movies marketed to adults and children and designed to lull moviegoers into a state of nostalgic, infantile bliss.[42]

The popularity of stories about white male adventurers, vigilantes, and business executives was attributable to the role these narratives played in mediating the meaning of success during the 1980s. In the wake of the recessionary economic conditions and anemic cultural morale of the 1970s, movies about the white male's redemption of the success ethic mobilized Reagan-inspired fantasies about America as a land of second chances and fluid individual economic and cultural mobility.

Incumbent in Reagan's role as a spokesman for an emerging Cold War culture of moral and economic self-governance and suburban conformity was a philosophy of success that balanced economic self-reliance with a commitment to the values of moral and material progress. While the natural aristocrat of the Reagan era was an exemplar of competitive individualism, he or she was also a responsible husband and father or wife and mother, according to a success philosophy that distinguished between the male sphere of public competition and the private female sphere of domestic and affective ties. The nuclear family, ordered on the basis of biologically circumscribed gender roles, became a site for the reproduction of values that enabled a middle class of self-governing individuals to reproduce itself from one generation to the next.

Reagan's clear-cut distinction between moral and immoral blacks and ethnics, the individual and the collective, and men's and women's roles provided a template for Hollywood's construction of the success ethic in movies of the 1980s. The biracial buddy movie incorporated aspects of race, gender, and class difference that proved absorbable into the neoconservative ideologies of Reagan-era culture by invoking literary classics like *The Adventures of Huckleberry Finn* and studio-system-era westerns about white frontier conquerors and Indian sidekicks who propagate the advancement of civilized values by violently exterminating evil racial and ethnic others. Joel Silver, producer of *48 Hrs.* (1982), *Lethal Weapon* (1987), *Lethal Weapon II* (1989), *Die Hard* (1988) *Die Hard 2: Die Harder* (1990), and *The Last Boy Scout* (1991), asserted "any great action movie owes something to the western."[43] The western's simple distinction between forces of good and evil proved especially appealing in action-adventure buddy movies because it facilitated the incorporation of the Reagan administration's rhetorical focus on inner-city crime and the maintenance of boundaries between cultures defined as "black" and "white."

Trading Places and *Beverly Hills Cop* attempted to maximize their crossover appeal by incorporating this ideology into stories that relate black experience from a white point of view. Inherent in these movies is an agenda of striving for the broadest possible appeal by promoting multiple readings of the relationship between race and class mobility. Celebrating a post–civil rights era philosophy of blacks and whites teaming up to overthrow inner-city criminals, government and economic elites, and international terrorists, which Reagan identified as threats to a meritocratic society, the premise of a black or ethnic costar's integration into a dominant white society had box-office appeal because it allowed these issues to be easily resolved through humor or sentimentality.[44]

MTV music-video movies such as *Flashdance* and *Footloose* similarly celebrated a Reagan-inspired culture of marriage and family in which adherence to traditional gender roles results in successful rites of courtship and a couple's integration into self-governing middle-class families. The link between patriarchal authority, upward mobility, and the restoration of the nuclear family is evident in *Fame, Flashdance, Staying Alive, Footloose,* and *Dirty Dancing*. The musical historically has linked rituals of courtship and marriage with men's and women's conformity to proper gender roles, even as it abstracts the proper ordering of gender roles by portraying male singers and dancers as feminized objects of a male gaze.

Kramer vs. Kramer's focus on the middle-class family also echoed the neoconservative contention that the feminist movement had jeopardized the nuclear family's moral and economic stability by encouraging women to attempt to balance a career with child-raising responsibilities. Simultaneously, it implied that men needed to be more actively involved in the child raising process. Shared rites of consumption and a workplace philosophy based on charm and personality are key themes of *The Big Chill* (1983) and *The Secret of My Success* (1987), both of which celebrate Reagan's conflation of consumption and earned class prerogative. *Risky Business* (1983), *Ferris Bueller's Day Off* (1986), *The Secret of My Success* (1987), and *Big* (1988) also successfully connected with a teenage audience by juxtaposing an adult world of repressive self-discipline with an adolescent world in which work is transformed into a form of play based on role-playing, personality, and charm rather than hard work and humility.[45]

Hollywood's focus on fantasy and spectacle-driven movies about redemptive entrepreneurs, patriarchs, and violent white redeemers appealed to audiences because they addressed issues of racial equality, the family, and individual economic and cultural mobility during a period in which Reagan had successfully used neoconservative rhetoric to mobilize traditional Republicans and to woo working-class and black voters away from the Democratic party. This rhetoric proved powerful amid a culture of widespread middle-class downward mobility in which multinational corporations' enfeeblement of labor unions marginalized working-class white males alongside women and minorities in minimum wage, often part-time service sector jobs. Reagan-era cinema continued to thrive both at home and abroad under these conditions of concentrated ownership and global expansion as yuppie comedies like *Look Who's Talking* (1989) and *Home Alone* (1990) and biracial action-adventure movies such as *Die Hard II* (1990) and *Lethal Weapon II* (1989) dominated *Variety*'s annual lists of top-grossing movies over the 1990s.

NOTES

1. Bernard Weinraub, "On the Set with Sylvester Stallone: All Right Already, No More Mr. Funny Guy," *New York Times*, 9 June 1993, sec. C1.

2. Rex Burns, *Success in America: The Yeoman Dream and the Industrial Revolution* (Amherst: University of Massachusetts Press, 1976), 3.

3. Richard Slotkin, *Regeneration Through Violence* (Middletown, Conn.: Wesleyan University Press, 1973).

4. Ibid., 646.

5. Christopher Sharrett, "Afterword: Sacrificial Violence and Postmodern Ideology," *Mythologies of Violence in Postmodern Media*, ed. Christopher Sharrett (Detroit: Wayne State University Press, 1999), 415.

6. Lee Walczak, "Sharp Contrasts with Carter's Economics," *Business Week*, 31 March 1980, 94.

7. Box-office figures throughout the text refer to domestic grosses for the United States and Canada and are taken from variety.com and worldwideboxoffice.com, 15 July 2002.

8. Ronald V. Bettig, *Copyrighting Culture: The Political Economy of Intellectual Property* (Boulder: Westview Press, 1996), 50.

9. "Rebel With a Cause," *Broadcasting*, 19 May 1980, 35.

10. Vertical integration involves the expansion of a business enterprise through the control of its operations from the point at which raw materials are acquired to the point of sale of the final product. A vertically integrated system of film and television entertainment incorporates the production of the movie or program, its distribution, and its final presentation. Horizontal integration similarly refers to a high concentration of ownership in a particular medium.

11. Garry Wills, *Reagan's America: Innocents at Home* (Garden City, N.Y.: Doubleday, 1987), 262.

12. Tino Balio, "Introduction to Part II," *Hollywood in the Age of Television*, ed. Tino Balio (Boston: Unwin Hyman, 1990), 273.

13. Thomas Schatz, "The New Hollywood," *Film Theory Goes to the Movies*, ed. Jim Collins, Hilary Radner, and Ava Preacher Collins (New York: Routledge, 1993), 19.

14. Justin Wyatt, *High Concept: Movies and Marketing in Hollywood* (Austin: University of Texas Press, 1994), 8.

15. Laura Landro, "Sequels and Stars Help Top Movie Studios Avoid Major Risks," *Wall Street Journal*, 6 June 1989, sec. A1.

16. Aljean Harmetz, "Now Showing: Survival of the Fittest," *New York Times*, 22 October 1989, sec. 2, 1.

17. Douglas Gomery, "The Reagan Record," *Screen* (winter/spring 1989) 97.

18. Aljean Harmetz, "Hollywood Battles Killer Budgets," *New York Times*, 31 May 1987, sec. 3, 1.

19. ———. "Figuring Out the Fates of 'Cop II' and 'Ishtar,'" *New York Times*, 4 June 1987, sec. C1.

20. Steve Pond, "$100 Million Mania: 9 Films in 9 Figures," *Washington Post*, 4 January 1991, sec. D6.

21. Joe Mandese, "Hollywood's Top Gun," *Media & Marketing Decisions*, March 1988, 109.

22. R. Serge Denisoff and William D. Romanowski, *Risky Business: Rock in Film* (New Brunswick: Transaction Publishers, 1991), 213.

23. Ibid., 219.

24. "Rebel With a Cause," 35.

25. Douglas Gomery, "Vertical Integration, Horizontal Regulation: The Growth of Rupert Murdoch's US Media Empire," *Screen* 27, no. 3–4 (1986): 83.

26. Michelle Hilmes, "Pay Television: Breaking the Broadcast Bottleneck," *Hollywood in the Age of Television*, ed. Tino Balio (Boston: Unwin Hyman, 1990), 306.

27. Schatz, "The New Hollywood," 21.

28. Ronald Reagan to Lou Greenspan, 1966 personal correspondence, published in Helene Von Damm, *Sincerely, Ronald Reagan* (Ottawa, Ill.: Green Hill Publishers, 1976), 20.

29. Harmetz, "Hollywood Battles Killer Budgets," 1.

30. John Izod, *Hollywood and the Box Office: 1895–1986* (New York: Columbia University Press, 1988), 135.

31. Landro, "Sequels and Stars," sec. A1.

32. Henry Jenkins, "Historical Poetics," *Approaches to Popular Film*, ed. Joanne Hollows and Mark Jancovich (New York: Manchester University Press, 1995), 116.

33. Wyatt, *High Concept*, 8.

34. Sut Jhally, "The Political Economy of Culture," *Cultural Politics in Contemporary America*, ed. Ian Angus and Sut Jhally (New York: Routledge, 1989), 78.

35. Janet Maslin, "Film: 'Footloose,' Story of Dancing on the Farm," *New York Times*, 17 February 1984, sec. C12.

36. Wyatt, *High Concept*, 196.

37. Thomas Jefferson, *The Portable Thomas Jefferson*, ed. Merrill D. Peterson (New York: Penguin Books, 1975), 536.

38. Sylvia Nasar, "Fed Gives Evidence of 80s Gains by Richest," *New York Times*, 22 April 1992, sec. A1.

39. Robin Wood, "Ideology, Genre, Auteur," *Film Genre Reader*, ed. Barry Keith Grant (Austin: University of Texas Press, 1986), 164.

40. Thomas Schatz, *Hollywood Genres: Formulas, Filmmaking, and the Studio System* (New York: Random House, 1981), 31.

41. Ibid.

42. Robin Wood, *Hollywood from Vietnam to Reagan* (New York: Columbia University Press, 1986), 164.

43. Jack Garner, "The Screening Room," Gannett News Service, 10 May 1989.

44. Ed Guerrero, *Framing Blackness: The African American Image in Film* (Philadelphia: Temple University Press, 1993), 128.

45. Elizabeth G. Traube, *Dreaming Identities: Class, Gender, and Generation in 1980s Hollywood Movies* (Boulder: Westview Press, 1992), 21.

Chapter 2

The Reagan Era and Hollywood's Political Economic Structure

The Protestant ethic historically has rationalized corporate practices of consolidation and conglomeration as a means of improving business efficiency and democratizing affluence. The industrial age's celebration of the businessmen as the quintessential American individualist revealed that the ability to incorporate, to mobilize, and to centralize capital and productive resources was the surest path to great wealth. The rationale of free-market economics and deregulation that promoted this trend of incorporation propagated a mythology of business efficiency that conflated Hollywood's domestic consolidation and overseas expansion with ideals of democratic economic and social freedom. Proponents of the studio system that prevailed in Hollywood between the 1920s and 1950s contended that an assembly-line method of moviemaking enabled the industry to democratize the availability of movies both in the United States and abroad. This rationale also guided policies that resulted in Hollywood's virtual return to a studio system during the 1980s.

Supporters of Reaganomics and deregulation argued that free-market competition and government's retreat from industry would promote the ascendance of media moguls most capable of competing in a self-governing marketplace and provide consumers with greater choice. However, liberal political economists contend that Hollywood's vertical and horizontal reintegration over the 1980s curtailed the diversity of its output by concentrating ownership and control over monolithic communications companies in the hands of an international investment class of bankers and businessmen who promoted economies of scale in movie production, distribution, and exhibition. Reaganomics and deregulation also spurred the maturation of a post-Fordist trend that integrated movies further than ever before into an emerging service industry economy.

New technologies, their colonization by multinational conglomerates, and escalating moviemaking costs resulted in the ascendance to power of business-trained executives in Hollywood. As intermediaries between the industry's media barons and its audiences, television-trained movie studio executives actively participated in the transformation of movies into commodities designed to address the theme of success in lifestyle terms rather than in terms of broader public significance. It was amidst that trend that movies became further interwoven into the process of commodity production and exchange as they were reshaped into promotional texts designed to harness the tightly diversified media conglomerate's integrated structure.

THE FORMATION OF THE MOTION PICTURE INDUSTRY

The filmed entertainment industry has been an oligopoly virtually since its inception. The earliest attempt to control the film industry was Thomas Edison's formation of the Motion Picture Patent Company (MPPC) along with a handful of member companies. The MPPC controlled the manufacture of motion pictures and equipment and the access to film stock during the early 1900s. It also used its control of motion picture exhibition to classify theaters according to their locations and success in drawing audiences. This arrangement became known as the run-zone-clearance system and established the concept of cinema as a time-based business in which newer product had greater earning power.[1]

While the MPPC was successfully disbanded in 1918 under the antitrust provisions of the Sherman Act, it nonetheless fostered developments that had a long-lasting impact on the film industry's growth. The company's success revealed that cinema was a potentially much larger business than had once been thought and centralized what had begun as a highly disorganized industry. The MPPC also proved that the industry could be run much more efficiently and profitably on the basis of a strategy of vertical integration which allowed a single company or group of closely meshed companies to control at least two functions within the three principal activities of production, distribution, and exhibition.[2]

The investment required to organize these operations necessarily demanded that their owners raise production financing and corporate funding from banks. The purchase of theaters provided these companies with tangible assets, which banks accepted as loan collateral. The banks involved also secured their loans by taking seats on the management boards of these emerging movie companies, where they imposed much greater standardization on the film industry than would otherwise have developed.

The standardization of film production, distribution, and exhibition led to the cultivation of a nationwide domestic market for movies, which enabled the filmed entertainment industry to rent out films abroad on much cheaper terms than local manufacturers in foreign countries. The First World War created a crucial opportunity for the cultivation of overseas markets for American movies because it so disrupted European production that overseas film industries could only make simple, inexpensive movies. Conversely, American markets remained firm sources of revenue for filmmakers during this period, enabling Hollywood to make expensive productions that played well abroad. Improvements in U.S. shipping facilities also promoted Hollywood's overseas exportation activities.[3]

The American film industry's coalescence into a vertically structured industry provided it with the additional advantage of negotiating as a cartel in its business dealings with foreign markets. The approximately ten companies that had established themselves by 1925–26 supplied each other's needs for films almost exclusively. By supporting each other in this fashion, they also weakened independent companies and anticipated the system of joint cooperation through which the major studios have historically colluded to limit competition within their ranks.

Hollywood's cultivation of the overseas market drew attention to film's power as an instrument of marketing and propaganda. By 1912, cinema had emerged as an agent of consumerism as exporters realized that the exhibition of Hollywood films brought in their wake demand for American goods. This theme was promoted through the architecture of Hollywood's early movie palaces, the lifestyles of its stars and studio bosses, and through the films themselves.

While movies had by the 1920s become a vehicle for celebrating a culture of consumption, the coming of sound further solidified the filmed entertainment industry's relationship with major financiers and banking interests. The advent of sound in 1927–28 required such massive capital investment in order to wire theaters, acquire additional ones, build studios, and convert them for sound that Hollywood's relationship with Wall Street was further solidified. Simultaneously, the cost of implementing sound had by 1929 caused smaller companies to either disappear or be absorbed by larger corporations and theater chains. Warner Bros., Twentieth Century Fox, and RKO joined Paramount and MGM in the first tier of movie studios with power and influence, while Universal, Columbia, and United Artists remained in the second rank of the industry. Only by differentiating their offerings from those of the first-tier studios did the smaller studios sustain profitability and survive the cartel conditions of the studio system.[4]

Each studio's focus on particular film genres had the additional benefit of making its offerings attractive to other major studios looking to rent alternative offerings to keep their theaters in business. No major studio could keep its screens full without the movies made by its rivals. Simultaneously, the major studios' reliance on their competitors' movies enabled them to exclude independent studios from the filmed entertainment industry. United Artists, Universal, and Columbia similarly ensured their survival and profitability by supplying films that were needed to fill the major studios' screening schedules. Since the minor studios owned few theaters, their role as producers-distributors was integral to their longevity.

While the future of the major studios was placed in jeopardy in the wake of Wall Street's crash in October, 1929, the vast loan commitments made by banks and other financiers for theater purchase and conversion to sound forced them to secure their investments by refinancing and reorganizing the major studios that had fallen on hard times—Twentieth Century Fox, RKO, and Paramount. Financiers were appointed to the governing boards of these companies because of Hollywood's reliance on external financing and joint-stock corporations.

The federal government's implementation of the Code of Fair Practice for the Motion Picture Industry as part of the National Industrial Recovery Act (NIRA) tightened the major studios' status as a collusive cartel by condoning the vertical integration of the major studios, allowing block-booking and blind-bidding, and confirming the practice of run-zone-clearance exhibition. The onset of World War II enabled Hollywood to further establish distribution offices abroad. The war curtailed production in the single biggest film producing country—France—and enabled American exporters to fill the gaps in supplies to former French client countries. The coalescence of an oligopoly at home provided Hollywood producers with the capital necessary to amortize overseas operations, giving the United States a unique advantage over other film-producing countries.

REAGAN AND POSTWAR HOLLYWOOD

One of postwar Hollywood's primary goals was the expansion of overseas markets for American movies. As leaders of the most powerful nation on earth, American government and business officials undertook political, economic, and cultural measures to jump-start the reconstruction of a global economy and to pave the way for American business's overseas growth after World War II. Their convictions were fueled by their recognition that American government and business possessed the capital necessary to reconstruct and incorporate spheres of economic activity in Western Europe. Cooperation between American business and government became crucial for seizing these opportunities.[5]

President Harry Truman, the Motion Picture Industrial Council (MPIC), and MPIC member Ronald Reagan were united in their belief that the cultivation of overseas markets for American movies depended on unfet-tered free-market enterprise. Their agenda focused on two prevailing con-cerns. One concern was that tighter restrictions were being placed on the importation of American films abroad. The other, raised by Congressional hearings in 1947, involved what role the industry would take in the Cold War. Here, as was often the case in Hollywood (and in Ronald Reagan's career), patriotism and self-interest converged.[6]

Reagan assumed a highly visible role in Hollywood's formation of gov-ernment policy, proposing that recovery assistance to Britain be contin-gent on the relaxation of quotas. He suggested that the State Department have authority to withhold financial relief assistance from any nation that unreasonably impeded the free interchange of ideas by restricting movies and other forms of communication. He argued that films were ambassa-dors and that Hollywood contributed to the nation's well-being.[7]

As a member of the MPIC, Reagan also participated in the formulation of a plan with the Department of State to make cinema a vital weapon in the Korean War's ideological battle against Communism.[8] He and the committee believed that movies played an important role in winning wars, but that Communist movies failed because of their heavy-handed propaganda. For this reason, Reagan rejected the notion that the work of the MPIC was even remotely similar to the work of Soviet propagandists. "We scorn the nonsense about 'aggressive imperialism,'" the group de-clared.[9]

Hollywood's and the government's efforts to cultivate foreign markets for American movies allowed the industry to act as a cartel abroad at a time when it had suddenly been prevented by the Paramount decree of 1948 from doing so at home. Under the direction of its new president, Eric Johnston, the Foreign Department of the Motion Picture Producers and Distributors of America (now the Motion Picture Association of America, or MPAA) was reorganized in 1945 as the Motion Picture Export Associa-tion (MPEA) under provisions of the Webb-Pomerene Export Trade Act of 1918. The act permitted the MPEA to act as the exclusive export agent for Hollywood movies, to set prices and terms of trade for films, and to over-see distribution abroad.

In bringing together the major studios and allowing them to act in con-cert through a single organization, the MPEA presented a united front to other nations and through coordinated legal collusion precluded poten-tially detrimental competition between American film companies over-seas.[10] Johnston was a free-market conservative whose ideas paralleled many of Reagan's own beliefs about movies' economic and cultural roles abroad. He believed that movies could help American business fill the economic void in countries devastated by war and that they could serve as global showcases for American techniques, products, and merchandise.[11]

Under Johnston's direction and with State Department assistance, the MPEA secured the 1948 Franco-American Film Agreement. The agree-

ment allowed U.S. firms to both withdraw $3.6 million annually in earn-
ings from France and to invest remaining funds in the joint production of
films with French companies, construction of new studios, acquisition of
distribution and story rights, and other related activities. Under the lati-
tude the agreement provided, American companies were soon organizing
offices overseas and cultivating a free market for dumping U.S. movies
abroad.[12]

These measures gave rise to runaway production, or overseas production, of films by Hollywood moviemakers. The major studios found that
runaway production offered the advantage of lavish sceneries that enabled them to distinguish their productions from television. Overseas production charges, particularly for the hire of skilled technicians and of
extras, also cost less than in California. Since the major studios preferred
to invest in runaway production where they could find efficient labor, not
all overseas countries were equally favored. The tax benefits of this
arrangement were also advantageous because the major studios were only
liable for funds generated overseas when they converted them into U.S.
currency.[13]

These advantages resulted in runaway production's popularization
during a period of rising filmmaking costs. While 19 runaway films were
produced in 1948, 183 were produced in 1968. The share of American film
industry earnings generated overseas also rose from 40 percent of theatrical revenue in the 1950s to about 53 percent in the early 1960s. Approximately 80 percent of those overseas rentals were earned in Europe. The
growth of runaway production provided production companies with
much greater control over domestic employment opportunities within the
film industry. Hollywood trade unions rapidly declined in membership
from about 22,000 in 1949 to 12,500 in 1956. While the unions' protests led
to a Congressional inquiry in 1961–1962, their efforts proved relatively fu-
tile because the major studios had by then found a new form of runaway
production with even greater financial incentives.[14]

This new form of runaway production took advantage of discreet subsidy schemes established by several European governments to protect
their national film industries from unequal American competition. The
generous support offered by European governments to their native film
industries' production efforts often helped finance works by European
production companies owned by American parent company distributors.
Many of François Truffaut's 1960s films, for example, were partially financed by the French government's patronage of the company Les
Artistes Associes, a subsidiary of United Artists.[15]

The Hollywood major studios enjoyed dramatic cost reductions
through runaway production. By the end of the 1960s, the volume of
American films financed abroad had risen to about 60 percent of the total
output of US producers. Thomas Guback writes that government subsidy

schemes enabled the American major studios to annex Europe's movie industries. American business capital was also expanding overseas, multiplying ninefold between 1950 and 1973.[16]

Reagan provided the major studios with significant control over a post–Paramount decree workforce by helping them achieve cartel power in their overseas production and distribution efforts. However, Reagan helped the major studios and independent producers to police the post–studio era workforce in other ways as well. The success of independent producers and studios in controlling a workforce that was no longer directly employed by a studio system of management was contingent upon having discretion over who worked and who didn't work. This discretion was achieved through the active cooperation of the government and the Hollywood studios in ferreting out actual and suspected Communists and leftist sympathizers working within the movie industry.

Ronald Reagan was an active agent in this drive for reform of the movie industry. While he had aligned himself with the left-of-center Hollywood Independent Citizens Committee of the Arts, Sciences and Professions (HICCASP) before World War II, he became increasingly conservative during and after the war. He provided information to the FBI about the organization, using the code name T–10.[17] As a board member of the Screen Actors Guild (SAG) in 1946, Reagan also began carrying a pistol in order to protect himself against threats against his life during a tense standoff within the guild over a strike.[18]

As a friendly witness before the House Un-American Activities Committee and president of SAG, Reagan also actively cooperated in the formation of a blacklist of unemployable movie personnel. The studios' exploitation of this threat enabled them to further control a pool of talent that depended upon them for work. By working together in the wake of the Paramount decree, the studios discovered that they could circumvent the intentions of the decree and perpetuate their control over the industry guilds. Ronald Reagan was an integral participant in this process, using his position as president of SAG to join industry management in implementing an industry-wide ban against some of the guild's members.[19]

Access to key talent was also crucial in Hollywood's post–World War II era because the Paramount decree's separation of movie production from distribution and exhibition had shorn the studios of guaranteed audiences for their productions. Stars, producers, and directors became important for successfully marketing a movie, enabling them to bargain for greater recognition—either in cash or artistic independence. As television and movie production became a matter of assembling a package of talent, agents who had access to key personnel became increasingly powerful. While Reagan's level of involvement in the deal has been questioned, it was during his presidency of SAG in 1952 that the union granted Music

Corporation of America (MCA) an exclusive waiver that allowed the company to act as both television producer and talent agent, providing it with a tremendous competitive advantage in the emerging field of television production.

The arrangement was a clear conflict of interest because it allowed MCA's talent agency to employ its own clients in television productions made by MCA's television production company, Revue, Inc. In this way, MCA functioned both as management and as representative of labor. As agent, its responsibility was to get as much money for its clients as possible. As producer, however, its incentive was to hold salaries to a minimum. The agreement enabled MCA to act as producer and agent, casting actors whom it represented in television productions, which it sold to networks and advertising agencies.[20] As a result, the company gained tremendous negotiating flexibility and profited both from its cut of its clients' salaries for starring in its productions and from its sale of television productions to networks and ad agencies.

Reagan directly shared in the advantages he helped engineer for MCA when the company hired him in 1954 to host and act in episodes of the TV show *General Electric Theater*, produced by MCA's Revue, Inc. The appointment proved to be a windfall for the former Warner Bros. contract actor because he was heavily in debt to the Internal Revenue Service and was in the process of divorcing actress Jane Wyman.[21]

The Reagan-led SAG also proved integral in helping MCA to exploit the emerging market of television production by allowing the company to forgo payment of residuals to actors who starred in MCA-owned movies broadcast on television. The contract required the actors to forfeit all claims for residual payments for television showings of movies made before 1960. The studios in turn agreed to create a pension and welfare fund for actors with a one-time contribution of $2.65 million. Actors were also entitled in the future to 6 percent of all future gross sales to television of theatrical movies made after 1960—after the deduction of distribution costs, which sometimes were as high as 40 percent.[22]

After resigning as SAG president in 1960, Reagan became a partner in the ownership of *General Electric Theater*. By 1961, Hollywood was turning out far more hours of TV programming than feature films, having reactivated its B-movie production process to feed TV's voracious appetite for shows. The income MCA derived from its production activities launched it on a skyrocketing course of prosperity, with its income from production soon surpassing that earned from its agency fees. Just ten years after the waiver that brought the company into production on a large scale, it controlled 60 percent of the entertainment industry, while the original talent agency accounted for only 10 percent of its income.[23] Reagan shared in the revenue, eventually securing from MCA a 25 percent share of all of *General Electric Theater*'s proceeds.[24]

In 1961 the Justice Department forced MCA to discontinue its role as both producer and agent. However, MCA retained the television production facilities it had bought from Universal in 1959, and augmented them with its purchase of Universal Studios and Decca Records. While the company had divorced itself from its original agency business, it became in its new form (as owner of a television production company, a large studio facility, one of the major distributors, and an important record label) well equipped to take eventual advantage of the multimedia culture of production that arose during the 1970s.[25]

GOVERNOR REAGAN AND HOLLYWOOD

Through his association with a powerful corporate class of Hollywood executives, including those at MCA, Reagan gained the financial capital necessary to run for the office of Governor of California. MCA executive Taft Schreiber helped organize Reagan's campaign for California governor in 1966. Schreiber, with the assistance of MCA founder Jules Stein, coordinated the sale of Reagan's ranch in the Santa Monica Mountains to Twentieth Century Fox, providing Reagan with the financial security necessary to enter gubernatorial politics. Fox paid $8,000 an acre for Reagan's ranch, although Reagan had purchased it fifteen years earlier for only $293 an acre and the studio resold it to the state of California during Reagan's incumbency as governor for only $1,800 an acre.[26]

Amidst Hollywood's near insolvency in the unstable mid-1960s, Governor Reagan actively used state influence to effect partial repayment of a debt to Hollywood executives who had helped him get elected. In 1968, Governor Reagan signed a state bill, which Governor Edmund G. "Pat" Brown had vetoed, that gave the major studios—including MCA's Universal—$3 million to $4 million each in tax breaks on their film inventories.[27] It was during this period that multinational companies snapped up Hollywood's major studios because of the under valuation of their film libraries.[28]

The studios' devotion of their resources during the 1964–1968 period to a series of lukewarmly received big-budget movies like *Cleopatra* (1963), *Dr. Dolittle* (1967), *Star!* (1968), and *Hello Dolly!* (1969) left many exhibitors desperate for product and the studios searching for hits. The primary role of independents like New World, and American Independent Pictures had previously been to fill in gaps in the production schedules of the major studios and the exhibition schedules of the theater owners. The major studios, emboldened by the replacement of the production code by a much looser system of rating movies individually, responded by offering independent moviemakers and young producers even more opportunities to make films.

Independent companies thrived for several reasons. They did so because the demise of the studio system provided stars, producers, and directors with unprecedented control over their movies in the New Hollywood. Through more explicit discussion of drugs and sexuality, young talent spoke to the tastes of an underserved youth market. The Motion Picture Association of America's replacement of the production code with a ratings systems, made possible by the Supreme Court and sold to the public as a response to changing times, also enabled mainstream filmmakers to engage in more explicit treatment of issues of the 1960s. Filmmakers used sexual explicitness to differentiate their product from the more strictly regulated shows on television.[29]

Independents also prospered during the late 1960s and early 1970s through their innovative use of separate exhibition opportunities to avoid competing with the major studios for circuit theaters. While drive-ins provided an opportunity to target young crowds, "four walling" enabled distributors to target indoor working-class and family audiences as well. Four walling is a practice whereby the distributor rents the theater outright. Although four walling placed greater onus on the distributor because the exhibitor received the theater rental up front, it also enabled the former to retain the majority of the box-office revenue generated by a hit film. Four-wall exhibition was vastly different from more traditional methods of film scheduling because it limited movies to one- or two-week runs and required immediate audience awareness and interest. *Billy Jack* (1971) demonstrated the profitability of four walling when it was re-released on May 9, 1973. Armed with a generous advertising budget after his successful litigation of a case against Warner Bros. for breach of a distribution contract, writer/director/producer/star Tom Laughlin rented theaters in key locations across the country and released *Billy Jack* on a four-wall basis. During its first week, the movie grossed $1.02 million in southern California, $1.45 million in New York, $710,000 in Philadelphia, and $600,000 in Chicago. Eventually, *Billy Jack* returned more than $30 million in domestic film rentals.[30]

As Laughlin's example illustrates, independent producers of the period who used four walling relied heavily on saturation television advertising campaigns aimed at specific audiences on the basis of market pretesting. Separate ads foregrounded specific themes designed to reach a broad spectrum of moviegoers. Laughlin rented a large number of theaters within the region of the television signal, maximizing the convenience of attending the film. Promotion for *Billy Jack* played upon romance, Native American countercultural sentiment, action-adventure, and martial arts.[31] Companies like Cinema V, often cited as a model for later 1990s independents such as Miramax and New Line Cinema, also distinguished themselves by focusing on and promoting art-house fare with bold, stylish advertising campaigns. The poster for Robert Downey's satire of the advertising industry, *Putney Swope* (1969), displayed a scantily clad girl replacing the title character's raised middle finger.

While directors of countercultural movies differentiated their films by focusing upon exploitation and teen film marketing techniques, they also turned moviemaking formulae upside down in order to thumb their noses at the established order. In *McCabe and Mrs. Miller* (1971), for example, Robert Altman sets up the former character as a typical western hero, ruggedly individualistic and a founding father of a pioneer town, then exposes him as a weakling and a loser. Incumbent in the movie is a blurring of representational and thematic boundaries distinguishing heroes from villains. Protagonists in *The Wild Bunch* (1969), *Butch Cassidy and the Sundance Kid* (1969), *Easy Rider* (1969), and *Midnight Cowboy* (1969) are similarly condemned as anachronisms and glorified as throwbacks to better times who refused to concede to the changes imposed by progress.[32] *The Graduate* (1967), *Midnight Cowboy* (1969), *Easy Rider* (1969), *Putney Swope*, *Little Big Man* (1970), *M*A*S*H* (1970), *Watermelon Man* (1970), *They Shoot Horses, Don't They?* (1971), *McCabe and Mrs. Miller* (1971), *Sweet Sweetback's Baadasss Song* (1971), and *The Spook Who Sat By the Door* (1973) mixed or undermined generic conventions that had in the previous era reified cultural institutions such as government and business. Michael Ryan and Douglas Kellner argue that these subversions of generic form suggested the exhaustion of genres as modes of ideological legitimation. They further argue, however, that the failure of attempts to assert alternatives to these forms left the discovery of a positive alternative to conservatives.[33]

While these films often garnered critical favor and commercial success, they also sometimes failed at the box office. In the wake of near bankruptcy, Hollywood discovered that the audience had stabilized in size, and that the market could only support a few productions. The major studios cut production in half in response to this stagnation in demand. Hollywood also learned from the success of early blockbusters such as *The Godfather* (1972; $135 million) that a few movies capture the majority of annual box-office receipts. Another lesson the studios learned was that aggressive marketing and promotion tactics could offset the risks of production.[34]

The takeover of the major studios by multinational companies only a few years earlier resulted by the mid-1970s in a period of restructuring and belt tightening during which their bankers and financiers forced them to streamline their operations, reduce overhead, share overseas distribution networks, and temporarily discontinue making big-budget movies. As Guback observes, this shift marked the investment community's effort to impose accountability on the process of moviemaking.[35] The integration of a major studio into a parent company often prefigured Hollywood's reintegration of movie production and distribution with exhibition. Paramount Pictures' acquisition by Gulf & Western Industries in 1966, for example, integrated the studio with Famous Music Corporation, Simon and Schuster Publishing House, a sports arena, and Famous Players Limited (the second largest theater chain in Canada).

Under the auspices of creating more jobs for laborers amidst scaled-down production schedules, Governor Reagan offered these multinational companies the tax breaks provided to other manufacturing industries, enabling parent companies to offset the growing financial risk involved in making movies in a time of rising costs and uncertain audience tastes. The Revenue Act of 1971, for example, enabled companies to reduce their income tax 7 percent in proportion to their investment in tangible property, which included theatrical films and television programs.[36] No matter how unsuccessful it was at the box office, each movie's costs generated a tax credit. Metro-Goldwyn-Mayer was able to reduce its statutory tax rate from 48 to 37 percent in 1975, from 46 to 27 percent in 1980 and to only 3 percent in 1982. Columbia Pictures lowered its rate from the statutory 46 percent to an effective rate of 24 percent in 1980. From 1979 to 1983, MCA's average tax rate was less than 22 percent, while the statutory rate was 46 percent.[37]

The Tax Reduction Act of 1975 and the Tax Reform Act of 1976 offered other forms of public subsidy for corporation owners and executives. Both measures encouraged employee participation in company stock purchase plans and sanctioned the usage of a percentage of their contributions for corporate income tax credit. Guback contends that this corporate subsidization was essentially "welfare for the wealthy."[38] Conversely, it did little to increase movie production or relieve chronic unemployment in the film industry.

The deduction for interest on corporate debt has long been part of the United States tax code. Businesses in a post–World War II economy had borrowed money to build plants, buy equipment, and make new products, thereby creating new jobs. Under this arrangement, it made sense to allow companies to write off the full interest expense on their tax returns in order to promote long-range industrial productivity in a culture of durable goods manufacturing.

The application of this depreciation principal to the film industry through the reclassification of filmmaking and marketing as a manufacturing activity, however, failed to promote the long-range growth of jobs in Hollywood. Instead, it served as a form of corporate welfare by reducing the risk of financing movies. Under the provision, films and television programs that flopped still generated a substantial tax credit. Carry-forward provisions of the tax law also allowed companies to stockpile credit that could be used to reduce future federal income tax.[39]

While income tax credit provided one means of curbing financial risk during a period of shaky balance sheets and rising filmmaking costs, the federal government's deregulation of the communications industry sparked investment in new technologies. The cultivation of cable, video-cassette, and satellite for purposes of movie distribution and exhibition provided further means of spreading the risk of the big-budget film-making that was becoming a preferred mode of production by the mid-1970s.

DEREGULATION OF NEW COMMUNICATIONS TECHNOLOGIES IN THE 1970s

While the Nixon administration deregulated the guidelines for owner-ship and operation of cable and satellite, it undertook greater regulation of the television industry during the early 1970s via its implementation of the fin-syn (Financial Interest and Syndication) rules and the PTAR (Prime Time Access Rule). The networks had for years used their control of television distribution to exact part ownership of the programs they put on the air. Without actually owning and operating the production fa-cilities in which television programs were made, the networks nonethe-less achieved, according to David Prindle, "vertical integration by contract."[40]

New technologies like cable television, which had existed since the 1940s, arose to challenge the networks' domination of the broadcast air-waves with the release of the Federal Communications Commission's 1972 Report and Order on Cable Television. The 1975 launch of the SAT-COM I telecommunications satellite made pay-cable a major player in an-cillary movie distribution by giving rise to Home Box Office (HBO), the nation's first nationwide "movie channel."[41]

Sony's 1975 introduction of the Betamax videotape recorder and Mat-sushita's release of the video home system (VHS) also then launched a home video revolution. Matsushita's VHS format prevailed because it was less expensive (though technically inferior), more flexible, and offered ef-ficient off-the-air recording. Matsushita was also more successful in ac-quiring the rights to popular movie titles, providing it with the means of pushing its VHS format.

Liberalization of entry into communications technologies coalesced during the Carter administration because of business investment in new communications technologies and contradictions in regulations designed to protect conventional broadcasters. During the tenure of Carter-appointed FCC Chairman Charles Ferris from 1977 to 1981, the commis-sion deregulated cable television and initiated efforts to foster new broad-cast services including direct broadcast satellite, multi-point distribution services, and low-power television.[42]

POLITICAL ECONOMIC REFORM
AND THE CONSERVATIVE AGENDA

While liberals argued that the deregulation of the communications industry would foster greater participatory democracy and programming diversity in broadcast culture, conservatives contended that deregulation would sever the tie that had developed between government broadcast agencies and their regulated industries. The conservative criticism of government regulation's hobbling influence on economic development and consumer choice had considerable public support during a period in which America's postwar economic boom between 1948 and 1972 ground to a halt under the effects of stagflation, economic recession, and mounting competition from industrializing nations like Japan. The government's attempt to halt inflation by raising interest rates exposed excess production capacity in Western countries, while OPEC's decision to raise oil prices and the Arabs' decision to implement an oil embargo against the West led to demands for less government intervention in the private sector. However, deregulation betrayed liberal hopes by unleashing the forces that regulatory controls sought to check in the first place.

The deregulatory measures undertaken by the Carter administration gained momentum as corporations formed political action committees (PACs) which enabled business and trade associations to act in unison to depose a federal government dominated by liberal Democrats. General Electric, for example, maintained during the 1980s a PAC that pressed company employees to make contributions to political candidates that it supported. The top-down structure of large corporations like GE is well suited for the execution of grass-roots regional lobbying campaigns.

Control over television network programming provided large corporations like GE with great influence over local and national news programming among affiliate stations. The influence media companies were able to exert over U.S. election campaign reporting placed pressure on elected officials to serve local broadcasters well. Members of Congress involved in broadcast policymaking, through FCC involvement or lawmaking, were inclined to favor the interests of this important media sector. In embracing Reagan's pro-business agenda, for example, television simultaneously failed to report on the skyrocketing federal deficit, the impact of tax cuts on social spending, the growing gap between rich and poor, and Reagan's covert wars throughout the world.

PACs, particularly ones organized by businesses to complement their lobbying activities, thus played a key role in the 1980 election campaign and in introducing a climate of business-friendly government reform.[43] Major corporations also shaped legislative debates over tax policy by politicizing management-level employees and stockholders. While only about 15 percent of Americans owned stock in the late 1970s, those who did were in upper-income brackets. Therefore, they had no direct interest in the expansion or maintenance of domestic spending programs, but considerable interest in lower tax rates.[44]

The business community's effectiveness in helping elect Reagan president, along with the sweeping reforms Reagan enacted once in office, exemplified big business's strategy of acting as a class by submerging competitive instincts in favor of joint, cooperative action in political reform. Once elected, Reagan implemented tax cuts, a lax antitrust enforcement environment, and further FCC deregulation which tilted patterns of ownership and control within the communications industry in favor of multinational media barons and their top management personnel.

Reagan nonetheless argued that the rise of new technologies such as cable television promised to end spectrum scarcity by democratizing access to the broadcast airwaves. Incumbent in this scenario was a conflation of entrepreneurial investment in new communications technologies and the renewal of a mythical frontier from which the self-styled entrepreneur extracts new wealth. As Garry Wills observes, supply-side economics conflated the resurrection of a culture of frontier individualism and freedom from government regulation with a return to values that made America great.[45]

Conservative think tanks funded by large corporations proliferated during the 1970s as big business sought to formulate political and economic strategies that could be pitched to conservative government policymakers during a period of ascendant political conservatism and pro-business sentiment. The leaders of think tank groups were in several cases appointed to policymaking positions in the Reagan administration upon the president's election to the White House. For example, in 1982 Reagan appointed Martin Feldstein, professor of economics at Harvard and leader of the National Bureau of Economic Research from 1978 to 1982, to chair his Council of Economic Advisers. Major Fortune 500 corporate donors funded the bureau's operating budget, which amounted to $5.8 million in 1983.[46]

CONCENTRATION, CONSOLIDATION, AND REAGAN-ERA HOLLYWOOD

With Ronald Reagan's election as president in 1980, the deregulatory, merger-friendly climate endorsed by conservative think tanks and PAC contributors gathered startling momentum. Reagan's election was the result of coordinated action on the part of big business interests that supported his pro-business agenda. Reagan administration revisions of federal tax law, including the 1981 Economic Recovery Tax Act, created an investment climate highly conducive to the interests of communications company owners and stockholders.

Cuts in corporate tax rates paralleled skyrocketing expenditures on national defense. During his 1980 campaign, Reagan called for a 5 percent increase in the Pentagon budget. In the aftermath of President Carter's failed attempt to rescue American hostages in Iran, the outgoing presidential administration itself raised defense costs by 5 percent in its 1981 budget. Over six years, the Reagan military budget experienced a real growth of 10 percent, ending up with a 160 percent higher outlay in 1989 than in 1983.[47]

The overwhelming majority of the tax reductions resulting from the cut enacted by Reagan went to capital-intensive businesses. Cuts in corporate income taxes were made possible by a provision that allowed corporation buyers to deduct from their taxes interest paid on borrowed money. The tax savings provided by these measures freed up tremendous amounts of investment capital for multinational conglomerates involved in diversifying their media interests through acquisitions and takeovers. The act also provided an enormous boon to banks and investors earning interest on the borrowing of multimedia conglomerates.

Guback writes that while shares in media companies are widely dispersed among public stockholders, power over as little as 5 or 10 percent of their stock can provide working control over their operations. He observes that in 1985 the officers and members of the boards of directors of Warner Communications held 2.5% of its stock; Coca-Cola Company (Columbia), 7.9%; Walt Disney Productions, 7.5%; MCA (Universal), 10.6%; and Gulf & Western (Paramount), 6.2%.[48] Consolidation of political and economic power occurred through the concentration of stock ownership of large companies in the hands of banks and interlocking boards of directors. Acting in unison, these executives used their collective financial capital and influence to develop and colonize new communications media.

The advantage of top-down leadership provided by the concentration of ownership among top management executives proved integral for establishing a record of box-office successes during a period of great emphasis on cost control. In 1982, for example, the average movie cost about $9 million to make and an additional $6 million for advertising and prints.[49] By observing strict cost control strategies, the Warner Bros. management team of Terry Semel and Bob Daly racked up a series of box-office hits between 1982 and 1999, including *Chariots of Fire* (1981; $58 million), *Risky Business* (1983; $63 million), *Lethal Weapon* (1987; $65 million), *Driving Miss Daisy* (1988; $106 million), and *Batman* (1989; $251 million).

Frank Mancuso, a twenty-four-year veteran of Paramount's sales and marketing division who became chairman of the studio in 1984, enjoyed an outstanding track record with *Footloose* (1984; $80 million), *Terms of Endearment* (1983; $108 million), *Beverly Hills Cop* (1984; $234 million), *Beverly Hills Cop 2* (1987; $153 million), *Pretty in Pink* (1986; $40 million), *Top Gun*

(1986; $176 million), and *Ferris Bueller's Day Off* (1986; $70 million). Mancuso's marketing background showed in the studio's use of seven different ad campaigns for *Top Gun*, each pegged to a different audience, and its decision to mail ads for youth-oriented movies such as *Pretty in Pink* to teens taking college entrance exams.[50]

The FCC's repeal of regulations on broadcast property ownership and broadcast content facilitated Hollywood's focus on reaching suburban teen audiences by encouraging the major conglomerates to purchase or negotiate partnerships with cable networks and enabling them to cross-market blockbuster and A-list titles in theaters and on cable television. The Reagan administration's implementation of the Cable Communications Policy Act of 1984 provided multiple system operators (MSOs) with a wish list of provisions that allowed them tremendous discretion over every program and service they carried. The act promoted horizontal integration by taking all power over the granting of franchises from municipalities and giving it to cable oligopolies like ATC (American Television and Communication) and TCI (Telecommunications Inc.).[51] Under Reagan, power thus shifted away from the public and cities and toward cable operations. [52]

The Reagan administration FCC also loosened restrictions on the number of television stations any one firm could own in 1984, raising the limit from seven to twelve. ABC, NBC, and CBS changed hands in 1985–86 under this relaxation of ownership regulations. By integrating Twentieth Century Fox, a chain of independent television stations, and various print publications, Rupert Murdoch created a fourth television network and a studio to supply it with programming. Antitrust concerns ultimately led the FCC to block several takeovers. ITT's proposed takeover of ABC was blocked because ITT's political activities threatened the network's news integrity.[53]

Under these conditions of vertical and horizontal integration, the major studios struck lavish production deals with stars, producers, and directors with proven track records of box-office performance. Writer/producer/director John Hughes (who made *Mr. Mom* [1983], *Sixteen Candles* [1984], and *The Breakfast Club* [1985] for Universal) signed a contract with Paramount in 1985 that resulted in the box-office hits *Pretty in Pink* and *Ferris Bueller's Day Off*. Universal paid $10 million for 20 percent of director Ron Howard's production company, Imagine (*Cocoon* [1985], *Parenthood* [1989]), and served as the headquarters for director Steven Spielberg's Amblin Entertainment (*Raiders of the Lost Ark* [1981], *E.T.: The Extra-Terrestrial* [1982], *Back to the Future* [1985]). Disney maintained a partnership with Interscope (*Three Men and a Baby* [1987], *Cocktail* [1988]). Jerry Bruckheimer and Don Simpson enjoyed an exclusive production contract with Paramount that offered them offices on the studio's backlot and a $375,000 annual advance.[54]

These arrangements enabled Universal, Disney, and Paramount to develop movies on a cost-controlled basis and to offer a steady stream of releases. Columbia TriStar, which maintained non-exclusive "first look" deals that provided it with only first right of refusal on a star's project, enjoyed several hits after its purchase by Coca-Cola in 1982 (including *The Karate Kid* [1984; $90 million] and *The Karate Kid II* [1986; $115 million]) but subsequently faltered, in part because it lacked exclusive deals with major stars and directors.[55]

Reagan had long supported Hollywood's return to a system of organization in which key personnel worked under long-term contract to the major studios. In his 1989 autobiography, *An American Life*, Reagan argued that "each studio was like a big family" that gave Hollywood performers, writers, and directors a sense of belonging. The studio system also promoted choice. "You had seven companies who were always competing with each other to turn out a better movie than the guy down the street, and if people didn't like a picture, they'd show it by voting with their feet."[56]

The Reagan administration FCC similarly argued that the revision of federal regulations on media ownership promoted greater competition by providing more opportunities for independent production. Viewers, in turn, were to benefit from healthy rivalries between the film, television, and cable industries by enjoying more convenient access and greater programming diversity. The net effect of policy reform was ostensibly a better informed, more educated, and happier public.[57] In reality, the absorption of these media into multinational conglomerates provided the major studios with the distribution clout necessary to expand globally. Terry Semel, president of Warner Bros. studios in 1989, declared "we'll grow because there are fewer distributors able to bring product to the marketplace for theaters, cable, and television."[58]

Cable television proved to be a lucrative avenue of ancillary programming for Hollywood's major studios, generating annual revenues of $3 billion. The FCC's passage of Must-Carry rules requiring cable systems to carry every television station within their franchise areas, and the Prime Time Access Rule (PTAR), forcing the networks to open up one hour of prime-time programming each evening for affiliates, provided an additional shot in the arm for Hollywood by increasing demand for syndicated movies and series. Syndication prices skyrocketed, providing another windfall for those studios producing TV series.[59] Paramount, for example, drew record prices in 1984 for its off-network syndication of the 1950s-inspired television shows *Happy Days* and spin-off series like *Joanie Loves Chachi* and *Laverne & Shirley*.[60] The studio also earned $200 million in 1987 by syndicating *Cheers* and *Family Ties*, network television's number two and number three shows.[61]

The networks attempted to bolster their flagging profits and reverse cable television's growth by campaigning for repeal of the fin-syn rules, which had been instated in the early 1970s. While the major networks heavily lobbied the FCC for repeal of the fin-syn rules, the studios that had supported Reagan's political aspirations also weighed in with their own opinions. Opposed by the president and Congress, the FCC put off reconsideration of the rules until 1990.[62] The major networks' audience share eroded under the combined assault of videocassette and cable. The price of a VCR (videocassette recorder) fell by two-thirds between 1975 and 1985, making it almost as common as a television in the American living room. Providing an additional boost to the emerging videocassette industry and VCR sales was a 1984 Supreme Court ruling that home taping of television shows did not constitute a violation of copyright laws.[63] The networks so shriveled under the competition that in 1990 the three networks' combined portion of the prime-time television audience had dwindled to 65 percent.[64] As Pepsi's placement of an advertisement on the *Top Gun* videocassette revealed, advertisers increasingly utilized new media to propagate their messages as television networks experienced an ongoing loss of audience shares.[65]

The success of blockbuster movies with multimedia potential was the driving force behind Hollywood's economic recovery in the 1980s. Action-adventure blockbusters carved out new ancillary markets, while the expansion of the global entertainment market dramatically increased Hollywood's theatrical rentals and sent secondary markets like cable and home video into overdrive. *Lethal Weapon* became the second highest-selling video in Warner Home Video history, selling 38 million units in twenty-three months.[66] Reflecting the integrated structures of their parent companies and designed with the marketplace in mind, the flexibility of movies like *Lethal Weapon* as multimedia texts facilitated their distribution and exhibition across multiple release windows on the basis of carefully coordinated marketing and promotion campaigns.

Incumbent in Hollywood's focus on suburban multiplex, cable-television audiences was an attempt to make movies that appealed to this demographic while maintaining crossover appeal. The mass media serve as a seductive inducement to consume in a post-Fordist society in which the reproduction of capital depends on consumption more than production. While Reagan-era Hollywood focused on movie cycles with share-ability across multiple media and global audience appeal, its careful attunement to marketplace trends and its reliance on advertising and marketing to promote new movies was emblematic of a multinational corporate order's growing reliance on product evanescence for the reproduction of wealth.

Corporate wealth was reproduced in a Fordist economy through the manufacture and sale of durable goods and the use of advertising to conflate products with conformity to an emerging lifestyle of suburban affluence. In a post-Fordist economy, manufacturers attempt to stabilize fluctuations in consumer demand by accelerating consumption turnover times through a heavy reliance on advertising and promotion to both cultivate and capitalize on fleeting trends in consumption.[67] Hollywood's focus on movie narratives which promoted fleeting lifestyle trends and its marginalization of stories which couldn't be conceptualized in such terms was disturbing, given the media's historically pivotal role in promoting the free and open flow of information.

MULTIPLEXES

The successful theatrical release of a movie became integral during the 1980s for its subsequent success in secondary markets like cable television, videocassette, and overseas release. The Reagan administration's lax enforcement of antitrust laws enabled media conglomerates to purchase existing theater chains and build new ones. Gulf & Western purchased the Mann Theater chain of more than 350 screens in October 1986, and sold a 50 percent interest in it to Warner Communications the following year. While Warner, as well as MGM and Fox, had been barred from owning domestic theaters under the Paramount decree of 1948, the U.S. District Court provided the company with a modification that allowed Warner to acquire theaters as long as they were held by a separate subsidiary.[68] Under these conditions, the multiplex rapidly replaced the downtown movie theater over the 1980s. In 1980, there were 17,590 movie screens in the United States. By 1987, the total ballooned to 23,555 screens. In 1990, the number grew slightly to 23,689 screens.[69]

Ownership of a theater chain enabled the major studios to maximize the potential for a successful theatrical debut and retain the majority of its profits. Chains enabled the major studios to set admission prices, retain all box-office earnings rather than sharing them with exhibitors, and gain more direct market control over the retail end of the business by operating important circuits. As well, distributors gained more control over release patterns and did not have to bargain in adversarial ways with theater operators.[70]

Through theater ownership distributors also gained a means of circumventing anti–blind bidding laws in twenty-four states and dictating licensing terms to exhibitors.[71] The major studios' monopolistic control over first-run exhibition in large cities matters because cinema is a time-based business in which the newest films often have the greatest earning power. First-run theaters benefit from the movie audience's habit of seeking out the newest movies.

The major studios further strengthened their control of the first-run market during the 1980s through their aggressive replacement of large auditoriums with multiplexes. Movies that proved successful could be moved from a smaller to a larger auditorium while those that proved unsuccessful could be conversely moved from a larger to a smaller venue. According to Guback, however, the concentration of ownership of multiplexes in so few hands meant that there were simply more locations to view a handful of movies rather than more movies playing on more screens.[72]

The proliferation of locations in key suburban areas provided the major producer–distributors with virtual monopolies over the release of their movies in large urban areas, facilitating a strategy of saturation release that became indispensable in the 1980s for the marketing of blockbuster movies. The growing number of screens offered distributors the opportunity to achieve very broad release for some of their pictures.

E.T. grossed a staggering $12 million in a single weekend upon its nationwide release in June 1982. Box-office figures for the week of June 9, 1982, alone were $96.9 million, nearly double the figure of the previous year's opening summer week.[73] Released during winter, 1982, the A-list movies *Reds* and *Absence of Malice* made money, but were dwarfed by *Rocky III*'s gross of $49 million during its first three weeks of release. *Footloose* earned $8.5 million over the 1984 President's Day holiday weekend after opening in 1,384 theaters.[74] During its first twelve days of release at 2,326 theaters, *Beverly Hills Cop 2* sold $64 million worth of tickets.[75]

Hollywood's promotion and distribution of a handful of releases curtailed the variety of movies available to patrons. During the 1986 Christmas holiday, the five most widely distributed films played in a third of all theaters in the country. Five other pictures played in a quarter of the theaters.[76] It was on the basis of this saturation release strategy that Paramount claimed the three top movies of 1987 (*Beverly Hills Cop 2* [$153 million]; *Fatal Attraction* [$156 million]; and *The Untouchables* [$76 million]) and a 20 percent share of the U.S. market.[77] Sleeper releases, which needed time to develop an audience, benefited from exhibition in studio-owned or affiliated theaters that held them over after a slow opening weekend. The senior vice president of marketing and distribution for Vestron Pictures observed that while *Dirty Dancing* did not have a big opening weekend it was consistent in its box-office performance, dropping off slightly from week to week but never more than 10 percent in its worst week. Launched in 800 theaters across the United States in August 1987, the film was still playing in 156 theaters in March 1988.[78]

Vestron also struck a deal with the AMC Theater chain through which it got 150 of its 800 promotional screenings of *Dirty Dancing* free.[79] Guback summarized the implications of Reagan-era theater ownership and construction for independent chains showing alternative offerings by observing that the trend towards vertical integration would ultimately erode the bargaining power of independent chains in their negotiations with a distributor who owned a competing circuit.[80]

A single developer's ownership of many malls, sometimes all over America, also made it possible for a movie studio to achieve national exposure by dealing with just one or two companies. This pattern of national ownership also facilitated formal partnerships between developers and studios. Control by one conglomerate over movie production, distribution, and exhibition, and merchandise tie-in and licensing intensified the threat of one kind of movie being promoted and marketed for the mall environment and mall customers to the exclusion of other kinds. In July 1983, Twentieth Century Fox launched a promotion for *Return of the Jedi* in conjunction with Lucasfilm in 150 malls across the nation.[81]

Mallwide promotions held on a single day across the country also became a means of garnering free television news publicity. Warner Bros. rolled out a fifty-mall promotion in June 1983 for *Superman III* which included displays, merchandise, and prizes for Clark Kent and Lois Lane look-alike contests held on mall courts. Movie studios also garnered free publicity by coordinating radio station–sponsored ticket giveaways to attract customers to prerelease screenings in malls. Paramount promoted *Staying Alive* at selected malls by giving prerelease screening passes to the first fifty people who asked for them at a certain mall store after being alerted by a radio announcement.[82]

The mall multiplex's replacement of the downtown movie theater in the midst of this trend shaped Reagan-era Hollywood's construction of success ideology. As Justin Wyatt argues, high-concept cinema's emphasis on consumerism and lifestyle operates in recuperative fashion by defusing countercultural social trends identified by Reagan as threats to America's recovery of a mythical conservative past.[83] As an indigenous outgrowth of postwar suburbia, the mall similarly provides an environment in which shared rites of consumption unite a moviegoing audience of families and teenagers into a class-circumscribed community ostensibly free of the tainting effects of crime, juvenile delinquency, and other forms of immoral behavior.

During a reporter's visit to Minneapolis' Mall of America, the largest mall in North America, a surveillance camera apprehended a pair of bored shoppers fornicating in the front seat of a car in the parking lot. "If they want to have sex, they'll have to go elsewhere," a guard stated. "We don't have anything against sex, per se, but we don't want it happening in our parking lots."[84] In this way, the Mall of America represents a sanitized form of community interaction designed to satisfy consumers' acquisitive drives without burdening them with the larger panoply of activities, both disruptive and constructive, that typify public spaces. Reagan-era movies ranging from *An Officer and a Gentleman*, to *Dirty Dancing*, to *Immediate Family* (1989) similarly distinguish between a suburban morality of chaste, middle-class postadolescent sexuality and a deviant teen culture of casual sex, unplanned pregnancy, and abortion.

The mall itself is also "a kind of theater," *American Film* noted in 1983, "an image-filled place, designed to attract consumers and sell products and services to them."[85] In an environment engineered to promote consumption, movies achieved an uneasy resemblance to big-screen advertisements that targeted a carefully researched swath of consumers rather than a mass of moviegoers drawn from the general public. Market research revealed to *Star Wars* (1977) director George Lucas the existence of both adult and child audiences for the soundtrack album and toys advertised by the film. Appeals to family values of patriotism provided a means of reaching both audiences. In this way, *Star Wars* represented a return to values of heroism and old-fashioned individualism and "revived a kind of Manichean, back-to-basics moral fundamentalism suggestive of the Reagan era yet to come," observed Peter Biskind.[86]

CABLE TELEVISION

While the Hollywood studios initially saw cable as a competitor for movie production and distribution rights, the two entities ultimately recognized their mutual interdependence. In the late 1970s, Hollywood attempted to strangle the cable industry by withholding new movies from cable exhibition. However, cable television offered home exhibition of uncut movies twenty-four hours a day for the price of three or four movie tickets per month. Cable television's broadcast of studio-era Hollywood classics complemented its exhibition of new movies and promoted viewer familiarity with stars and directors. It thus represented a lucrative new avenue for studios seeking to maximize the shelf life of new movies and renew the lifespan of old studio-era classics.

It was because of these advantages that cable television operators and the major studios recognized that cooperation yielded greater long-range benefits than competition. The result was cable television's maturation into a horizontally and vertically integrated industry on the basis of cross-ownerships, distribution contracts, preproduction deals with movie studios, and shared ownership arrangements.[87] In 1984, for example, Paramount signed a contract with Showtime/The Movie Channel, Inc. that provided the programming service with exclusive pay cable rights to virtually every theatrical film the studio produced over the following five years. The contract was estimated to be worth between $600 million and $700 million for Paramount.[88] In this way, cable distribution became a means of cross-promoting new movie releases and of creating a subsequent release window for them. Vestron produced a six-minute documentary entitled "The Making of *Dirty Dancing*" that aired on HBO for two months during the film's theatrical exhibition.[89]

Vertical integration within the cable industry was complemented by horizontal integration of cable distribution outlets. The multiple system operators that own most cable franchises have large groups of subscribers. ATC (American Television and Communication), Time's vast franchise of cable systems around the U.S., controls a legal monopoly in each municipality from coast to coast. ATC has the sole right to deliver cable services into households in its franchise territory.[90] Telecommunications Inc. (TCI) holds a similar monopoly that commands nearly 5 million subscribers. TCI's subscriber base also consists of the same audiences that attend the suburban multiplexes that sprang up in the 1980s—well-placed suburban households highly valued by pay and basic cable companies and advertisers.[91]

A new vertically integrated structure arose as large companies like Time, Inc., Teleprompter, and Viacom financed and distributed programming to guaranteed exhibition outlets in monopolistic cable systems nationwide.[92] The competition from the new distribution technologies put enormous pressure on network profitability and on network managements that were historically unaccustomed to managing in a competitive environment.

Cable television, once a financially shaky, tightly regulated industry, became network TV's greatest competitor during the 1980s on the basis of its enormous economic influence over the mass communications industry.[93] Time, Inc. took in $1.5 billion in 1987 from its ownership of HBO and Cinemax, two of the top five pay television channels, and a share of Ted Turner's Broadcasting Service and the Black Entertainment Television cable channel.[94]

The FCC rationalized deregulation as a means of spurring innovation and creating greater viewer choice through healthy competition. However, cable's reliance on subscription revenues and its ability to guarantee prime demographic audiences to advertisers resulted in a glut of recycled and narrowly focused programming. Cable spokespeople countered that they introduced television classics to a new generation of viewers, noting that audiences often preferred them to network programming.[95] As pay-television channels established workable business relationships with the major studios, assuring a steady stream of big budget films for broadcast, they also became more conservative in their interactions with independent distributors.

While the initial cost of setting up a cable system is high, cable's initiation of very little programming and its relatively low equipment costs make ownership of a cable system a very profitable long-term endeavor. Cable operators retain a large portion of their subscription revenues (as much as 80 percent), while paying the remainder to program suppliers. Operators also profit from other revenues, including the sale of advertising, installation, converter and remote control rentals, pay-per-view, fees from shopping channels, expanded basic service, and other services.[96] With cable television's overseas expansion, advertising has become the fastest growing source of cable revenues, providing multinational manufacturers of goods and services with highly efficient means of creating new overseas markets for their products.

The FCC's placement of control over cable rates in the hands of large cable monopolies also enabled such operators to introduce tiered price structures. Tiered price structures offered the perception of choice while limiting programming to a narrow range of blockbuster hits, studio library holdings, and in-house-produced programming. In this way, the number of channels and program offerings on cable television proliferated while offering very little content diversity.

The FCC condoned this arrangement on the basis of the rationale that cable television's broadband method of transmission had ended spectrum scarcity. Surveys ostensibly designed to ferret out monopolistic conditions instead rationalized them by counting the number of distribution outlets and conduits in local markets rather than assessing the diversity of the content transmitted over cable.[97] While cable's establishment of cross-ownerships, exclusive distribution contracts, and preproduction deals with the major studios curtailed the diversity of its programming, studies of ownership patterns and consumer accessibility overlooked these considerations. More recent innovations in cable transmission have further promoted uneven access to new services and programming, given the high cost of wiring communities for cable television. Those communities unable to help shoulder the costs of such an investment are likely to be denied innovations in cable television on the basis of the industry's treatment of the public as consumers whose right to view is based on an ability to pay.

The homebound leisure culture of cable television viewing is traceable to the postwar era, during which Americans relocated from the city to the suburb. Incumbent in this trend was an attempt by the middle class to distance itself from the crowded mixture of races and classes that populated the nation's urban areas and to form communities of homeowners bound by shared habits of work and leisure. Reagan's familiarity to audiences as a postwar spokesman for a culture of suburban affluence and Cold War patriotism aligned him with this culture of leisure and relaxation.

Hollywood's focus on the suburban audiences with the rise of cable television resulted in movies that underscored these themes of class-circumscribed community. In *The Big Chill*, for example, countercultural holdover Nick (William Hurt) chastises Harold (Kevin Kline) for cajoling a local policeman into letting Nick go after he is apprehended for speeding. When Nick accuses Harold of selling out to the establishment, Harold responds that he is a homeowner and a member of the local community. "I'm dug in," he fires back. "And that cop has kept this house from getting ripped off."

HOME VIDEO

The concurrent introduction of cable and the VCR was significant in terms of each innovation's sales, growth, and cultivation of consumer buying behaviors. The major movie studios were at first threatened by video's potential for eroding the size of the theater audience and undercutting the cost of going to the movies. These fears seemed to be justified when the Supreme Court's decision to uphold the First Sale Doctrine in its disposition of a case between Universal and Sony gave rise to mom-and-pop video stores. The doctrine freed retailers to sell outright or rent a videotape to their customers. In short, the Supreme Court's decision affirmed the right of video shops to sell or rent the videotapes they stocked.[98] However, by 1980 all of the major Hollywood studios had created divisions or joint ventures to manufacture and distribute prerecorded entertainment, and they offered selected movie titles directly (or through various other distribution outlets, such as record stores) to consumers for $50 to $75 a title.[99] The major studios made purchase of presale rights for videocassette distribution of new movies a condition for the manufacture and sale of them on video.

It was through their control of distribution channels that the major studios influenced the terms of preproduction deals. During home video's infancy, independent producers often maintained control of video rights. As the major studios launched video distribution companies, however, home video rights became a standard component of distribution deals.[100] Early on, production companies like Vestron did very well by producing and distributing small films like *Dirty Dancing* because there was little competition for video rights. As the video store industry developed, however, consumers showed a primary interest in hits, favoring the major studios over smaller companies like Vestron.

Beverly Hills Cop 2, for example, racked up sales of 500,000 videocassettes in 1988, setting a new record for annual videocassette sales before being topped later in the year by *Three Men and a Baby*'s sale of 550,000 units. *Variety* observed in 1988 that only a year earlier it had been widely believed that higher-priced A-list titles could not sell more than 300,000 units annually.[101] The major studios often launched the videocassette release of A-list titles with huge multi-million dollar promotions. Pepsi and MCA, for example, teamed up to put $25 million worth of promotion behind *E.T.*[102] Vestron was unable to marshal the resources necessary to make and promote A-list movies and began laying off employees in 1987 and went out of business completely in 1991.

Home video rights became increasingly profitable as the major studios' retail video outlets focused on blockbuster and A-list titles and audience demand for these titles escalated. By 1988, those films grossing over $10 million at the box office (almost always distributed by the major studios) represented 70 percent of wholesale video revenues.[103] The major studios' concentration on acquiring the distribution rights to hits provided fewer and fewer film producers with more and more production capital. *Video Marketing Newsletter* reported in 1986 that 45 percent of all revenue received by a film producer was from the video marketplace.[104] In 1984, for example, *Supergirl's* North American rights sold for $3.25 million and CBS/Fox Video bought video rights to *The Empire Strikes Back* for $15 million.[105]

The major studios also achieved dominance in the emerging sell-through market of videocassette sales through tie-in deals that offset their cost, enabling them to encourage volume sales by cutting prices. *Sell-through* refers to a strategy whereby video distributors capitalize on demand for a particular videocassette title by enabling audiences to own it for an affordable price. A tie-in deal between Paramount and Pepsi, for example, enabled the studio to offer *Top Gun* in 1986 for $26.95 instead of $29.95. By the end of 1987, nearly three million units had been sold, and according to *Variety* the movie had " . . . reestablished the viability of low-priced blockbuster films and made sure the industry's first major experiment with a commercial on a film cassette was a huge success."[106] Cable television, videocassette, and soundtrack album sales exploded after Paramount offered a so-called double take discount that allowed *Top Gun's* pay-per-view price of $4.00 to $4.50 to be applied to the purchase price of the videocassette or CBS Records soundtrack. Participating cable operators were offered the videocassette at a wholesale price that enabled them to profitably package the *Top Gun* deal.[107] Nestlé's placed an advertisement prior to the beginning of *Dirty Dancing*. Jeep did the same with *Platoon* (1987). Research found that consumers were receptive to tie-ins, especially when they lowered the price of the tape.[108]

Although a lower price necessarily meant diminished revenue on a per-unit basis, the sell-through strategy offset this result through greater overall volume sales of the same title. The sell-through approach thus worked best for hit blockbuster movies.[109] With home video so prevalent, theaters that specialized in showing revival pictures or movies made at Hollywood's margins were forced to close or change their formats. One estimate concluded that the 200 movie houses in the United States in 1980 that showed revival fare had dwindled to a mere 15 sites by 1987.[110] The major studios' advantages of buying power, inventory rotation, shared advertising costs, and direct dealings with suppliers resulted in their domination of video retailing by the mid-1980s and distinct signs of horizontal integration.[111]

With the maturation of the video industry, video stores completed their purchases of older titles and library material, leading them to focus on the acquisition of blockbusters and A-titles in a strategy that proved highly advantageous to the major studios.[112] It was estimated that by the end of the 1980s, A-titles constituted 77 percent of the movies ordered each month by video store owners.[113] The biggest cable franchises also dominated investment in video store chains. Telecommunications, Inc. (TCI) and Cox Enterprises invested in Blockbuster stores, concentrating ownership of local cable outlets, theaters, and video outlets.[114]

The proliferation of VCRs in the home fueled demand for videocassettes. A 1988 report by pollster Lou Harris reveals that VCR ownership had increased 234 percent during the previous four-year period examined by the study. Bruce Austin also reveals that American households watched 6 billion hours of prerecorded video in 1988 and 221 billion hours of broadcast television in 1988. An executive at Columbia Pictures noted that the VCR had opened up an over-thirty audience for movie entertainment typified by "the couple with two infants who cannot get out. . . . We are making movies for them. They will not go to movie theaters," he observed.[115]

INDEPENDENT TELEVISION STATIONS

While the video industry and cable promoted each other's growth, the introduction of Must-Carry rules gave rise to hundreds of new independent television stations across America. Must-Carry rules required cable systems to carry every television station within their franchise areas regardless of the station's ratings and whether it duplicated another network or PBS affiliate. Must-Carry rules thus encouraged the startup of new UHF independent stations because owners of weak-signaled stations could improve transmission distance and quality through their carriage on cable systems.[116]

Independent television station owners gained immediate influence by buying stations in key urban markets. In 1985, Australian Rupert Murdoch's purchase of the former Metromedia chain of six television stations located in large urban areas gave him immediate coverage of more than 18 percent of all homes with television sets in the U.S. The markets under Murdoch's control included New York City (the largest U.S. television market), Los Angeles (second largest), Chicago (third), Dallas (eighth), Washington, DC (ninth), and Houston (tenth).[117]

Murdoch's purchase of the chain occurred weeks after his co-purchase of Twentieth Century Fox with oilman Marvin Davis, who sold his half-interest in the studio to his partner only months later. Murdoch's purchase of Twentieth Century Fox enabled him to use the company's film library and its film and television production endeavors to feed both his embryonic fourth TV network and his European satellite Sky Channel. On the average, satellite distribution costs 30% of normal television transmission, and even less than theatrical distribution.[118]

Twentieth Century Fox's assured access to key metropolitan audiences through its Metromedia stations and Sky Channel provided the conglomerate with additional advantages. In order to rent programs to nonnetwork TV stations, a studio like Fox must finance the show and then sell it on the basis of its prospective ability to generate viewer ratings. Rental undertakings are risky and may yield little profit. Assured access to key metropolitan audiences through Metromedia stations and the Sky Channel removed a great deal of the risk for Fox. A network of independent stations also provided an adequate basis for selling national advertising time.[119]

In this way, Murdoch's vertical integration of a production facility and movie library, a distribution network, and a series of delivery outlets reduced risk and costs. By vertically integrating, Fox no longer had to worry about being shut out of New York, Los Angeles, or four other major U.S. media markets. Murdoch horizontally integrated his planned film and television operations with his 1988 purchase of thirteen business and trade publications from Ziff-Davis, his introduction of U.S. and U.K. versions of *Elle*, the French fashion magazine, and his reformulation of the *Star* tabloid's look and content.[120]

Movie studios often coordinated promotional campaigns with independent stations by distributing electronic press kits to them for airing. Vestron sent out 150 such promotions for *Dirty Dancing* to major television markets and stations. Research reports indicated that 40 percent of the kits were used upon the movie's release and that subsequent airings occurred as the film became a box-office hit.[121] Paramount's coproduction of *Entertainment Tonight* and *Solid Gold* similarly enabled it to cross-promote new movies and hit soundtrack songs from its movies on network television.[122]

Paramount gained access to network television by coproducing *Entertainment Tonight* and *Solid Gold* with two independent television station groups, Cox Broadcasting and Taft, enabling the studio to launch a promotional campaign of fifteen-second TV advertising spots six months before its release of *Beverly Hills Cop 2*. These spots proved integral to its huge first-weekend gross over the four-day Memorial Day weekend.

Other conglomerates bought independent stations in large markets. Universal bought the powerful New York independent station WWOR (not affiliated with one of the three networks), found on many cable systems. Disney also bought a similarly large independent, KHJ, based in Los Angeles. The price of stations rose accordingly, further limiting entry into the television industry to investors with the resources to acquire stations and develop programming and distribution.[123] Independent television stations, like cable TV and videocassette, thus became another avenue for exhibiting studio libraries and recent A-list and blockbuster movies.

The growing importance of shareability between television and movies created by this trend resulted in Hollywood's focus on presold television stars with proven appeal to audiences valued by advertisers. Eddie Murphy's familiarity to television audiences as a cast member of the otherwise all-white *Saturday Night Live* resulted in his makeover into a movie star carefully situated in comedy roles in which his abbreviated standup routines were extended into two-hour stories in which he was similarly cast in white cultural settings. MTV music video movies were similarly a modular series of montages, inspired by TV commercials, that sold chic lifestyle trends on the basis of a carefully coordinated match of music and image. Michael J. Fox was elevated from the star of *Family Ties* to A-list movies such as *Back to the Future* and *The Secret of My Success.* Yuppie movies invited viewers to indulge in fantasies of suburban utopia conceptualized in terms of advertising-inspired lifestyle trends.

NOTES

1. John Izod, *Hollywood and the Box Office, 1895–1986* (New York: Columbia University Press, 1988), 20–109.

2. Jeanne Thomas Allen, "The Decay of the Motion Picture Patents Company," *The American Film Industry,* ed. Tino Balio (Madison: University of Wisconsin Press, 1976), 123.

3. Kristin Thompson, *Exporting Entertainment* (London: British Film Institute, 1985), 62.

4. Izod, *Hollywood and the Box Office,* 63.

5. Thompson, *Exporting Entertainment,* 28.

6. Steven Vaughn, *Ronald Reagan in Hollywood: Movies and Politics* (New York: Cambridge University Press, 1994), 194.

7. Ibid., 195.

8. Ibid., 196.

9. Ibid., 201.

10. Izod, *Hollywood and the Box Office,* 117.

11. Vaughn, *Ronald Reagan,* 200.

12. Thomas H. Guback, "Hollywood's International Market," *The American Film Industry,* ed. Tino Balio (Madison: University of Wisconsin Press, 1976), 397.

13. Izod, *Hollywood and the Box Office,* 159.

14. Ibid., 160.

15. Ibid.

16. Guback, "Hollywood's International Market," 408.

17. Vaughn, *Ronald Reagan,* 130.

18. Ibid., 140.

19. Jon Lewis, "Money Matters: Hollywood in the Corporate Era," *The New American Cinema,* ed. Jon Lewis (Durham: Duke University Press, 1998), 89.

20. David F. Prindle, *The Politics of Glamour: Ideology and Democracy in the Screen Actors Guild* (Madison: University of Wisconsin Press, 1988), 78.

21. Ibid., 79.

22. Dan E. Moldea, *Dark Victory: Ronald Reagan, MCA, and the Mob* (New York: Viking Penguin, 1986), 142.

23. Garry Wills, *Reagan's America: Innocents at Home* (Garden City, N.Y.: Doubleday, 1987), 266.

24. Ibid.

25. Ibid.

26. Moldea, *Dark Victory,* 268–269.

27. Wills, *Reagan's America,* 304.

28. Tino Balio, "Introduction to Part I," *Hollywood in the Age of Television,* ed. Tino Balio (Boston: Unwin Hyman, 1990), 40.

29. Jon Lewis, "Money Matters: Hollywood in the Corporate Era," *The New American Cinema,* ed. Jon Lewis (Durham: Duke University Press, 1998), 90.

30. Justin Wyatt, "Marketing/Distribution Innovations," *The New American Cinema,* ed. Jon Lewis (Durham: Duke University Press, 1998), 75.

31. Ibid.

32. Robert B. Ray, *A Certain Tendency of the Hollywood Cinema, 1930–1980* (Princeton, N.J.: Princeton University Press, 1985), 310.

33. Michael Ryan and Douglas Kellner, *Camera Politica: The Politics of Ideology in Contemporary Hollywood Film* (Bloomington: Indiana University Press, 1988), 79.

34. Tino Balio, "Introduction to Part II," *Hollywood in the Age of Television,* ed. Tino Balio (Boston: Unwin Hyman, 1990), 260–261.

35. Thomas Guback, "Government Financial Support to the Film Industry in the United States," *Current Research in Film: Audiences, Economics, and Law,* Vol. 3, ed. Bruce A. Austin (Norwood, N.J.: Ablex Publishing Corporation, 1987), 100.

36. Ibid., 101.

37. Ibid.

38. Ibid.

39. Ibid.

40. David F. Prindle, *Risky Business: The Political Economy of Hollywood* (Boulder: Westview Press, 1993), 36.

41. Thomas Schatz, "The New Hollywood," *Film Theory Goes to the Movies,* ed. Jim Collins, Hilary Radner, and Ava Preacher Collins (New York: Routledge, 1993), 21.

42. Robert Britt Horwitz, *The Irony of Regulatory Reform: The Deregulation of American Telecommunications* (New York: Oxford University Press, 1989), 245.

43. Erik Barnouw, *Tube of Plenty: The Evolution of American Television,* 2nd ed. (New York: Oxford University Press, 1990), 484.

44. Thomas Byrne Edsall, *The New Politics of Inequality* (New York: W.W. Norton, 1984), 116.

45. Wills, *Reagan's America,* 365.

46. Edsall, *The New Politics,* 116.

47. Garry Wills, "It's His Party," *The New York Times Magazine,* 11 August 1996, 52.

48. Thomas Guback, "Patterns of Ownership and Control in the Motion Picture Industry," *Journal of Film and Video* (winter 1986): 19.

49. Tom Nicholson, David T. Friendly, and Peter McAlevey, "Hollywood's Socko Summer," *Newsweek,* 28 June 1982, 63.

50. Ronald Grover, "Paramount's Hot Streak is Untouchable—For Now," *Business Week,* 14 September 1987, 153.

51. Douglas Gomery, "The Reagan Record," *Screen* (winter/spring 1989): 94.

52. Ibid.

53. Barnouw, *Tube of Plenty,* 510.

54. Frank Lipsius and Christopher Lorenz, "Small Unit Style for Making Big Films," *The Financial Times Limited,* 2 January 1985, 22.

55. Aljean Harmetz, "Now Showing: Survival of the Fittest," *New York Times,* 22 October 1989, sec. H1.

56. Ronald Reagan, *An American Life* (New York: Simon & Schuster, 1990), 117.

57. Janet Wasko, *Hollywood in the Information Age: Beyond the Silver Screen* (Austin: University of Texas Press, 1994), 5.

58. Harmetz, "Now Showing: Survival of the Fittest," sec. H1.

59. Thomas Schatz, "The New Hollywood," *Film Theory Goes to the Movies,* ed. Jim Collins, Hilary Radner, and Ava Preacher Collins (New York: Routledge, 1993), 21.

60. "Paramount's Program for Success: Program for Many Media," *Broadcasting,* 16 January 1984, 90.

61. Grover, "Paramount's Hot Streak," 153.

62. Prindle, *Risky Business,* 40.

63. J. Hoberman, "Ten Years That Shook the World," *American Film,* June 1985, 59.

64. Ronald V. Bettig, "Who Owns Prime Time? Industrial and Institutional Conflict over Television Programming and Broadcast Rights," in *Framing Friction: Media and Social Conflict,* ed. Mary S. Mander (Urbana: University of Illinois Press, 1999), 148.

65. Dennis Hunt, "'Top Gun': Pepsi Ad Fires First Shot," *Los Angeles Times,* 23 January 1987, sec. 6, 1.

66. PR Newswire Association, "Blockbuster Sequel 'Lethal Weapon 2' Crashes into Home Video Feb 8 at $24.98 Suggested List Price," 13 November 1989.

67. David Harvey, *The Condition of Postmodernity* (Boston: Basil Blackwell, 1989), 156.

68. Thomas Guback, "The Evolution of the Motion Picture Theater Business in the 1980s," *Journal of Communication* 37, no. 2 (1987): 73.

69. Will Tusher, "Nation's Screen Tally Reached a New High in '90," *Variety,* 28 January 1991, 3.

70. Guback, "The Evolution of the Motion Picture Theater Business in the 1980s," 73.

71. Ibid., 76.

72. Ibid., 72.

73. Nicholson et al. "Hollywood's Socko Summer," 63.

74. Southwestern Newswire, "Paramount Pictures' Motion Picture Division Sets New High for February Box Office Totals, Grosses $13 million," 23 February 1984.

75. Aljean Harmetz, "Figuring Out the Fates of 'Cop II' and 'Ishtar,'" *New York Times*, 4 June 1987, sec. C1.

76. Guback, "The Evolution of the Motion Picture Theater Business," 75.

77. Joe Mandese, "Hollywood's Top Gun," *Media & Marketing Decisions*, March 1988, 109.

78. Michael Wiese, *Film & Video Marketing* (Ann Arbor, Mich.: Braun-Brumfield, 1989), 173.

79. Ibid., 178.

80. Guback, "The Evolution of the Motion Picture Theater Business in the 1980s," 72.

81. William Severini Kowinski, "The Malling of the Movies," *American Film*, September 1983, 53.

82. Ibid.

83. Justin Wyatt, *High Concept: Movies and Marketing in Hollywood* (Austin: University of Texas Press, 1994), 195.

84. David Guterson, "Enclosed. Encyclopedic. Endured." In *Harper's*, August 1993, 55.

85. Kowinski, "The Malling of the Movies," 55.

86. Peter Biskind, "Blockbuster: The Last Crusade," *Seeing Through Movies*, ed. Mark Crispin Miller (New York: Pantheon Books, 1990), 118.

87. Wasko, *Hollywood in the Information Age*, 80.

88. "Paramount's Formula for Success," 90.

89. Wiese, *Film & Video Marketing*, 158.

90. Wasko, *Hollywood in the Information Age*, 309.

91. Ibid.

92. Ibid., 80.

93. Ibid.

94. Gomery, "The Reagan Record," 94.

95. Wasko, *Hollywood in the Information Age*, 73.

96. Ibid.

97. Ibid.

98. Bruce A. Austin, "Home Video: The Second-Run 'Theater' of the 1990s," *Hollywood in the Age of Television*, ed. Tino Balio (Boston: Unwin Hyman, 1990), 329.

99. Ibid., 331.

100. Tom Bierbaum, "Year of Growth for Homevid; Eyed $10-Bil in Retail Biz," *Variety*, 11–17 January 1989, 89.

101. Ibid.

102. Ibid., 333.

103. Wasko, *Hollywood in the Information Age*, 138.

104. Eric Gelman et al., "The Video Revolution," *Newsweek*, 6 August 1984, 50.

105. Wasko, *Hollywood in the Information Age,* 135.

106. Business Wire, Inc., "Paramount Pictures Television Group Will Promote Pay-Per-View and Videocassette Sales Simultaneously," 24 February 1987.

107. Austin, "Home Video," 341.

108. Ibid., 338.

109. Ibid., 340.

110. Ibid., 341.

111. Austin, "Home Video," 336.

112. Ibid., 340.

113. Ibid., 342.

114. Ibid.

115. Austin, "Home Video," 342.

116. Douglas Gomery, "Vertical Integration, Horizontal Regulation: The Growth of Rupert Murdoch's US Media Empire," *Screen* 27, no. 3–4 (1986): 80.

117. Ibid., 153.

118. Gomery, "The Reagan Record," 93

119. Gomery, "Vertical Integration, Horizontal Regulation," 80.

120. Ibid., 81.

121. Weise, *Film & Video Marketing,* 157.

122. "Paramount's Program for Success: Program for Many Media," 90.

123. Gomery, "The Reagan Record," 95.

Chapter 3

Reagan-Era Hollywood and the Recuperation
of the Success Ethic

While institutional changes in Hollywood shaped Reagan-era cinema's ideological recuperation of the success myth, the shift toward conservative race, gender, and class themes in movies of the 1980s was also a product of shifting cultural conditions. According to Wood, *The Texas Chainsaw Massacre* (1974), *Taxi Driver*, and *Cruising* (1980) are all incoherent texts that sprang from a breakdown in American cultural identity during the era of the Vietnam War and Watergate. During the late 1970s and early 1980s, however, the blockbuster movies of George Lucas and Steven Spielberg papered over the fissures and cracks created by the counterculture, gay rights, and feminist movements, encouraging audiences to buy into constructions of success that celebrated themes of reassurance and renewal, themes promoted by President Reagan.[1]

Ryan and Kellner observe that the period of the late 1960s to the early 1980s exemplifies a progression from film's role as a bearer of radical possibilities in form and content to its role as a symbolic restorer of conservative values. Three movements, they write, demarcate the ideological shifts that occurred between the late 1960s and early 1980s: "the fruition and further vicissitudes of the social movements of the sixties, the failure of liberalism in the seventies, and the triumph of conservatism in the eighties."[2]

A key influence on Reagan-era cinema's symbolic recuperation of the success ethic was the high-concept mode of production embraced by Hollywood during the 1980s. High concept's emphasis on product differentiation was linked to the rise of industry conglomeration. Product differentiation resulted in a focus on marketplace tastes that wedded self-conscious aesthetic style with a highly exploitable storyline. In the wake of *The Big Chill* (1983), *The Breakfast Club* (1985) was dubbed "The Little Chill" on the basis of its recontextualization of the former movie's premise for a teenage audience. While both movies explored rites of communal bonding between groups united by shared musical tastes and coming-of-age experiences, their choices of age-appropriate settings, stars, and soundtrack songs exemplified their attempts to appeal to differing market segments. While the characters' consumption habits and musical tastes can be read as a form of bonding between family members, these habits of conspicuous consumption are also representative of a sense of community defined in terms of shared lifestyle.

The function of movies as ritualistic affirmations of values such as family provides a means of exploring how popular movies yoke generic form and ideology. Restoration of the community's stability through the symbolic affirmation of ideals such as the family is one way in which genres of integration, such as the musical and the screwball comedy, and genres of order, such as the western, the gangster movie, and the detective movie, achieve narrative closure.[3] The differing treatments of the theme of middle-class ideological reproduction from one generation to the next across genres is attributable to the intersecting influences of an auteur with a specific artistic vision and a prevailing constellation of cultural themes.[4]

Different genres thus represent different narrative strategies for dealing with common ideological conflicts within the success ethic. Genres of order and genres of integration dramatize these tensions through their exploration of race, gender, and class differences between principal characters. Genres of order like the sports success movie and the detective movie focus on a single protagonist, usually male, who resolves conflicts between opposing value systems through the violent elimination of a threat to the social order.[5]

Genres of integration such as the musical, the screwball comedy, and the family melodrama focus on a couple or collective, usually dominated by the female, and trace the integration of the central characters into a familial community. However, considerable overlap exists between these categories. Genres of order address the possibility of social integration by exploring the politics of the lone hero's compromise of his individuality through his temporary assimilation into the community. Genres of integration similarly explore the conflicts and frictions between members of the community that ultimately must be resolved for social order to be restored.[6] Their celebration of these themes historically has made them powerful mediators of contradictions within the success ethic.

COUNTERCULTURAL REVOLUTION

During the late 1960s and early 1970s, a confluence of factors in Hollywood and American culture provided an opportunity for the dramatization of progressive screen images of race, gender, and class relations. As part of Hollywood's attempt to appeal to an increasingly youthful audience attuned to the anti–Vietnam War movement, the civil rights movement, and the drug culture of the 1960s, filmmakers self-consciously explored genres of the studio era in order to address changing tensions in cultural relations. Incumbent in this process of evolution was an innovative interrogation of generic form and content that resulted in the genre movie's self-conscious criticism of the ideological assumptions underlying its stylistic form and narrative content.[7]

John Cawelti's influential essay on the generic transformation of studio-era film genres is instructive in its delineation of various modes of self-conscious critique. According to Cawelti, four modes of burlesque and parody subvert generic form and content in movies. In each of these modes, elements of a convention or formula are situated in altered contexts that use ironic commentary or an inversion of audience expectation to provoke reflection on the ideological underpinnings of classic film genres.[8] While Cawelti traces these storytelling devices to Greek tragedy and nineteenth-century literary classics, their usage as devastating critiques of dominant political, economic, and cultural beliefs in movies of the late 1960s and early 1970s provides a striking instance of their ongoing viability.

Equally striking during the countercultural era was the openness of audiences to devastating critiques of modern political and ideological institutions. Stars and directors in touch with a burgeoning youth movement were able to score box-office hits consistently during a period in which costly epics and musicals, approved by an old-line generation of studio heads, flopped. In paying homage to both classical Hollywood genres and European cinema's personal style of filmmaking, directors Arthur Penn, Robert Altman, and Francis Ford Coppola deconstructed the ideological assumptions of studio-era genres in a period of cultural upheaval during which audiences widely questioned inherited norms of success. Made for modest sums, these movies gained critical acclaim and appealed to an increasingly youthful audience. While Hollywood did not devote serious attention to market demographics until the 1970s, Jim Hillier writes that a 1957 survey revealed that 52 percent of the moviegoing audience was under twenty, and 72 percent was under twenty-nine. Thus, a group that constituted only 40 percent of the country's whole population constituted at the time about three-quarters of the moviegoing public.[9]

Of integral importance to Hollywood's often explicit portrayal of the counterculture movement of the 1960s was the replacement of the production code with a ratings system in 1968 by the Motion Picture Association of America (MPAA). In two decisions handed down the same day (*Ginsberg v. New York, Interstate Circuit v. Dallas*), the U.S. Supreme Court ruled that local communities could establish their own censorship guidelines regulating the definition of obscenity. The decision immediately prompted the MPAA to introduce a ratings system (G, PG, R, X) in order to provide guidelines for lawmakers and movie audiences.

By clearly distinguishing films from one another in terms of potentially objectionable content, Hollywood hoped to preclude any attempts by local governments to establish their own censorship guidelines. Conversely, the ratings system widened the definition of acceptable content by providing categories for films that never would have received seals of approval in the past.[10] Filmmakers used this leeway to differentiate their product from the more strictly regulated shows on television.[11] In this way, countercultural constructions of genre challenged the ideological assumptions inherent in genres ranging from the screwball comedy to the western.

Screwball comedies of the studio era celebrated the family as a self-sufficient unit in which a son's achievement of hard-earned respect from a real or surrogate father figure dissolved differences between generations, and marriage united men and women into a community. *The Graduate* challenged this construction of gender and class relations by openly criticizing inherited middle-class norms of success. *Bonnie and Clyde* similarly dissected the gangster movie's romanticization of violence. Revising the conventions of the road movie and the western, *Easy Rider* self-consciously undercut assumptions about the relationship between freedom and individualism espoused by these genres.

A commercially successful cycle of movies about urban black culture also reworked and recast traditionally white stories, plots, and character types for African-American audiences, addressing the concerns of the Black Nationalist community in the early 1970s in unprecedented fashion. Critics of this cycle complained that because whites directed movies such as *Black Caesar* (1972), they merely perpetuated stereotypes of black as pimps, drug dealers, and criminals. However, the popularity of blaxploitation with an underserved black audience revealed that the genre's dramatization of the black criminal as a heroic outlaw resonated with countercultural youth. *Variety* estimated that 70 percent of the rental income of Ossie Davis's *Cotton Comes to Harlem* (1970) came from black audiences, whereas only 30 percent of the audiences for crossover vehicles like *In the Heat of the Night* (1967) were black.[12] The box-office success of *Shaft* (1971), *Sweet Sweetback's Baadasssss Song*, and *Superfly* (1972), albeit modest by contemporary standards, confirmed the marketability of movies with urban black themes and characters to inner-city audiences. The commercial success of these movies led to the assertion that it was possible to make movies specifically for black audiences without worrying too much about what the rest of the public would think.[13]

While *Bonnie and Clyde*, *The Graduate*, and *Easy Rider* were critical hits that yielded modest revenues during their theatrical debuts, they failed to pull Hollywood from a steady downward spiral in box-office receipts that resulted in a film industry recession in 1969. Under these conditions, the major studios retrenched. Hollywood learned from the recession that attendance had stabilized in size, that a handful of annual releases garnered the majority of box-office receipts, and that defensive production and marketing tactics were necessary to maximize these movies' box-office potential.[14]

By the early 1970s, the waning popularity of youth pictures resulted in their eclipse by movies with greater appeal to multiple audience segments. Hollywood's focus on crossover audiences was motivated by the proliferation of suburban multiplexes, the expansion of the black middle class with the opportunities created by the civil rights movement, and network television's focus on thematically black programs. Surveys revealed that as much as 35 percent of the audience for the blockbuster hits *The Godfather* ($134 million) and *The Exorcist* (1973; $204 million) was black.[15] The box-office success of *The Godfather II* (1974; $102 million) also revealed that audiences were most interested in blockbuster movies based on presold properties and heavy promotion on television.

Jaws' (1975) commercial success signaled the reinvention of movie genres as multimedia texts marketable to multiple audience segments on the basis of the carefully coordinated mobilization of theatrical exhibition, cable television, videocassette, and network TV advertising. *Jaws'* focus on the threat to society posed by a monster, which weakens social institutions and emasculates traditional authorities by threatening a seaside town's tourist trade, summarized the spirit of other crisis films of the 1970s ranging from *Dirty Harry* (1971) to *Network* (1976). While acknowledging the breakdown of middle-class institutions such as the family, the white-collar workplace, and the government, vigilante crime dramas, detective movies, westerns, and corporate conspiracy movies also contained an implicit longing for redemptive leadership in these areas. Inherent in the vigilante crime dramas *Dirty Harry* and *Death Wish* (1974) are both criticisms of the outlaw who restores community order and celebrations of vigilante cops and fathers as lone upholders of law and order in decaying cities overtaken by black street hoods, drug dealers, and countercultural terrorists.[16] However, these films' right-wing critiques of liberal laws which protect criminals at the community's expense were simultaneously dependent upon their acknowledgement of a disintegrating society in which problems had grown so complex that individuals were no longer capable of rectifying them.[17]

THE REBIRTH OF CONSERVATISM

The box-office popularity of the modestly budgeted *Rocky* reveals that by 1976 viewers were tiring of downbeat stories about the collapse of individual autonomy amid a pervasive system of public and private economic and cultural corruption. Shot on a meager $1 million budget, *Rocky* was a dark horse that metamorphosed into a runaway box-office smash on the basis of Sylvester Stallone's canny exploitation of a culture of bicentennial pride, white backlash against the civil rights initiatives of the 1960s, and humble economic expectations associated with President Jimmy Carter's emphasis on resource conservation. Stallone effectively intertwined his own story of rags-to-riches struggle in Hollywood with *Rocky*'s second-chance shot at self-respect and economic mobility.[18] Insisting that downbeat movies had run their course, Stallone predicted that all his future movies would be uplifting stories about heroes who redeem fundamental American success values.

Rocky's box-office popularity was attributable to its celebration of national renewal, a theme declared by the born-again Jimmy Carter in his bid for the presidency. Carter focused on the country's need for spiritual rebirth in a standard speech about a government as good as its people, and juxtaposed himself with Nixon by stressing the importance of character. By 1978, however, Carter's public approval ratings had plummeted as the silent majority's tolerance of liberal criticism evolved into a triumphant, conservative reaffirmation of success values like meritocracy, black integration into a dominant white society, and women's reembrace of the roles of wife and mother.[19]

Carter espoused a populist Democratic agenda that advocated government reform of the automobile industry, the cultivation of new energy sources as alternatives to foreign oil, and limited involvement in foreign military affairs. An ally of integrationist civil rights leader Andrew Young, Carter was popular among the black middle class that arose following the implementation of affirmative action. Carter's election revealed him to be the direct beneficiary of the rise of a New South that arose in the wake of the Johnson administration's elimination of racial segregation and implementation of Great Society reform programs. As Lester Maddox's gubernatorial successor in Georgia, Carter stood in direct contrast to an Old South based on Reconstruction-era racism and Jim Crow laws. As the one-term governor of Georgia, Carter was also perceived as an outsider untainted by Washington scandal.

Rocky's resituation of the black and white buddy motif in a 1940s sports success melodrama romanticized the Carter culture of downscale economic expectations amid economic recession and energy conservation. The title character's goal of simply "going the distance" against the black champion Apollo Creed was an endorsement of simple survival rather than over-the-top triumph. However, *Rocky* also anticipated an emerging culture of Reagan-era racial conservatism by romanticizing its working-class hero as a symbol of traditional American values that had been left behind by a leftward-leaning counterculture.[20] Inherent in this inflection of race relations was the suggestion that interracial harmony stems from minority self-help and marketplace talent rather than affirmative action or welfare.

President Carter's rhetoric paralleled the writings of culture critics like Christopher Lasch and Tom Wolfe, who termed the 1970s the "me decade." Carter argued that Americans' self-indulgence in hedonistic consumerism threatened the nation's moral purpose and sense of resolve. *Saturday Night Fever* explored this tension by romanticizing a 1970s culture of sexual liberation while simultaneously predicating Tony Manero's maturation on his concern for his future. The movie's glorification of disco life and the culture of celebrity ignited a dance club craze across the country among young singles.

The condemnation of traditional norms of masculinity in liberal incarnations of the war movie and studies of working-class ethnic culture reflected the popularization of a so-called new man in movies of the mid-to-late 1970s. Also presaging a critical examination of men and women's traditional roles within the family was the visibility of the gay rights movement. While *Saturday Night Fever* disassociated disco culture from its countercultural origins in New York's underground gay nightclub scene, it simultaneously condemned traditional working-class masculinity as a form of familial dysfunctionality fed by the pressures of capitalism. When Tony gets a raise, his laid-off construction worker father vents his frustration as a breadwinner by belittling him. Burdened by Catholic guilt, Tony's mother cries when her other son, "Father Frank," fails to call her. Only in his relationship with Stephanie does Tony find a sense of freedom that liberates him from the constrictions imposed by working-class definitions of what it means to be a man.

Traditional gender roles are called into question in *Girl Friends* (1978) when a friendship between two women is destroyed when one of them marries and is forced by the demands of home, husband, and child to reorganize her priorities.[21] *Girl Friends* takes up a marriage-versus-career theme typical of the woman's melodrama, yet ends with a rueful contemplation of the formation of the heterosexual couple rather than an affirmative celebration of it. Marriage becomes "patriarchy's means of containing and separating women," according to Wood. *Chilly Scenes of Winter* (1980) also resurrects the "comedy of remarriage" genre but reconfigures it in unexpected ways. In studio-era examples of the genre like *The Awful Truth* (1937) and *Philadelphia Story* (1940), the reunion of the estranged couple is guaranteed from the outset because they're already married when we meet them.[22] In *Chilly Scenes,* however, the female lead rejects both the ex-husband and a rival suitor.[23]

Fast Times at Ridgemont High (1982) also constructs for the female viewer a spectator position that avoids both subordination and masochism.[24] Wood suggests that while most examples of this coming-of-age teen comedy genre are obsessed with male sexual desire and anxieties, *Fast Times* explores young women's desires and criticisms of male presumption. Mark's (Brian Backer) romantic pursuit of Stacey (Jennifer Jason Leigh) becomes an exploration of his sexual reticence as a virgin rather than a hypermasculine fantasy of getting laid and becoming a man.[25]

The critical and commercial drubbing dealt to Michael Cimino's *Heaven's Gate* has in retrospect often been cited as a pivotal moment in the filmed entertainment industry's condemnation of artistically ambitious film school auteurs and a return to a culture of bottom-line cost consciousness in its choice of which films to make and release. According to Peter Biskind, however, *Heaven's Gate* was merely a watershed symbol of changes that had been building since *The Godfather*'s illustration of the importance of promoting a movie on the basis of a presold literary property and saturation release.[26]

Hollywood complemented its marketing plan of preselling movies and utilizing television advertising to front-load audience attendance patterns with a strategy of using TV to cultivate movie stars and genres. Shaped by the patterns of cross-ownership that coalesced in the wake of President Reagan's election in 1980, this practice resulted in the industry's reinvention of movie genres as high-concept narratives based on episodic television programming's ideologically recuperative story structures.

Reflecting a rightward shift in popular taste, Hollywood also championed white male individualists in comic book fantasies like *Superman* (1978), conservative recuperations of the Vietnam War such as *The Deer Hunter* (1978), in which a returning veteran finds solace in his working-class hometown's steadfast faith in patriotic tradition, and sports success stories like *Rocky II* (1979). *Urban Cowboy* (1980) also reappraised *Saturday Night Fever*'s progressive critique of gender and class relations by equating its protagonist's pummeling of a rival for his wife's affections with his restoration of his role as head of the household.

These movies appeared as conservative reappraisals of the Carter administration, characterizing it as weak, indecisive, and ineffectual. Carter's failure to revive a stagnant American economy and his vacillation as a foreign policy leader led Richard Nixon to lambaste him in his 1980 assessment of the presidency. Among Carter's perceived failures were his return of control over the Panama Canal to the Panamanians, the Soviets' invasion of Afghanistan almost immediately after his concessionary negotiation of the SALT II arms limitation agreement, and his failure to win the freedom of Americans held hostage in Iran.

Rocky II's ($85 million) success in the wake of *Rocky*'s ($117 million) unanticipated popularity made it evident that cable-wired suburban and multiplex audiences craved stories about heroic underdogs who successfully reestablished boundaries between the individual and the collective, different races, and men and women's public and private roles. Wood contends that the ideological function of this style of filmmaking was to defuse social threats to patriarchal, bourgeois society remaining from the 1960s. These influences resulted in a ritualized quality that embodied an ideological agenda of reassurance.[27]

THE REAGAN ERA

Beneath superficial distinctions, seemingly discrete Reagan-era genres champion common philosophies of racial integration, conformity to proper gender roles, and meritocratic economic mobility. The growing cooperation implicit in the overlap between movies and television influenced the movies' generic form and content in significant ways. Amid rising moviemaking costs incurred by market research, rising promotional costs, skyrocketing star salaries, and saturation release strategies, television-trained executives assumed control over the process of moviemaking during the 1980s. Television's reliance on advertising sponsorship and its organization of programs on the basis of fixed time slots and episodic story structures molded Hollywood's choice of stories, as a high-concept mode of production led producers and studio executives to seek movies that conformed to a narrow set of themes that could be easily summarized in a fifteen-second advertising spot or print campaign.

What proved fascinating about high concept was its success in incorporating art cinema and avant-garde conventions into Hollywood's genre- and star-based system of entertainment. High concept's self-conscious visual design borrowed heavily from European art cinema by foregrounding authorial expressivity in conventions of character, mise-en-scène, and editing, departing from classical Hollywood style's premise of narrative and stylistic invisibility.[28] However, high concept also represented an extension of classical Hollywood cinema's system of moviemaking by luring audiences on the basis of a tight match of star, genre, and movie premise.

The ritualized quality of high concept's formulaic and ideologically recuperative narrative style resulted in Reagan-era cinema's focus on a narrow range of themes with broad popular appeal and the reiteration of them across multiple genres. Craig Baumgarten, an executive at Paramount during Don Simpson's stint as a producer, observed that under Simpson's leadership the studio began "issuing blueprints" governed by his dictation of script details from beginning to end.[29] The marketplace-driven, style-conscious design of high concept resulted in an inherent ideological conservatism that made it an effective vehicle for dramatizing Reagan's construction of American identity in terms of moral absolutes of good versus evil.

Invoking Reagan's distinction between races, genders, and classes, Hollywood churned out movies incorporating long-standing mythological tropes conflating whiteness and civilization, biological determinism and gender identity, and economic standing and individual moral merit. Reagan actively traded on these ideologies as well, aligning himself in his condemnation of the Soviet Union with a frontier mythology of Manifest Destiny, which argued that America's moral regeneration and material progress was contingent upon white society's reclamation of hostile lands and its redemption of savage peoples. Drawing upon this philosophy of white hegemony, economic progress, and moral self-help, Reagan contended that the entrepreneur's creation of new jobs would redeem the inner cities from poverty and moral depravation by rebuilding them and putting their citizens back to work. Men jockeying for competitive favor in a workplace of equal opportunity would be recharged by a leisure culture of earned affluence and a culture of affective familial ties. Conspicuous consumption was in turn a sign of secular grace in this moral universe, an earned emblem of merit available to anyone willing to work for it through a sustained agenda of hard work and self-discipline.

A champion of the people molded by practical experience rather than formal learning, Rocky Balboa is a Reagan-era incarnation of the natural aristocrat who achieves class mobility by redeeming the hostile racial other and the inner city from moral depravity. Over the course of the *Rocky* series, the fighter becomes a Christ-like martyr whose capacity for violence and withstanding physical suffering becomes a catalyst for the redemption of race, gender, and class relations. Reagan's own body became a parallel symbol of national redemption after John Hinkley's near-fatal assassination attempt on the president's life in 1981. The attempt boosted Reagan's popularity ratings, which had been lukewarm during his first year in office, as the president equated the restoration of his own health with an upswing in the nation's economic health in a speech before Congress.

High concept's emphasis on style conflated this hard body motif with action-adventure spectacle, resulting in the biracial buddy movie's preoccupation with the hero's restoration of a colorblind meritocracy through his violent extermination of racial and ethnic others. While the biracial buddy formula proved most popular in action-adventure blockbusters such as *Rocky, Beverly Hills Cop, 48 Hrs.,* and *Lethal Weapon,* the high-concept theme of interracial triumph over class corruption and racism permeated a variety of genres, including the family melodramas *Places in the Heart* (1984) and *Driving Miss Daisy* (1989), the screwball comedies *Trading Places* and *Brewster's Millions* (1985), and the road movie musicals *Blues Brothers* (1980) and *Crossroads* (1986). Inherent in each of these movies' focus on narrative closure is a common fantasy of blacks and whites teaming up to overthrow conspiratorial forces of racial and ethnic others who threaten the ideal of racial equality and classlessness.

Dramatizations of blacks and whites uniting to combat the threats to racial equality posed by political and economic elites and immoral street criminals had tremendous appeal during a backlash against groups perceived as beneficiaries of economic privilege and government charity. While liberalism may have worked during the period when America was industrializing, the new postindustrial era of inflation, limited resources, and unemployment suggested to many that the welfare state did not work. The shift from industrialism to postindustrialism was characterized by the relocation of heavy manufacturing jobs from urban areas to cheaper Third World labor sources and the parallel rise of a service economy which resituated displaced workers in part-time jobs in which they often weathered lower pay, longer hours, and cyclical unemployment. The middle class, in particular, became increasingly resentful over seeing its tax dollars funding government programs from which it seemed to gain little or nothing given its own downward mobility.

Reagan's belief that private industry, rather than government, was responsible for creating new wealth, new jobs, and individual upward mobility became a fundamental premise of his campaign to downsize government. Washington D.C.'s Urban Institute predicted, in a published report, a drop of $18 billion in donations between 1981 and 1984. Reagan, however, argued that market incentives and public spirit would provide the money lost through taxation. "You are that tough little tug that can pull our ship of state off the shoals and out into the open water," he told a gathering of business executives in 1984.[30]

In an era of ostensibly greater individual accountability, Reagan drew upon a binary rationale of individual responsibility versus immorality in arguing his case for tougher treatment of criminals, and he traced the breakdown of the criminal justice system to countercultural liberalism and government spending.[31] The values that underlay these conditions were, in turn, transmitted by a liberal and permissive society that coddled poor blacks.[32] Sociologist William Julius Wilson conversely argued that class-based economics rather than race-based values were the source of mushrooming inner-city poverty during the 1980s. Racism waned at the same time as opportunity in education, employment, and housing opened to blacks.[33]

High-concept cinema's reliance on a sleek, stunning visual style and its corollary establishment of clear-cut dividing lines between a middle-class lifestyle of patriarchal, bourgeois conformity and otherness results in an equation of whiteness and class affluence with affluent, high-tech settings and institutions in the biracial buddy movie. *Beverly Hills Cop* juxtaposes a neon-lit, street-level Detroit culture defined as working-class and black with Beverly Hills, an icon of wealth and conspicuous consumption defined as white and wealthy. Exemplary of high concept's glossy, high-sheen visual style, *Beverly Hills Cop* constructs this setting of ubiquitous affluence and class distinction as an image-conscious world of mirrored building surfaces, clean architectural lines, and minimalist hues of blue, gray, and black.

While settings of white affluence are equated with middle-class respectability, they also harbor political elites who use invisible high-tech avenues of multinational capital exchange to execute illicit terrorist conspiracies. In its evocation of high technology, *Beverly Hills Cop* constructs its namesake setting as a world of impenetrable mirrored surfaces and cold, discrete colors that camouflage a late capitalist money-laundering conspiracy between a foreign government and the rich and powerful elite of American society. While *Beverly Hills Cop*'s storyline is driven by its black and white buddies' attempts to reclaim this world of white privilege from corrupt forces of otherness, it also dramatizes the genre of integration's theme of interracial brotherhood by celebrating Axel Foley's assimilation into a world coded as bourgeois and white. The formation of father-and-son, fraternal, and conjugal relationships across lines of color is also a thematic focus of *An Officer and a Gentleman, The Toy* (1982), *Trading Places, Brewster's Millions*, and *Soul Man* (1986).

Within this context, black characters were relegated to supporting roles in white cultural contexts in which they were cast either as villains who threatened the social order or as trusted sidekicks who reaffirmed the existing order through their loyalty to it. *Rocky, Beverly Hills Cop, 48 Hrs., Trading Places, The Toy, Lethal Weapon, Die Hard*, and *Driving Miss Daisy* are examples of this motif. The coding of blacks and foreigners who fail to conform to these norms as villains conversely suggests that racial and ethnic difference can be a threat to a color-blind, classless society. Reagan-era cinema's use of contrasting settings often orders this distinction between black and ethnic heroes and villains.

The high-concept visual motif of icy, metallic colors and spare lines defines the interior of the high-rise Nakatomi Building in *Die Hard* as a setting of multinational corporate finance. The high-concept motif also molds the movie's construction of the designer suit–wearing German terrorist Hans and his sidekick, a black computer wizard named Theo, as elite terrorists who hold the company family hostage by manipulating a sophisticated computer-driven infrastructure of security and telecommunications. As members of a corrupt intelligentsia, they are ideological antitheses of the tank top–wearing, working-class John McClane (Bruce Willis) and his amiable black sidekick, policeman Al Powell (Reginald VelJohnson). McClane relies on intuition rather than intellect to negotiate the building's thirty-nine floors of air ducts, elevator shafts, and empty office spaces, while Powell relies on primitive two-way radio communication with him to foil the terrorists' high-tech plan to crack the corporation's computerized safe.

While *Beverly Hills Cop* and *Die Hard* equate the black buddy's integration into a white, middle-class culture with his redemption, other biracial buddy movies conversely characterize the white hero's immersion in a working-class culture defined as ethnic or black as the basis for his achievement of an intuitive bond between mind and body that facilitates his overthrow of black street hoods and conspiratorial elites. *Rocky III, Flashdance,* and *The Karate Kid* focus on underdogs who achieve class transcendence through their redemptive embrace of a culture of exotic otherness defined as black or Asian. Often, this formula celebrates the crossover of white hipsters into exotic cultures coded as other. *Blues Brothers, The Karate Kid, Crossroads,* and *Soul Man* portray non-white cultures as stereotypically earthy or mystical in order to draw in shorthand fashion upon reductive aspects of African-American and Asian cultures. In each case, the white protagonists are purged of rigid, neurotic qualities associated with Protestant middle-class norms of self-control and reason by embracing qualities of rhythm, intuition, sensuality, and emotion.[34]

The buddies within these films are also characterized as mismatched on the basis of opposing characteristics of black and white, masculine and feminine, and working class and middle class. Martin Riggs (Mel Gibson) of *Lethal Weapon* is a working-class Vietnam veteran and suicidal vigilante, while Roger Murtaugh (Danny Glover) is an aging middle-class family man and the butt of several jokes about impotence. John McClane of *Die Hard* is also a street-tough New York cop, while Al Powell is a Los Angeles beat cop who has been unable to fire his weapon since killing a child by accident.

The high-concept motif of the white male hard body provides a means of constructing the avenging heroes of *Rocky III, Lethal Weapon,* and *Die Hard* as patriarchal protectors of the so-called soft bodies of black buddies, wives, and children.[35] During the 1980s, physical fitness became an expression of elite class standing as a variety of exercise products and services proliferated in order to take advantage of the marketing opportunities afforded by the Reagan era's conflation of fitness and moral and economic renewal. Fitness became an index of social rank, especially among the upwardly mobile middle class, as body size and shape became a declaration of moral abstinence and clean living.[36] In *Rocky, Die Hard,* and *Lethal Weapon,* exaggerated musculature becomes a defining trait of the action-adventure hero and his redemption of race, gender, and class relations through violent macho exploits.[37] Sylvester Stallone's cartoonishly pumped-up physique in *Rocky III* stands in stark contrast to his more modest physical stature in *Rocky* and *Rocky II* and becomes a symbol of his role as patriarch in his defense of his wife and family from the black Clubber Lang.

While the hard body hero's overt masculinity becomes a visual expression of his virility as husband and father, it also serves as an index of racial difference that distinguishes between blacks and whites. Almost invariably white, the male hard body is a product of a culture of meritocratic individualism that restores boundaries between a moral middle class and criminals who threaten its sanctity. In contrast, the black costar symbolizes qualities of family and femininity.[38] Rocky's achievement of hard body status in *Rocky III* is directly dependent on former nemesis Apollo Creed's domestication into a supportive trainer and manager.

Drawing upon genres of order, this mythological formula dramatizes the buddies' quest for the restoration of law and order in a large urban setting through the violent elimination of racial and ethnic others, a typical narrative convention of adventure stories laden with assumptions about a colonizing race's moral, social, and physical mastery of a colonized race.[39] Critics have contended that the formula merely perpetuates a long-standing system of coding and rationalizing the racial hierarchy and interracial behavior.

Paramilitary movies like *Raiders of the Lost Ark, First Blood* (1982), *Uncommon Valor* (1983), *Missing in Action* (1984), and *Rambo: First Blood Part II* (1985) conflate the white male's physical efficaciousness as a hard bodied defender of values of democracy and family with his retrieval of precious natural resources or helpless women and children from hostile enemies in Third World countries.[40] In *Rambo: First Blood Part II*, for example, a phallic knife that John Rambo holds in his hand becomes an extension of the warrior-like physicality that distinguishes him as a one-man army.

These movies also strongly evoke *Treasure of the Sierra Madre* (1948) and *The Searchers* (1956) in their characterizations of their male leads as fortune hunters and out-of-time anti-heroes who venture into dangerous territories and brave hostile enemies in order to achieve fortune or to recover a prisoner held captive by a violent and hostile ethnic other. However, the proliferation and commercial popularity of movies about the United States' recovery of precious resources and helpless hostages from evil Third World countries during the Reagan administration's implementation of a full-scale military buildup and a much more aggressive foreign policy agenda suggests that *Raiders of the Lost Ark* operated as a symbolic condonement of Reagan-era militarism rather than simply as a nostalgic homage to Hollywood's studio era.[41]

While Hollywood's high-concept mode of production fetishized the pumped-up male body as an emblem of Reagan-era masculine heroism, it conflated women's economic and cultural mobility with their physical makeover on the basis of class cues of style and fashion. The MTV music video movie's use of stylistic excess to objectify male and female bodies during dance sequences complements the biracial buddy movie's fetishization of the male body during action-adventure spectacles of violence. Tony Williams, citing Lance Henrikson, draws a direct parallel between dance movement in the Hollywood musical and the violent choreography of the action-adventure movie, noting that Hong Kong director John Woo's earliest cinematic influences were *West Side Story* (1961) and musicals starring Gene Kelly and Fred Astaire.[42] Sylvester Stallone establishes a parallel between song and dance performances in the musical and macho violence in action-adventure movies by proclaiming in *The Official Rocky Scrapbook* that he and Carl Weathers (Apollo Creed) strove to "become the Fred Astaire and Ginger Rogers of the pugilistic world" during their choreographed fight scenes.[43]

While Stallone's sculpted body in *Rocky III* illustrates high concept's practice of defining characters on the basis of the Reagan-era cultural trend of physical fitness, a loose-fitting sweatshirt and baggy sweats, standard aerobics fashion accessories during the 1980s, serve as integral aspects of *Flashdance's* characterization of Alex as a fashion icon. Flashdancing, a combination of urban hip-hop and aerobic dance, defines Alex as a street-smart breakdancer-stripper who distinguishes herself as a natural aristocrat by using her talent rather than her boss Michael's (Michael Nouri) contacts to break into the world of legitimate dance.[44]

Similarly, Ren McCormick's (Kevin Bacon) penchant for vintage 1950s-looking new wave clothing aligns him with androgynous MTV musical icons such as David Bowie, to whom his mother playfully compares him as he peruses his look in the mirror in feminine fashion before leaving for school. While *Footloose* in this way recognizes the musical's fetishization of the male body in female terms, it nonetheless distinguishes between men and women's roles when Ren physically defends Lori from her abusive former boyfriend, anticipating their integration into a well-adjusted heterosexual couple and, ultimately, a family.

Reagan-era cinema's ideological recuperation of feminism through its characterization of wives and mothers as heroines was exemplified by its construction of the young widow as a defender of children in family farm melodramas. Farm movies used the family farm crisis of the 1980s to explore gender relations in the working-class family. They include *Country* (1984), *The River* (1984), *Places in the Heart* (1984), and *Field of Dreams* (1989). *Places in the Heart* interweaves a populist critique of corporate capitalism with a romanticization of its heroine as a defender of the home. Widowed after a drunken young black man (evocative of the coon stereotype) accidentally shoots her sheriff husband, Edna Spalding (Sally Field) faces foreclosure on her farm by the local bank. While the young black man is summarily lynched, a black drifter named Moses (Danny Glover), whom Edna forgives for petty thievery, guides her through the planting and harvesting of a cotton crop that enables her to save the property. In this way, *Places in the Heart* suggests that capitalism readily assimilates honest hard-working blacks and punishes those who transgress boundaries of law and order.

A cycle of melodramas about housewives guarding their families from predatory single women complemented the family farm cycle's characterization of wives and mothers as household saviors. *Tender Mercies* (1983), *Terms of Endearment* (1983), *Moonstruck* (1987), and *Someone to Watch Over*

Me (1987) juxtapose saintly homemakers with independent career women coded as man-stealing home wreckers. These films evoke family melodramas of the 1940s in their focus on themes like the false happiness of wealth, the goodness of nuclear family values of monogamy, trust, and devotion, and the obligation to punish women who transgress the roles of homemaker and mother. In doing so, they affirm both an ascendant white upper middle class's preoccupation with its own private concerns and the solace offered by familial attachments in a predatory free-market economy.

Body Heat (1981), *Against All Odds* (1984), and *Fatal Attraction* (1987) revive 1940s film noir's preoccupation with the threat posed by ambitious, independent woman to innocent white-collar men and their families. Inherent in these movies is a criticism of the incompatibility of the roles of career woman and wife and mother, a theme also taken up by a cycle of yuppie workplace comedies like *Mr. Mom* (1983), *Broadcast News* (1987), *Baby Boom* (1987), and *Working Girl* (1988).

A cycle of movies about cross-dressing, including *Tootsie* (1982), *Victor/Victoria* (1982), and *Yentl* (1983), explores the relationship between men and women's conformity to proper gender roles and the restoration of heterosexual institutions of courtship and marriage. These movies investigate gender roles by using cross-dressing as a motivation for celebrating both the reeducation of sexist men and the empowerment of enfeebled women. The treatment of cross-dressing in this two-way fashion opens the cycle to liberal and conservative ideological readings. However, biologically inscribed forms of sexual differentiation ultimately prove insurmountable, as characters of both sexes ultimately revert to their original gender identities after being apprehended by suitors or female confidantes.[45]

Movies of the 1980s about class also erect categorical distinctions between genders by predicating the restoration of a culture of economic autonomy on men and women's adherence to traditional gender roles. *Rocky, Rambo, Die Hard, Lethal Weapon,* and *48 Hrs.* are about strong and honest working-class white men who restore a culture of classlessness by vanquishing corrupt and greedy aristocrats who threaten meritocracy, even though the characterization of them as natural aristocrats simultaneously defines them as champions of individual rights. *Die Hard* conflates John McClane's overthrow of German terrorists who hold his wife hostage and kidnap his children with his role as a protector of the community, while his working-class aversion to white-collar norms of conformity and his single-handed rescue of the Nakatomi Corporation's workforce align him with values of self-sufficiency and individualism. Reagan's rhetoric resurrected a longstanding antagonism between working people and idle elites, shaping a style of right-wing populism designed to appeal to popular resentment of bureaucratic authority.

While blaming government bureaucracy for stripping the middle class of discretionary control over its income, neoconservatives contended that the feminist movement had also cheapened men's role as breadwinners. Reagan disciple George Gilder suggested that men are sexual nomads whose submission to the taming influence of female institutions of marriage and family renders them more responsible breadwinners. However, he simultaneously suggested that women who support themselves without help from their husbands undercut the family's stability by subverting men's moral and financial authority.[46]

While Reagan-era cinema defines the hardbody warrior as a working-class redeemer of the workplace and the family, high concept's preoccupation with conspicuous consumption also made style a primary determinant of Hollywood's characterization of the white-collar entrepreneur and corporate executive as a natural aristocrat. Evoking Reagan's declaration that he wanted America to remain a country where someone could always get rich, the young urban professional became a spokesperson for a media-manufactured baby boomer demographic trend that conflated one's consumption of pricey lifestyle goods with membership in a white-collar natural aristocracy.

As Barbara Ehrenreich suggests, extravagant consumption became a symbolic form of compensation for the yuppie's singular commitment to a lifestyle of professional busyness, which distinguished the natural aristocrat from the beneficiary of inherited class wealth.[47] A December 1980 *New York Times Magazine* cover story on fashion designer Oscar de la Renta and his wife, François, announced that the working upper crust had eclipsed the "leisure-oriented jet set" in America.[48] The story equates style, class distinction, and entrepreneurial savvy by observing that de la Renta's reputation as an internationally successful fashion designer and his glorification of style were complementary reasons for his close friendship with the Reagans.[49]

Movies about yuppies frequently use high concept's shorthand style of characterization to conflate affluence with achievement. A pair of Ray-Ban Wayfarer-style sunglasses becomes in *Risky Business* a high-concept fashion statement about the moral blankness that enables so-called future enterpriser Joel Goodson to secure admission to an Ivy League college. However, yuppie movies also assuage the ironic incongruities that accompanied Reagan-era culture's conflation of earned class prerogative and conformity to expensive norms of style. Ehrenreich described the yuppie's compulsive consumption as a surrender to hedonism and a means of easily labeling an ostensibly self-made success hero as nothing more than a caricature of individualism.[50] Movies about yuppie life address contradictions inherent in the promotion of the Reagan-era natural aristocrat as the product of self-made economic stature within a white-collar environment in which mobility requires conformity to impersonal codes of dress and behavior.

The yuppie movie's characterization of the white-collar workplace as an intrinsically unfulfilling environment in which mobility is dependent on personality rather than character led to a cycle of corporate-suburban narratives which romanticize suburban leisure culture as a respite from the corporate rat race. A group of college friends reunite in *The Big Chill* and discover a sense of renewal through their recovery of shared lifestyle and leisure tastes. Closely aligned with this focus on the suburban culture of leisure and relaxation are movies which focus on yuppies with children. *Kramer vs. Kramer* initiates the cycle by juxtaposing workplace and domestic responsibilities and suggesting that the yuppie lifestyle of competitive materialism can encourage young professionals' neglect of their responsibilities to spouses and children. Mothers who go to work learn that they must choose between career and family, while fathers who adopt the role of caretaker must learn the responsibilities involved in raising children. Suburban luxury is defined as an earned prerogative for nuclear families in which moms and dads conform to their natural roles, while poverty and maternal sacrifice through divorce are constructed as the logical outcome of moral irresponsibility.

Incumbent in yuppie movies is the construction of suburbia as a self-sufficient community of individual families that is restored to stability through the elimination of the threat posed by external forces like the state, bureaucracy, science, rationalism, and capitalist greed. The rejection of these forces is predicated on an affirmation of ecological and spiritual values identifiable with the New Age movement of the 1980s. *Close Encounters of the Third Kind* (1977), *E.T.: The Extra-Terrestrial* (1982), and *Poltergeist* (1982), for example, predicate the family's redemption on the assistance of Christ-like mediators.

The contradictions inherent in the celebration of the yuppie as a redeemer of the myth of classlessness stemmed from the downward mobility experienced by many middle-class families during the 1980s. The borrowing binge undertaken by corporate America in the 1980s created debts that required companies to divert massive sums of cash into interest payments, resulting in less money to spend for new plants and equipment, and research and development.[51] This trend resulted in the exportation of U.S. manufacturing jobs to cheaper overseas sources. As blue-collar jobs that paid enough to support a family evaporated, unions lost bargaining power in their relations with management, especially given the antilabor convictions Reagan demonstrated in his firing of striking air traffic controllers in 1981.

Interest payments on the national debt incurred by the lightening of corporate taxes were heaped onto individual taxpayers. While corporations were reducing their tax burden, the middle and lower classes were being saddled with greater tax bills. The share of taxes paid by corporations dwindled to 17 percent, while the share paid by individuals ballooned to

83 percent.[52] A U.S. Federal Reserve study indicated that the share of wealth held by the richest 1 percent of U.S. households increased under Reagan-Bush monetarist policies, from 31 percent in 1983 to 37 percent in 1989. The report also indicated the wealthiest 1 percent of U.S. households achieved these gains through their ownership of 49 percent of publicly held stock, 62 percent of business assets, and 45 percent of nonresidential real estate.[53] The distribution of wealth indicated by the study was also directly linked with the distribution of annual income over the 1980s.

A Congressional Budget Office report further revealed that the annual income share of the top 1 percent of U.S. families was 12 percent in 1989, up from 7 percent in 1977. Redistribution of income over the period was the product of tax policies, which benefited the wealthiest Americans. The 600,000 families earning over $310,000 per year took 60 percent of the growth in average after-tax family income between 1977 and 1989, and 75 percent of the increase in pretax income over that time. At the same time, the tax burden rose after 1977 for families in the lowest income decile and fell for families in the highest income decile.[54]

Wood argues that Reagan-era movies acted as blandishments of reassurance in the midst of seismic shifts in economic mobility.[55] As representations of American values like rugged individualism and self-help, Reagan-era movies were thus pivotal in mediating economic and cultural relations in the 1980s. Hollywood's construction of economic and cultural relations in neoconservative terms paralleled its return to profitability in the wake of an interim during which it had given free rein to genre movies that systematically undermined these assumptions. The biracial buddy movie was key to Hollywood's reascendent profitability. In turn, the genre's popularity was traceable to its reactionarily conservative portrayal of race relations in a post–civil rights era of ostensible economic equality.

NOTES

1. Robin Wood, *Hollywood from Vietnam to Reagan* (New York: Columbia University Press, 1986), 164.

2. Michael Ryan and Douglas Kellner, *Camera Politica: The Politics and Ideology of Contemporary Hollywood Film* (Bloomington: Indiana University Press, 1988), 7.

3. Thomas Schatz, *Hollywood Genres: Formulas, Filmmaking, and the Studio System* (New York: Random House, 1981), 35.

4. Robin Wood, "Ideology, Genre, Auteur," *Film Genre Reader*, ed. Barry Keith Grant (Austin: University of Texas Press, 1986), 68.

5. Schatz, *Hollywood Genres*, 35.

6. Ibid.

7. Ibid., 36.

8. John Cawelti, "*Chinatown* and Generic Transformation in Recent American Films," *Film Genre Reader*, ed. Barry Keith Grant (Austin: University of Texas Press, 1986), 199.

9. Jim Hillier, *The New Hollywood* (New York: Continuum, 1994), 14.

10. John Belton, *American Cinema/American Culture* (New York: McGraw-Hill, 1994), 288.

11. John Izod, *Hollywood and the Box Office, 1895–1986* (New York: Columbia University Press, 1988), 188.

12. Hillier, *The New Hollywood*, 144.

13. Hillier, *The New Hollywood*, 145.

14. Tino Balio, "Introduction to Part II," *Hollywood in the Age of Television*, ed. Tino Balio (Boston: Unwin Hyman, 1990), 261.

15. Ed Guerrero, *Framing Blackness: The African American Image in Film* (Philadelphia: Temple University Press, 1993), 105.

16. Robert B. Ray, *A Certain Tendency of the Hollywood Cinema, 1930–1980* (Princeton, N.J.: Princeton University Press, 1985), 306.

17. Ryan and Kellner, *Camera Politica*, 81.

18. Sylvester Stallone, *The Official Rocky Scrapbook* (New York: Grosset & Dunlap, 1977), 21.

19. Ryan and Kellner, *Camera Politica*, 77.

20. Peter Biskind and Barbara Ehrenreich, "Machismo and Hollywood's Working Class," *American Media and Mass Culture: Left Perspectives*, ed. Donald Lazere (Berkeley: University of California Press, 1987), 206.

21. Wood, *Hollywood from Vietnam to Reagan*, 121.

22. Schatz, *Hollywood Genres*, 163.

23. Wood, *Hollywood from Vietnam to Reagan*, 215.

24. Ibid., 220.

25. Ibid.

26. Peter Biskind, *Easy Riders, Raging Bulls: How the Sex-Drugs-and-Rock 'n' Roll Generation Saved Hollywood* (New York: Simon & Schuster, 1998), 401.

27. Wood, *Hollywood from Vietnam to Reagan*, 163.

28. Justin Wyatt, *High Concept: Movies and Marketing in Hollywood* (Austin: University of Texas Press, 1994), 61.

29. Biskind, *Easy Riders, Raging Bulls*, 402.

30. Milton Goldin, "Ronald Reagan and the Commercialization of Giving," *Journal of American Culture* (1990),: 31.

31. Diane Bohlcke and Sandra Harper, "The Interplay Between Media Rhetoric and Administration Rhetoric: An Examination of the Image of the American Criminal Justice System," *Visions of Rhetoric: History, Theory and Criticism*, ed. Charles W. Kneupper (Arlington, Tex.: Rhetoric Society of America, 1987), 255.

32. Myron Magnet, *The Dream and the Nightmare: The Sixties' Legacy to the Underclass* (New York: William Morrow, 1993), 32.

33. William Julius Wilson, *The Truly Disadvantaged: The Inner City, the Underclass, and Public Policy* (Chicago: University of Chicago Press, 1987), 57.

34. Guerrero, *Framing Blackness,* 123.

35. Susan Jeffords, *Hardbodies: Hollywood Masculinity in the Reagan Era* (New Brunswick, N.J.: Rutgers University Press, 1994), 24.

36. Barbara Ehrenreich, *Fear of Falling: The Inner Life of the Middle Class* (New York: Pantheon Books, 1989), 233.

37. Jeff Yanc, "'More Than a Woman': Music, Masculinity, and Male Spectacle in *Saturday Night Fever* and *Staying Alive," The Velvet Light Trap,* 1996, 46.

38. Jeffords, *Hardbodies,* 13.

39. Stuart Hall, "The Whites of Their Eyes: Racist Ideologies and the Media," *Silver Linings: Some Strategies for the Eighties,* ed. George Bridges and Rosalind Brunt (London: Lawrence and Wishart, 1981), 39.

40. Gina Marchetti, "Action-Adventure as Ideology," *Cultural Politics in Contemporary America,* ed. Ian Angus and Sut Jhally (New York: Routledge, 1989), 189.

41. Ibid.

42. Tony Williams, "Woo's Most Dangerous Game: *Hard Target* and Neoconservative Violence," *Mythologies of Violence in Postmodern Media,* ed. Christopher Sharrett (Detroit: Wayne State University Press, 1999), 32.

43. Sylvester Stallone, *The Official Rocky Scrapbook* (New York: Grosset & Dunlap, 1977), 32.

44. Wyatt, *High Concept,* 57.

45. Chris Straayer, "Redressing the 'Natural': The Temporary Transvestite Film," *Film Genre Reader II,* ed. Barry Keith Grant (Austin: University of Texas Press, 1995), 403.

46. George Gilder, *Wealth and Poverty* (San Francisco: Institute for Contemporary Studies, 1993), 80.

47. Ehrenreich, *Fear of Falling,* 231.

48. Francesca Stanfill, "Living Well is Still the Best Revenge," *New York Times Magazine,* 21 December 1980, 25.

49. Ibid., 20.

50. Ehrenreich, *Fear of Falling,* 239.

51. Donald L. Bartlett and James B. Steele, *America: What Went Wrong?* (Kansas City: Andrews and McMeel, 1992), 14.

52. Ibid., 20.

53. Sylvia Nasar, "Fed Gives Evidence of 80s Gains by Richest," *New York Times,* 22 April 1992, sec. A1.

54. U.S. Congress, Congressional Budget Office, *Measuring the Distribution of Income Gains,* CBO Staff Memorandum, Washington, DC: Congressional Budget Office, March, 1992: 3.

55. Wood, *Hollywood from Vietnam to Reagan,* 164.

Chapter 4

Race and the Biracial Buddy Movie

The biracial buddy movie rose to prominence during the 1980s because of changes in Hollywood's political economic structure, mode of production, and conditions of exhibition, changes which both preceded Ronald Reagan's rise to the presidency and accelerated under his administration. In the late 1960s and early 1970s, the conditions that gave rise to low-budget classics such as *Easy Rider* (1969) led to the popularization of movies such as *Sweet Sweetback's Baadassss Song* (1971). The major studios' curtailment of their production schedules left exhibitors desperate for movies while relatively modest moviemaking and promotion costs enabled independent production companies to successfully compete for movie audiences.

The relocation of the white middle class to the suburbs left urban black audiences as the primary patrons of older downtown movie theaters. According to a 1967 estimate, blacks accounted for about 30 percent of the moviegoing audience in the nation's cities, where the largest theaters were located.[1] The black power movement was expressed in Hollywood in terms of demand for more control over the representation of blacks in movies. While whites wrote and directed most blaxploitation movies, and most examples stereotyped inner-city blacks as pimps and drug dealers, their popularity nonetheless revealed that an undertapped urban black audience existed for Hollywood movies. Images of hip urban blacks replaced the image of Sidney Poitier ingratiating himself to his future white in-laws in *Guess Who's Coming to Dinner* (1967).

During the early 1970s, blaxploitation evolved into crossover movies such as *Uptown Saturday Night* (1974) and *Let's Do It Again* (1975), designed to appeal to black and white suburban audiences. The replacement of downtown movie theaters by suburban multiplexes was partially responsible for this trend. The decline of militant Black Nationalism that accompanied the visible formation of an African-American middle class also led black audiences to seek a more integrated view of themselves.

The assimilation of Hollywood's major studios into vertically and horizontally integrated media conglomerates intensified the industry's focus on casting blacks in movies with crossover appeal. Crossover movies maximized their appeal by relying on a few, isolated, big-name black stars. Black audiences, it was believed, could be drawn to movies designed to appeal to white audiences, but white audiences could not be guaranteed to attend movies aimed at black moviegoers. "I think the going wisdom in Hollywood is: 'They [blacks] come to our movies, so we don't have to cater to them,'" observed independent filmmaker John Sayles.[2]

Movies such as *Trading Places* (1983) and *Lethal Weapon* (1987) relate black experience from a white point of view by isolating an African-American character in a largely white cast and cultural setting and offering only token insight into his background. While Hollywood decision makers advocate egalitarian mobility in principal, there are in fact very few black executives in Hollywood. White executives' propensity for making deals with friends also disadvantages women and African Americans. However, blacks may also fail to reach positions of decision-making authority because of their lack of qualifications for particular jobs.[3] Indeed, the Writers Guild of America, West has a black membership of less than 2 percent.[4] The absence of blacks from the Writers Guild may in turn partially account for the narrowness of the parts black actors are offered in major Hollywood movies.

Attempts to broaden the breadth of Hollywood's representation of blacks are often vetoed on the basis of financial conservatism. International investors are frequently hesitant to invest in movies that relate minority experience from a non-white point of view. Leonard Schrader, screenwriter of *Blue Collar* (1978) and brother of director Paul Schrader, had a hard time raising money for the film because of the casting of blacks (Richard Pryor and Yapphet Kotto) in two of the three leading roles. Harvey Keitel rounded out the trio. [5]

Sylvester Stallone discovered two years after making *Rocky* (1977) that producing and directing a production involving a mostly black cast "could be a very costly sociological experiment." When writer-director Stallone attempted to cast *Paradise Alley* (1978) with mostly black actors, all of his backers vetoed the idea.[6] According to Stallone, "they said a black movie could only gross a certain amount of money and never had a chance to go into megabucks."[7]

Collette Wood, executive secretary of the Beverly Hills chapter of the National Association for the Advancement of Colored People (NAACP), noted in 1982, "there has been a steady decline in black employment in the industry since 1975."[8] In his own survey of cast lists for the 299 major films made between September 1979 and April 1982, Leroy Robinson, president of the Black Motion Picture and TV Producers' Association, estimated that blacks appeared in barely 3 percent of all speaking roles.[9]

Comedies originally written for a bankable white star most often provided opportunities for black actors to play leading or costarring roles. *Burglar* (1987) was written for Bruce Willis, *Beverly Hills Cop* (1984) for Sylvester Stallone, and *Lethal Weapon* (1987) for Nick Nolte. Hollywood made few such big-budget productions, however, and cast only a handful of black stars in them based on their ability to replicate the box-office appeal of white stars. Eddie Murphy's popularity, for example, elevated him from costar alongside Dan Ackroyd in *Trading Places* and Nick Nolte in *48 Hrs.* to star of the *Beverly Hills Cop* series.

The multiple readings of race relations that can be derived from a story about the fraternal bonds that form between men of opposing races as they engage in violent spectacles of conquest and adventure made the biracial buddy movie an effective vehicle for Hollywood's agenda of marketing movies to crossover audiences at home and abroad. However, Hollywood's penchant for casting blacks as sidekicks and comic minstrels in such movies suggests that they were most easily readable as stereotypical representations of black experience.

A primary reason for this symbolic truncation of African-American roles is the biracial buddy formula's focus on formulaic mythological representations of ethnic and racial identity. In its original formation, Frederick Jackson Turner's frontier hypothesis proclaimed that continual expansion into the frontier and the cultivation of resource-rich lands provided the basis for post–Civil War prosperity. Building on Thomas Jefferson's notion of the self-made agrarian yeoman, Turner argued that agriculture had provided the basis for all material wealth and that in America there was sufficient vacant land for everyone to free themselves from external necessity through hard work and self-discipline.

A central premise of James Fenimore Cooper's nineteenth-century literary series *The Leatherstocking Tales* was a hegemonic characterization of Indian removal policies as a form of regenerative violence through which American government and industry rationalized its mission of colonizing frontier lands and peoples. In this series, a mythical white frontiersman violently blazes a trail for Eastern civilization's westward expansion while simultaneously embodying values of self-sufficiency and respect for nature identified with the vanishing wilderness. Often, he must rescue a white hostage taken by Indians in order to redeem the values of civilization from the tainting effects of a culture described as both barbaric and beautiful in its natural simplicity.

Inherent in Cooper's studies of the cultural conflicts that arise at the frontier border of civilization and nature are the issues of individual property rights versus free access to game and land, the rough equality of humans in a state of nature versus the social stratification of people through unequal distribution of property and racial discrimination, and institutional religion versus the natural, intuitive theology of the frontiersman.[10] Cooper's most famous hero, Natty Bumpo, became a template for a series of novels written between 1860 and 1893 about hunters, trappers, and other frontiersmen who flee an encroaching civilization by moving further west, even as they carve out a path for its advancement. Over the studio era, Hollywood adopted this hero as a model for scores of alienated anti-heroes in westerns such as *Stagecoach* (1939), *Shane* (1953), and *The Searchers.*[11]

The biracial buddy movie also takes up these themes by pairing a white man and a black or ethnic sidekick as outcast agents of civilization who reclaim the late-twentieth-century urban landscape for meritocratic people of color and suburban families by violently eradicating hostile ethnic and racial others. This formula dramatized Reagan's conviction that a get-tough attitude toward criminals and welfare cheats was the key to inner-city economic reform. The hyperviolence of action-adventure movies such as *Rocky, Lethal Weapon,* and *Die Hard* stems logically from this attitude, especially in their romanticization of the hardbody white male as the Christ-like redeemer of a civilized middle-class community of women, children, and noble people of color.

THE BIRACIAL BUDDY MOVIE

Blacks have since the rise of the studio system made movies that both conform to and challenge mainstream Hollywood's representation of African-American identity. Blaxploitation arose in the late 1960s and early 1970s during a period of falling box-office receipts as gaps in the major studios' production schedules, the existence of an underserved black audience, and the civil rights movement provided black actors and directors with an opportunity to challenge dominant representations of them.

While blaxploitation provided employment opportunities for blacks as directors (Gordon Parks, Jr., Gordon Parks, Sr.) and actors (Richard Roundtree, Issac Hayes) they seldom participated in the substantial profits made by their films. Nonetheless, *Shaft* and *Superfly* mobilized the incendiary anger of urban blacks by dramatizing their belief that the white establishment allowed them few legitimate avenues of upward mobility. While not an example of blaxploitation, Melvin Van Peebles' *Sweet Sweetback's Baadasssss Song* went a step further by telling the story of a black revolutionary who flees from Los Angeles to Mexico after killing two white policemen he watched beating up a young black man. Shot in nineteen days on a budget of $500,000, the film eventually grossed approximately $15 million.[12]

While images of hip aggressive black males appealed to the Black Nationalist convictions of young African-Americans, the replacement of downtown one- and two-screen auditoriums frequented by urban black moviegoers by suburban multiplex chains resulted in the rise of crossover movies designed to appeal to both black and white audiences. *Uptown Saturday Night* (1974), *Let's Do It Again* (1975), *Car Wash* (1976), *Greased Lightning* (1976), *Bingo Long and the Traveling All-Stars* (1976), *The Greatest* (1977), and *Bustin' Loose* (1981) appealed to multiple, often diverse, suburban market segments on the basis of their comic celebrations of a black bourgeoisie and condemnations of Black Nationalism.

Piece of the Action (1977) celebrates black middle-class integration through the characterizations of Bill Cosby and Sidney Poitier as middle-class male role models for unruly black teens. As mentors, they teach the adolescents forms of behavior, dress, and self-presentation that enable them to become successful members of the world of white capitalism.[13] *Car Wash* also suggests that black and ethnic workers should cooperate with the system. Conversely, it also offers a Marxist assessment of the consequences of systemic oppression of the black working class.[14]

President Jimmy Carter, who balanced his support for social reforms such as affirmative action with a call for black economic self-help, echoed *Car Wash's* rejection of a philosophy of black power. However, the taxes imposed by the Carter administration's ongoing maintenance of welfare patronage for poor blacks and whites during a recessionary economy of stagflation generated a backlash of resentment among working-class whites who saw few benefits for themselves in such programs.

Rocky's appeal sprang from its focus on antagonisms between workers and blacks which stemmed from economic recession and white, blue-collar resentment of welfare and affirmative action. Inherent in *Rocky* is a celebration of the title character's bedrock faith in traditional values of self-help and piety, a theme declared by the born again Jimmy Carter in his focus on creating a government as good as its people. However, the film's characterization of Apollo Creed as a race-baiting showman also plays upon a conservative backlash against the progressive racial politics that Carter represented as a former governor of Georgia from the New South.

Rocky's family (Adrian, Mickey, and Paulie) is a collective that provides the fighter with the love, faith, and inspiration he needs to succeed. The family's natural self-sufficiency is nonetheless threatened by the intervention of technocratic, race-based government mandates in the workplace. *Smokey and the Bandit* (1977), *F.I.S.T.* (1978), *Blue Collar,* and *Rocky II* (1979) also criticize unions and affirmative action as forms of government interference in the private sector.[15] Implicit in such criticism is an indictment of social programs since they are funded by government borrowing and taxation that curtail investment and jobs and drive up inflation. While affirmative action and welfare continued to be constructed as threats to color-blind economic mobility after Reagan's election, the president also demonized fascist government terrorists and economic elites as additional threats to race and class mobility.

Hollywood's high-concept mode of production encouraged this truncated representation of race and ethnicity by underscoring racial differences through cinematic style. The motif of the hardbody serves as a synecdoche in *Rocky III* (1982), *Lethal Weapon,* and *Die Hard* that defines the white superhero as a redeemer of race and class relations whose moral selflessness makes possible a colorblind society that allows the deserving black sidekick to enjoy a middle-class standard of living.

PLOT: INTERRACIAL BROTHERHOOD, FAMILY, AND ERADICATING THE OTHER

Circumstance sets the biracial buddy movie plot into motion by throwing a black man and a white man together in a fashion that immediately establishes their mutual reluctance as a basis for exploring their shared similarities. Their mutual antagonism introduces the idea that in a nation based on pluralism, extreme differences are common and necessary.[16] The tension is heightened by the black cohero's and white hero's mistaken perceptions of each other on the basis of stereotypical assumptions linking race or ethnicity and morality. Initial hostilities are overcome, however, by the introduction of an other who threatens society's meritocratic, colorblind order. The pair's overthrow of the threat implies that black integration into white society is predicated on the former's assimilation of white cultural norms.

In *Silver Streak* (1976), for example, Richard Pryor plays a criminal in police custody whose freedom hinges on his exoneration of his white buddy (Gene Wilder) from murder charges. In revealing that international art thieves framed Wilder, Pryor helps overthrow conspiratorial elites who threaten a culture of racial and class equality. Inherent in the plot is a potentially radical critique of capitalism that suggests that racism and economic inequality stem from society's concentration of wealth in the hands of a white elite. However, *Silver Streak* equates the overthrow of elites with the reestablishment of interracial harmony. *Silver Streak* also establishes a link between interracial harmony and the formation of family as it conflates the elimination of the corrupt ring of art thieves with Wilder's romantic coupling with a female love interest (Jill Clayburgh) held captive by the thieves.

Pryor's introduction halfway through the movie reveals the extent to which the movie is told from Wilder's point of view. The biracial buddy formula's focus on white point of view serves several purposes. It implies that the achievement of interracial harmony depends upon the black character's integration into a dominant white society. It also prevents a more racial critique of capitalism that might arise from the suggestion that racism and economic inequality stem from an attempt to marginalize blacks who fail to assimilate a dominant white culture's norms. Certainly stories of different races achieving moral regeneration by teaming up to defeat forces which threaten their bond has historically exercised a powerful mythological appeal. Christopher Ames writes that incumbent in the motif is a so-called denial of history, which, in joining black and white buddies to eliminate a force which threatens both races, "expresses a powerful mythic longing to reverse or purge historical guilt."[17]

However, the linkage of proper racial and gender roles also had powerful appeal to a culture reoriented by the civil rights and feminist movements. *Rocky* and *Rocky II* play upon a backlash of racial conservatism by focusing on the ostensible threats to the white family posed by liberal civil rights initiatives and economic recession. In *Rocky II*, Rocky's dismissal from a meatpacking plant parallels Adrian's (Talia Shire) return to work, which in turn results in her near loss of the couple's baby. Conflating the proper ordering of race roles in the public sphere with the proper ordering of gender roles in the private sphere, the movie creates a parallel through crosscutting between Rocky's defeat of Apollo Creed and Adrian's successful delivery of a baby boy.

Rocky III (1982) shifts the focus of the series from affirmative action and workplace meritocracy to the threat posed by inner-city crime to the white suburban family. Idle wealth creates in Rocky a sense of moral complacency, causing him to suffer an embarrassing defeat in a charity match at Las Vegas' MGM Grand Hotel. While the setting is an obvious plug for parent company MGM/UA's vacation resort, it also reveals Rocky to be woefully surfeited and uncomfortable among the decadent trappings of wealth and fame. However, Clubber Lang's aggressive overtures towards Rocky's wife at a public ceremony honoring the champion as a city father force the champ back into a physically grueling training regimen that returns him to hardbody virility.

Drawing upon genres of order, *Rocky III* predicates the restoration of a culture of racial harmony on the black hero's assistance in helping the white hero violently eliminate a black challenger who threatens Rocky's family. Underlying such a motif is the suggestion that interracial harmony is the product of black self-help rather than federal assistance. Federal assistance, it is implied, breeds black street criminals like Clubber Lang (Mr. T) who threaten the white suburban family's sanctity. Incumbent in this assertion is an appeal to Reagan administration themes of law and order and family self-sufficiency.

The first half of *Rocky IV* (1985) further develops the theme of how government intervention in race relations threatens a culture of racial meritocracy and self-governing familial relations. Rocky's return to the ring is motivated by Russian champion Drago's vicious slaughter of Apollo Creed in the ring. Drago's Aryan features and robotic demeanor align him with a Communist culture of technocratic organization that distributes rewards on the basis of government engineering.

Upon arriving in Russia for the fight, Rocky begins an outdoor training regimen of working in a barn with farming equipment, chopping wood, and jogging in the wild. Drago, on the other hand, trains in a government-sponsored gym while tethered to state-of-the-art monitoring equipment by a tangle of wires. While *Rocky IV* identifies the white male hardbody with nature, it equates Drago's ethnic hardbody with forces of technocratic engineering, which threaten a self-regulating capitalist marketplace's distribution of rewards on the basis of natural deservedness.[18]

Beverly Hills Cop and *Lethal Weapon* also play upon the threat posed by foreign government officials and corrupt businessmen to a society of race and class meritocracy. In *Beverly Hills Cop*, white police misconstrue Axel Foley as a street criminal after they encounter him being thrown through a plate glass window. However, Foley ultimately helps the Beverly Hills Police Department apprehend a German money-laundering operation. Foley's integration into white society is signaled by the department's payment of his hotel bill in compensation for his detective services. In *Lethal Weapon*, the situation is reversed, with the renegade Martin Riggs (Mel Gibson) helping Roger Murtaugh and the Los Angeles police apprehend a ring of elite CIA-trained, drug-smuggling murderers. In *Die Hard*, Al Powell helps John McClane overthrow a German terrorist group. In both movies, the black buddy ensures the safety of his downed white counterpart in the face of a sudden final attack by firing his gun in a symbolic gesture of remasculinization and fraternal solidarity.

It is through this shared effort that the black and white buddies restore a culture of upward mobility based on merit and ability rather than race or class. In *48 Hrs.*, it is similarly the selfless sacrifice of the black costar that catalyzes the white star's redemption in the eyes of bureaucracy and capitalism. Reggie Hammond (Eddie Murphy) sacrifices his freedom in order to save his white partner Jack Cates (Nick Nolte) from being fired by the police department and murdered by members of Hammond's former gang. Hammond's achievement of moral awareness parallels his self-transformation from a sweatshirted prison con into an Armani-suited detective with a badge and a gun. In each case, the resolution is also contingent upon the black buddy's assimilation of middle-class traits of moral integrity and proper behavior.

Such a resolution is also dependent in the *Rocky* series, *48 Hrs.*, *Beverly Hills Cop*, *Lethal Weapon*, and *Die Hard*, on the elimination of villainous forces spawned by bureaucratic corruption or mismanagement. In *Lethal Weapon 2*, a group of South African drug smugglers who use diplomatic

immunity to launder drug money through U.S. banks embodies the tainting effects of bureaucracy on relations between business and the nation-
state. The characterization of the villains as members of a government
widely believed to be racist and imperialist underscores the plot's equation of bureaucracy and racist oppression. Resolution of the conflict between black and white and technocratic oppression and natural freedom
occurs when Riggs literally tears down the smugglers' palatial Hollywood
Hills headquarters and Murtaugh subsequently "revokes" the group
leader's diplomatic immunity by shooting him dead.

The restoration of a natural order between men and women depends on
the reestablishment of proper boundaries between gender spheres. Conflicts between men and women are set into motion by the patriarch's preoccupation with eliminating public threats to the family's welfare,
echoing the yuppie movie's suggestion that the father who is overinvested
in work is both the cause of and the solution to family conflict. In *Lethal
Weapon*, the leaders of an international drug cartel kidnap Murtaugh's
daughter. Reclaiming his identity as a father, Murtaugh rushes to a desert
rendezvous with the terrorists, alone in his battered station wagon, in
order to rescue his daughter from them.

In *Die Hard*, John McClane and Al Powell's defeat of a ring of foreign,
ex-military terrorists restores the stability of McClane's marriage when, in
the final scene, his wife (Bonnie Bedelia) reclaims her married name, dons
the protective masculine mantle of a warm police jacket, and agrees in the
wake of her kidnapping to resign her job and return with the detective to
the East Coast. In *Beverly Hills Cop*, Axel Foley's elimination of an international drug smuggling ring from Beverly Hills restores the stability of the
police department's family of cops.

While *Rocky*, *Beverly Hills Cop*, *48 Hrs.*, *Lethal Weapon*, and *Die Hard* uphold Reagan-era values like law and order, police camaraderie, and family, they also dramatize violent, vigilante solutions to what the Reagan
administration labeled as the chief threats to familial security and well-
being of 1980s America—terrorism, drug trafficking, and urban crime.
These incarnations of masculinity are reminiscent, Elizabeth G. Traube
writes, of the wild, masculine dime novel heroes who emerged in the nine-
teenth century and rebelled against the mechanization of society. Such a
version of masculinity has more recent roots in the antibureaucratic vigilante heroes of the early 1970s like Dirty Harry, who similarly rebel against
an abstract workplace order typical of late capitalist society.[19] Often, the
characters who symbolize threats of terrorism, urban crime, and drug trafficking are constructed in terms of ethnic or racial otherness.

The theme of throwing off the oppressive, class-imposed norms of a bureaucratic, technocratic society reveals the presence of class anxieties
within such films. Black and white buddies who foil attempts by government officials and wealthy elites to exploit those beneath them appeal to a

common antagonism to late capitalist society's abstract organization of economic relations. Fred Pfeil attributes the popularity of this theme to working-class resentment of post-Fordist trends in American culture, typified by a disappearance of high-paying factory labor and the proliferation of low-wage service industry labor.[20]

Lethal Weapon focuses on the need for black-white partnerships to defend against the threat posed by a racist South African government operating a money-laundering operation through its American consulate. A black panhandler and a white stockbroker team up to overthrow a pair of wealthy Wall Street brothers and a government agent in *Trading Places*. The biracial buddies mediate the tensions imposed by the attempts of civilized forces to govern natural forms of social and economic organization by overthrowing conspiratorial forces of control.

In *Trading Places*, the Duke brothers' (Ralph Bellamy, Don Ameche) corruption stems from their privileged class status, which is expressed on the basis of their idle gentlemen's bet over whether nature or socialization determines individual success or failure. *Trading Places* has been called a screwball comedy because Valentine and Winthorpe's (Dan Ackroyd) resolution of their class differences celebrates America's lack of class barriers. The film has also been so labeled because it criticizes capitalism's uneven distribution of rewards on the basis of birthright and privilege rather than meritocratic deservedness, while nonetheless eventually turning to such a system to resolve the principal characters' class and gender conflicts.[21]

Conversely, the film condemns information-age capitalism by suggesting that it promotes the same practices of hustling (through price rigging and illegal garnering of inside information) in both the heroic Valentine and Winthorp and the villainous Dukes. It thus condemns capitalism as a system that punishes the Dukes not for having illegal information but for having incorrect information. Alan Nadel suggests that *Trading Places* characterizes capitalism in terms of multiple white class positions. He observes that when Winthorp summarizes his belief that his social and financial plight can be blamed on blacks, he is "speaking not so much for the superrich as for the lower-middle-class whites who constitute what has been called 'Reagan Democrats,'" the same audience to which *Rocky*'s criticism of affirmative action appealed.[22] A picture on Winthorp's office credenza of a smiling Ronald Reagan standing before an American flag conversely vilifies wealthy big business executives and Wall Street investors as a self-serving cadre of economic elites that consolidated their control over private wealth during the Reagan era.

Trading Places suggests, through Valentine and Winthorp's successful partnership, that the system is capable of absorbing people of different race and class origins and that it in fact promotes both the creation of new money through the transcendence of such differences and the displacement of old money generated by the exploitation of such barriers. Capitalism thus results in the formation of a sort of family between Winthorp, Ophelia, Valentine, and Coleman, respective representatives of white male privilege, white female exploitation, black male exploitation, and old-world class stratification. It is through the black character's sacrifice that family is achieved. In *Trading Places*, Billy Ray Valentine sacrifices a position of economic affluence in order to save Winthorp from homelessness and poverty.

Trading Places' success inspired a thinly veiled rehash, *Brewster's Millions*, that cast white comedian John Candy alongside star Richard Pryor. In casting Pryor as the straight man, *Brewster's Millions* softens his comedy routine about growing up black and poor in an effort to increase his appeal to white audiences. The film pivots on the premise that a man is given thirty days to dispose of $30 million, and is required to have nothing to show for all his spending at the end of the time, in order to demonstrate that he knows, after all, that money isn't everything and to prove he is worthy of inheriting a $300 million fortune from his late, white grandfather.

Not only must Pryor's character spend the $30 million in thirty days, but he must also keep the reasons for his spendthrift behavior a secret from his friends or forfeit the inheritance. He uses the money to promote important but overlooked social causes, which are of course viewed as outlandish by others in the movie. He throws away a fortune during a New York mayoral campaign to persuade the public to vote neither for the Milquetoast, major-party candidates, nor for himself, in order to force a new election in which important issues will be discussed. Like *Trading Places*, *Brewster's Millions* thus suggests that in supply-side economic fashion while capitalism may distribute rewards unequally on the basis of race and class it nonetheless contains the mechanisms for its own moral and economic regeneration.

Soul Man (1986) similarly suggests that a beneficent white capitalist order reproduces itself through the distribution of opportunity on the basis of moral deservedness. Under the tutelage of a black law professor (James Earl Jones), a young white law student masquerading as black proves that he is worthy of a scholarship to Harvard Law School that is intended for a deserving black student. The resolution of racial conflict is contingent upon the integration of the white student and a black single mother into a family. However, the film was thoroughly criticized for its insensitive comedic treatment of racism. The upper-middle-class white student (C. Thomas Howell) supposedly learns what it's like to be black in a white institutional culture by inadvertently overdosing on tanning pills. Howell's character gets the scholarship because no other black students are qualified to win it. However, the film simultaneously suggests in neominstrelsy fashion that white men make the best blacks. Critics blamed the film's use of comedy, in its quest for a white audience, for its insensitivity.[23]

In the screwball comedy *The Toy* (1982), Richard Pryor and Jackie Gleason transcend class and race differences through Pryor's restoration of the latter's relationship with his son (Scott Schwartz). In the process, Pryor persuades Gleason, a rich Southerner, to sever his connections with the Ku Klux Klan. The movie concludes with Gleason offering Pryor a writing job on his corporation-owned newspaper, grateful for the return of his son. The change of heart depends on the black character's adoption of norms defined in terms of race, but definable in terms of class. In *The Toy*, Pryor thus evolves from a bankrupt publisher of a Black Nationalist newspaper into a reporter on a white, corporation-owned newspaper. The predication of black upward mobility on the black individual's assimilation of the manners of a middle-class society coded as white neatly avoids any discussion of class barriers to black upward mobility.

While *Trading Places* and *The Toy* revive the screwball comedy, *Places in the Heart* is a family melodrama. The film integrates Moses, a black drifter, with Edna Spaulding (Sally Fields), a white widow, into a family who join together to save her from economic ruin. Edna's uplifiting Christian influence transforms Moses from a drifter and a thief who steals her silverware into a good Samaritan, while Moses helps save the widow's home by working hard and guiding her in planting and harvesting a cotton crop.

The film ends with a dreamy and surrealistic church service during which Edna, her dead husband, Moses, and a black dead character named Wiley who was summarily lynched for accidentally shooting Edna's husband while drunk, are reunited in a ritual of reconciliation. In this way, the black characters are redeemed from lives of petty crime and immorality by the institution of Christianity. Ironically, such an ending reverses the causality of Edna's economic redemption, which is brought about by Moses' selfless sacrifice.[24]

Crossroads (1986) relates the history of Mississippi Delta blues through the eyes of a young white guitarist named Eugene Martone (Ralph Macchio). Resituating *The Karate Kid* in the Deep South, the movie uses intermittent black-and-white flashbacks to Robert Johnson's mythical encounter with Satan at a rural crossroads to frame the story of Martone's pilgrimage from Long Island to Mississippi. The flashbacks contextualize black history in terms of a mystical past to which Martone gains access by agreeing to help his mentor Willie Brown (Joe Seneca) escape a Harlem nursing home. A former associate of blues man Robert Johnson, the shaman leads the young white guitarist along Southern back roads where Martone absorbs lessons in poverty and hard living that transform him from a boy to a man. With only enough money for a bus ride to Memphis, the pair travel to Willie's hometown on the back of a pickup truck loaded with chicken coops, an experience that ostensibly provides Martone with a passkey to blues tradition.

Driving Miss Daisy (1988) similarly relates the history of the Civil Rights movement from a white point of view. Drawing on the family melodrama, a friendship between Hoke (Morgan Freeman), a black male chauffeur, and Miss Daisy (Jessica Tandy), his elderly white female employer, becomes a microcosmic celebration of postwar racial integration in the South. Casting its black supporting actors as servants in essentially voiceless roles that revolve around and flatter liberal whites, the film suggests that Miss Daisy is the most important person in Hoke's life. Class relations in the film construct working-class life as black and masculine and upper-class life as white and female.

Like *Driving Miss Daisy, Mississippi Burning* (1988) relates the era of civil rights reform from a white perspective. *Mississippi Burning* deals with the 1964 disappearance of three civil rights activists during Mississippi's so-called Freedom Summer. Rewriting the FBI's role in the civil rights movement, the movie focuses on a bureaucratic yankee agent's (Willem Dafoe) reconsideration of his orthodox style under the tutelage of a small-town southern agent (Gene Hackman) who is willing to bend the rules to serve racial justice. As in *Places in the Heart* and *Driving Miss Daisy*, black supporting characters are largely muted by white leads' interpretation of their experiences.

Field of Dreams also uses a white everyman's redemption under the tutelage of a black surrogate father figure as a lens through which to view the 1960s culture of Black Nationalism. Ray Kinsella (Kevin Costner), an Iowa farmer, hears voices that encourage him to build a baseball field in the middle of a cornfield. Kinsella's actions dumbfound his neighbors because his farm is in danger of being crushed by the competition posed by corporate agriculture. After completing the job, Kinsella compulsively travels to Boston to retrieve Terence Mann (James Earl Jones), an aging 1960s black radical author whose work deeply influenced the former student activist's ideals. Upon his return, Kinsella discovers that his father's baseball heroes have magically materialized on the field.

In one of the final scenes, Mann makes a stirring speech about baseball and the American dream as black and white, father and son, and radical and conservative unite by playing baseball together. Reworking the biracial buddy formula in a baseball movie, *Field of Dreams* conflates the healing of racial differences fanned by the flames of the 1960s with the baseball genre's celebratory themes of the rebirth of family and patriotic tradition. As the sun sets over his enchanted baseball field, Ray pensively plays catch with his deceased father in a rite of healing. In a final nighttime shot, the pair continue the ritual as a line of car headlights winds its way from a distant horizon to the sacred baseball diamond, forming a pilgrimage of true believers drawn by the field's healing transformation of the past into a bright future.

SETTING: WHITE AFFLUENCE AND BLACK POVERTY

Biracial buddy narratives often equate white characters' immersion in inner-city settings and black characters' exposure to affluent white cultural settings as the basis for the redemption of race relations. *Trading Places* and *Rocky III* chronicle a process whereby white men redeem a culture of meritocracy after their redemption by an urban culture coded as black. Conversely, movies such as *48 Hrs.*, *Beverly Hills Cop*, and *Field of Dreams* portray blacks as being morally redeemed through their exposure to an edifying, civilizing white culture.

Biracial buddy narratives are often set in large, modern, urban settings in which a culture of white, upper-class conspicuous consumption is juxtaposed with one of minority poverty and decay typified by crime and suffering. Movies that take place in a setting of determinate space achieve resolution through white repossession of a contested geographical area defined as black. Examples include *48 Hrs.*, *Beverly Hills Cop*, *Another 48 Hrs.*, and *The Last Boy Scout*. Typically, the violent quest to redeem wilderness involves the restoration of a culture of meritocratic conspicuous consumption. Such a quest codes sites of conspicuous consumption as white and ones of urban blight and poverty as black.

Oftentimes, biracial buddy movies use high-concept set design and art direction to code white settings as loci of power and influence. *Beverly Hills Cop* and *Die Hard*, for example, isolate their everyman working-class heroes in gleaming settings of reflective chrome and glass that imply a seemingly impenetrable world of high-tech sophistication and white-collar corporate gamesmanship. The Nakatomi Building security system that German terrorists use to hold John McClane hostage dramatizes the plight of blue-collar workers rendered powerless by a system of late capitalism that uses an infrastructure of satellites and computers to coordinate a worldwide labor force. Conversely, McClane's physical mastery of this environment provides a simple and attractive solution to the problems raised by multinational capitalism over the 1980s, especially for males socialized to rely on physical force despite the limited opportunities for using it.[25]

Beverly Hills Cop juxtaposes the decay of black working-class Detroit with the gleaming splendor of Beverly Hills art galleries, hotels, and restaurants. The movie opens with a montage chronicling inner-city urban blight in Detroit, but soon shifts to a focus on a white culture of conspicuous consumption typified by shots of Rodeo Drive, a Rolls Royce dealership, and the various luxury homes, hotels, and restaurants through which Axel Foley chases a group of German drug smugglers and money launderers. Defining class in terms of overt contrasts in physical appearance, *Beverly Hills Cop* juxtaposes Foley's dilapidated Chevy Nova with a California couple's European luxury car as the detective trades flirtatious glances with the female passenger at a stoplight. *Lethal Weapon 2* follows Murtaugh and Riggs through well-appointed luxury homes in the Hollywood Hills and other luxurious sites around Los Angeles.

The narrative isolation of the black star in a largely white, often affluent cultural setting is an attempt to idealize America as a democratic consumer society, both for audiences at home and abroad. As Josh Stenger observes, lavish settings of conspicuous consumption had huge appeal to international audiences because "the shopping mall has become a new locus classicus of consumer cultures around the world."[26] Such a strategy resulted in Hollywood's packaging of black buddies as integrated members of a culture of meritocratic mobility, erasing any recognition of the class politics involved in the definition of black identity.

Beverly Hills Cop conveys Axel Foley's mastery of a world of power and material exclusivity by celebrating his negotiation of a series of highly stylized settings associated with wealth and institutional corruption. Cold metallic silver and blue wash across the smooth white walls of the Beverly Hills police station, the villains' high-rise corporate offices, and a U.S. Customs warehouse. The modern architecture and interiors that pervade Beverly Hills serve as indexes for the wealth and mobility of the characters who occupy these environments. Foley's faded jeans, T-shirt, and pullover jacket clash sharply with the designer-clothing-clad men and women he encounters in these surroundings. Beneath the surface, however, Foley proves himself to be readily assimilable into Beverly Hills society. In this way, immersion in a white consumer culture deracinates blacks in such films. Mark Crispin Miller describes the various characters on *The Cosby Show* as "mobile display cases" for the family's affluent lifestyle, adding that "here affluence is magically undisturbed by the pressures that ordinarily enable it."[27] A curious lack of racial friction emerges from Billy Ray Valentine's immersion in polite New York society and Axel Foley's immersion in Beverly Hills culture. "A street-wise black Detroit cop is set loose in the national capital of conspicuous consumption, and all we get are jokes about the comic gentility of the local police force," David Ansen laments.[28]

The buddies' quest for the restoration of law and order in a large urban setting through violent conquest is a typical narrative convention of adventure stories laden with assumptions about racial superiority. *Rocky III* juxtaposes the inner-city culture of Los Angeles, coded as black, with suburban Philadelphia, defined as white. *Beverly Hills Cop* similarly contrasts a street-level Detroit culture defined as working-class and black with Beverly Hills, an icon of wealth and conspicuous consumption defined as white and wealthy, even though it simultaneously harbors an international criminal conspiracy involving multinational capitalism. The relationship between race, class, and the restoration of morality in the city is similarly open to multiple interpretations in *48 Hrs.* The movie inverts the characterization of street culture as black and middle-class culture as white when Reggie Hammond, dressed in an Armani suit, borrows Jack Cates' badge in order to interrogate a working-class bar's white patrons. In successfully passing himself off as a detective and gaining valuable information, Hammond reveals that he has internalized the white, middle-class norms of the law enforcement community. However, his return to jail at the end of his furlough substantiates his declaration that he represents the patrons' worst nightmare as he silences and frisks them. Hammond's reincarceration suggests that he is in actuality a threat to the well-ordered community which must be contained.

While the bar scene celebrates Hammond's internalization of white cultural norms, it also simultaneously implies his difference by characterizing him as an exotic other positioned as the object of the gaze of the men in the bar—and the white spectator. Hammond's exhibitionistic act of throwing a glass at a mirror in order to get attention from the white clientele is comparable to an earlier shot of a partially naked, white female go-go dancer that brackets the beginning and end of the barroom sequence.[29]

While black immersion in a culture of white civilization deracinates the black buddy, white immersion in an ethnic or black world of nature imparts to the white lead a sense of natural, atavistic masculinity. The ability of whites to integrate themselves into a stereotypical black culture serves as the premise of several biracial buddy movies, including *Blues Brothers* (1980) and *Crossroads* (1986), both of which use the road movie formula to celebrate white people's so-called blackness.

The establishment of an opposition between a sterile world of white middle-class suburbia and a tainted world of black or ethnic street culture draws upon a longstanding stereotype of non-white cultures as deviant and exotic. *Crossroads* traces its young white hero's journey from boyhood to manhood by charting his trip from a recital hall in New York's Julliard School of Music, where he plays classical guitar for a bespectacled professor in a bow tie, to a smoky Mississippi blues joint, where he joins his mentor for an impromptu jam in front of an all-black audience of admirers. Backlit in red, the barn-like trappings of the Southern roadhouse throw into relief the pale white sterility of the recital hall.

The Karate Kid II uses a small Japanese fishing village as an exotic backdrop for a *Rocky*-inspired story of father-son bonding through lessons of moral self-help. Like Rocky and Apollo Creed, Daniel (Ralph Macchio) and Mr. Miyagi (Noriyuki "Pat" Morita) train in a silhouetted two-shot against a majestic background, waves crashing on the Pacific Ocean beach at sunset. Flourishing Japanese gardens of waterfalls and bonsai plants and crowded street markets populated by vendors in silent supporting roles serve as stereotypically exotic settings for Daniel's preparation for a final fight against an evil rival who threatens the young hero's Japanese girlfriend. Daniel's defeat of the challenger, like Eugene Martone's defeat of a rival guitarist (Steve Vai, coded as "the devil") in *Crossroads*, signals the boy hero's maturation and the integration of white and other into a well-ordered community.

Similarly, exposure to a street culture defined as black masculinizes Louis Winthorp in *Trading Places*, while Billy Ray Valentine's reeducation by the white upper class renders him racially invisible. In this way, *Trading Places* illustrates that upper-class white culture draws upon the atavistic energies of a street culture defined as black, even as it struggles to disassociate itself from street culture. It does so by equating masculinity with entrepreneurial savvy and hunger. It is thus Winthorp who mediates these opposing cultures by serving as a missing link in the story of social (as opposed to biological) evolution.[30] Qualities associated with blackness like street savvy and masculinity serve as a platform for white upward mobility in the film, which in turn makes possible the trickling down of wealth to working-class people, white and black, male and female.

CHARACTERIZATION: "GOOD" VERSUS "BAD" BLACKS

A key reason for the biracial buddy movie's appeal to a crossover audience of blacks and whites is its message that racial differences are inevitable in a society based on cultural pluralism. On the one hand, the humor created by black actors' invocation of recognizable stereotypes arises from a perception of such caricatures as laughable anachronisms. On the other hand, the humor for some audiences arises from these movies' stereotypical affirmation of white privilege through their assertion of black inferiority.

By his own admission, Eddie Murphy's comic sensibilities spring from the world of television, in which advertising sponsorship often results in narratives that universalize white middle-class norms as natural and commonsensical. *I Love Lucy*, *The Honeymooners*, and *Batman* were some of Murphy's favorite shows during high school, and Elvis Presley was one of his greatest show business inspirations. John Landis, who directed Murphy in *Trading Places* and *Coming to America*, told *Time* magazine that "I grew up on TV, but Eddie is TV. His world experience comes from the tube."[31]

The *Chicago Tribune* noted that while growing up Murphy had directly benefited from the Great Society programs of the 1960s as a resident of a predominantly black, middle-class suburb, Roosevelt, Long Island. It noted that "what Americans of all sorts detect in Murphy's humor is a man who is saying that, for him, race is no longer a burden or even an issue but something to be toyed with—another 'fun' choice on the lifestyle menu that one may dig or not, as the mood takes you."[32]

While the biracial buddy formula tried to appeal to as broad an audience as possible through textual openness, the prevailing cultural conditions of the Reagan era arguably shaped its construction of race. Rocky's symbolic upset of the flamboyant and thoroughly affluent black champion Apollo Creed, modeled on Muhammad Ali, became intertextually associated with the white, working-class Stallone's own against-all-odds success within a financially sagging and gloom-obsessed film industry ravaged by an anemic American economy.[33]

While the biracial buddy movie romanticizes the white, working-class hero as a redeemer of racial and class equality, it simultaneously predicates black economic mobility on conformity to the demands of a dominant white society. Black characters who integrate themselves into a dominant white cultural order champion a middle-class strain of black identity. Typically, the black buddy's loyalty and respectability are predicated on his middle-class standing. Richard Schickel describes Roger Murtaugh, a suburban family man contemplating retirement in the *Lethal Weapon* series, as "the Cosby role"[34]; Apollo Creed of the *Rocky* series wears three-piece suits; and Billy Ray Valentine of *Trading Places* eases into the white-collar culture of Wall Street effortlessly. The black buddy's middle-class standing also stands in stark contrast to the working-class status of other black characters that populate biracial buddy movies. *Rocky III* juxtaposes the good Apollo Creed with the bad Clubber Lang; good Reggie Hammond of *48 Hrs.* is juxtaposed with a variety of street thugs.

While a muscular, working-class black male such as Clubber Lang symbolizes a threat to middle-class values of law and order, the working-class, hardbody white hero embodies the defense of these beliefs. To discourage erotic contemplation of the male body and underscore the screen male's mastery over his body, the biracial buddy movie often subjects the white hero to extreme physical threats, tests, and punishments. Simultaneously, displays of violence become connotative extensions of the hero's physical power and mastery of his surroundings.[35] Rocky Balboa recaptures the "eye of the tiger" by undertaking a pilgrimage, at Apollo Creed's insistence, to the downtown Los Angeles gym that molded Creed into a world champion. While a group of black fighters stare forebodingly at the white champion upon his entry into the dark, dank gym, Creed's exhortations to the Italian Stallion to push himself harder than ever before provide Rocky with the courage and strength to defeat Clubber Lang.

While the biracial buddy movie constructs working-class white masculinity as authoritarian and economically self-sufficient, it constructs middle-class black masculinity in converse terms. Manthia Diawara suggests that the biracial buddy formula "castrates" the black male by characterizing his asexuality as part of a process of cultural deracination and isolation that results in his integration into white society.[36] The white buddy often acts in fatherly fashion to redeem the black buddy from the feminine realm by restoring the former's sense of sexual agency. The completion of this process is typically signified by the black buddy's violent final defense of the pair from villains. In *Rocky IV*, Apollo Creed rises to Rocky's defense by stepping into the ring against a Russian challenger. In *Lethal Weapon 2*, Murtaugh redeems himself after numerous jokes about his flagging sexual prowess when he fires in Riggs' defense as his white buddy collapses in his arms. As a phallic fire hydrant spews a stream of water into the air, Murtaugh and Riggs hug each other in a final homoerotic confirmation of their interracial, all-male workplace family.

The lack of sexuality incumbent in *Lethal Weapon*'s characterization of Murtaugh and *Beverly Hills Cop*'s construction of Foley represents an attempt to transcend racist stereotyping. Even as Murphy repeatedly raises the issue of sex, identifying himself with street culture in his various biracial buddy roles, he is nonetheless rendered asexual. "Sexual superiority is warp and woof of the black myth," the *Washington Post* suggested in its attempt to explain why Foley's verbal preoccupation with sex went so chronically unfulfilled.[37]

Usually, the black hero's emasculation is tied to his inadequacy as a violent avenger. Sergeant Powell of *Die Hard* can't fire his gun; Detective Murtaugh uses an old service revolver that is (to his colleagues) laughably small. When Murtaugh shows Riggs his service revolver, Riggs responds, "a lot of old-timers carry these." When Cates and Hammond square off for a fistfight in *48 Hrs.*, Hammond takes the brunt of the punishment.

The categorical definition of the buddies' black nemesis as bad in such movies is open to challenge. Cultural studies scholar John Fiske suggests, for example, that the gold chains worn by Clubber Lang in *Rocky III* can be read as symbols of racial and class oppression or earned prerogative.[38] Publicity about Mr. T's rise from an inner-city childhood as the son of a mother on welfare, to a job as a Hollywood stuntman, to roles in *Rocky III* and *The A-Team* support the latter reading. However, the roles in which Mr. T appeared restricted the viability of such a reading by narrowly stereotyping him in terms of physical strength, size, and ferocity. Such qualities were either indexes of his usefulness to white authority figures (as in *The A-Team*), or indicators of his danger to white civilization.

It is arguable that the positioning of black and white partners as interlopers in each other's cultures also opens the biracial buddy movie to multiple readings of race and class relations. In *Trading Places*, Winthorp's descent into a street culture in which he lives with a prostitute (Jamie Lee Curtis) alongside Hispanics and blacks forces him to identify with capitalism's exploitation of working-class women and people of color. Conversely, Billy Ray Valentine's sudden ascent to wealth leads to his disdain for his black street friends, whom he kicks out of his luxurious home after reprimanding them for their lack of social refinement.

ICONOGRAPHY: VIOLENCE, INTEGRATION, AND THE REDEMPTION OF RACE RELATIONS

The biracial buddy movie uses a variety of symbols to convey themes of interracial harmony and the restoration of the community. Rocky's violent extermination of Clubber Lang in *Rocky III* and Riggs and Murtaugh's final embrace in *Lethal Weapon* illustrate how racially contextualized rites of integration and order are encoded into the biracial buddy movie's iconography. Violence in *Rocky, Beverly Hills Cop*, and *Lethal Weapon* is driven by lowest common denominator attempts to appeal to worldwide audiences. However, such spectacle is also freighted with cultural meaning because violence historically has been a means in American mythology through which the white hero redeems himself and the community. In each of these films, the hero has a special talent that enables him to do the moral bidding of a community which is too weak to defend itself. Incumbent in such violence is the restraint of forces that threaten the well-being of the biracial buddies and, by extension, the community.

NOTES

1. James A. Miller, "From Sweetback to Celie: Blacks on Film into the 80s," *The Year Left 2*, ed. Mike Davis, Manning Marable, Fred Pfeil, and Michael Sprinker (London: Verso, 1987), 141.

2. David Ansen, "A Revival of Black Movies?" *Newsweek*, 7 January 1985, 50.

3. David F. Prindle, *Risky Business: The Political Economy of Hollywood* (Boulder: Westview Press, 1993), 127.

4. Arthur Lubow, "Blacks in Hollywood: Where Have They All Gone?" *People*, 17 May 1982, 30.

5. Peter Biskind, *Easy Riders, Raging Bulls: How the Sex-Drugs-and-Rock 'n' Roll Generation Saved Hollywood* (New York: Simon & Schuster, 1998), 349.

6. Lubow, "Blacks in Hollywood," 30.

7. Ibid.

8. Ibid.

9. Ibid.

10. Henry Nash Smith, *Virgin Land: The American West as Symbol and Myth* (Cambridge: Harvard University Press, 1950), 62.

11. John Belton, *American Cinema/American Culture* (New York: McGraw-Hill, 1994), 211.

12. Stephen Holden, "Sweet Sweetback's World Revisited," *New York Times*, 2 July 1995, sec. H9.

13. Michael Ryan and Douglas Kellner, *Camera Politica: The Politics and Ideology of Contemporary Film* (Bloomington: Indiana University Press, 1988), 126.

14. Ibid., 124.

15. Ibid., 129.

16. Jeffrey A. Brown, "Bullets, Buddies, and Bad Guys: The 'Action Cop' Genre," *Journal of Popular Film and Television* 21, no. 2 (1993): 83.

17. Christopher Ames, "Restoring the Black Man's Lethal Weapon," *Journal of Popular Film and Television* 3, no. 20 (1992): 83.

18. Stephen C. LeSueur and Dean Rheberger, "*Rocky IV, Rambo II,* and the Place of the Individual in Modern American Society," *Journal of American Culture* (summer 1988): 27.

19. Elizabeth G. Traube, *Dreaming Identities: Class, Gender, and Generation in 1980s Hollywood Movies* (Boulder: Westview Press, 1992), 20.

20. Fred Pfeil, "From Pillar to Postmodern: Race, Class, and Gender in the Male Rampage Film," *The New American Cinema,* ed. Jon Lewis (Durham: Duke University Press, 1998), 150.

21. Belton, *American Cinema/American Culture,* 135.

22. Alan Nadel, *Flatlining on the Field of Dreams: Cultural Narratives in the Films of President Reagan's America* (New Brunswick, N.J.: Rutgers University Press, 1997), 32.

23. Ed Guerrero, *Framing Blackness: The African American Image in Film* (Philadelphia: Temple University Press, 1993), 124.

24. Jane Caputi and Helene Vann, "Questions of Race and Place: Comparative Racism in *Imitation of Life* (1934) and *Places in the Heart* (1984)," *Cineaste* 15, no. 4, (1987): 19.

25. Mark Gallagher, "I Married Rambo: Spectacle and Melodrama in the Hollywood Action Film" *Mythologies of Violence in Postmodern Media,* ed. Christopher Sharrett (Detroit: Wayne State University Press, 1999), 210.

26. Josh Stenger, "Consuming the Planet: Planet Hollywood, Stars, and the Global Consumer Culture," *The Velvet Light Trap* 40 (1997): 45.

27. Mark Crispin Miller, "Prime Time: Deride and Conquer," *Watching Television,* ed. Todd Gitlin (New York: Pantheon, 1986), 208.

28. David Ansen, "An Officer and a Comedian," *Newsweek,* 3 December 1984, 81.

29. Manthia Diawara, "Black Spectatorship: Problems of Identification and Resistance," *Black American Cinema,* ed. Manthia Diawara (New York: Routledge, 1993), 215.

30. Nadel, *Flatlining on the Field of Dreams,* 36.

31. Deborah A. Wilburn, *Eddie Murphy: Entertainer* (New York: Chelsea House Publishers, 1993), 28.

32. Larry Kart, "Eddie Murphy: Comedy's Supernova Sends Humor into a Different Orbit," *Chicago Tribune,* 7 April 1985, sec. C8.

33. Sylvester Stallone, *The Official Rocky Scrapbook* (New York: Grosset & Dunlap, 1977), 20.

34. Richard Schickel, "Bone Crack," *Time,* 23 March 1987, 86.

35. Ibid., 209.

36. Diawara, "Black Spectatorship," 214.

37. Paul Attanasio, "Box Office Breakthroughs: Moving Beyond Race in American Film," *Washington Post,* 31 March 1985 sec. G1.

38. John Fiske, *Television Culture* (New York: Routledge, 1987), 206.

Chapter 5

Gender and the MTV Music-Video Movie

Hollywood since the rise of sound in the 1920s has attempted to establish synergies between hit Broadway plays, film musicals, and other media such as radio and television. *The Jazz Singer's* (1927) introduction of on-screen sound provided a new method of marketing sheet music and radio performances to audiences. Over the 1930s, Warner Bros., MGM, and Paramount acquired music publishers so that they could participate in royalties from the sheet music industry. The film industry realized that a popular theme song could draw audiences into the theater, while a well-liked film could also promote the music in it. The film industry soon found that it could make a great deal of money from licensing radio to play music by popular composers like George Gershwin and Cole Porter.[1]

Hollywood's use of radio promoted other symbioses as well. Film stars gave interviews, hosted shows for sponsors and endorsed their products, and played in radio dramas sponsored by retail companies. For example, Paramount recruited Bing Crosby and Bob Hope from radio during the 1930s.[2] The filmed entertainment industry also controlled a substantial portion of the pop music publishing industry and derived substantial income from music royalties paid by the radio companies. The introduction of the long-playing record in the 1940s led to the musical's abandonment of sheet music for the original cast recording and prompted Hollywood to bankroll Broadway productions in order to gain the rights to plot, title, and music. Hollywood's shift from marketing sheet music to selling soundtrack recordings resulted in the musical's movement away from music written for live reproduction and towards songs written for phonograph and radio.[3]

Television's proliferation over the 1950s further altered the relationship between music and narrative that was once integral to the American film musical's use of song to tell stories about romance and courtship. With the rise of television, the musical became a vehicle for promoting the consumption of recorded soundtracks rather than the sale of sheet music for live singing along around the family piano. The musical's dance styles became increasingly idiosyncratic. The film musical thus increasingly capitalized on trends in popular fashion to mask its status as a mass medium, thereby encouraging audiences to relate to the onscreen characters through the consumption of soundtrack recordings and clothing styles rather than sing-along participation or home re-creation of the soundtrack music.[4]

Hollywood responded by prepackaging 1950s musicals that drew on the reputations of established Broadway plays and record industry stars. The beginning of this trend was evident in the films of Elvis Presley and beach blanket movies starring Frankie Avalon and Annette Funicello. However, *Saturday Night Fever*'s carefully coordinated roll-out strategy of theatrical release and staggered radio airplay represented a milestone in the musical's makeover into a marketing- and style-driven high-concept vehicle.

As a form of entertainment, the musical also takes on an additional function at the level of reception. Rick Altman suggests that entertainment over American history has been vilified by both business and religion, as a waste of time and a sin. He nonetheless suggests that this vilification of entertainment overlooks the role it plays in the re-creation of the worker for optimal workday performance.[5] The American film musical historically has served as an appropriate vehicle for promoting leisure-time activities of musical production and consumption because of its narrative focus on the role of entertainment in both facilitating the individual's achievement of class mobility and binding women and men of different classes into couples and families.

The values of economic individualism praised by the Reagan administration are incumbent in the music-video movie's focus on the theme of the individual's achievement of class transcendence through redemptive rites of physical competition and talent. In celebrating performing talent as a foundation for middle-class mobility, the music-video movie champions entertainment as a redemptive form of work that enables the male and female leads to distinguish themselves from other couples who fail to achieve class mobility because they lack the natural ability or moral character to do so. Character lifestyles are often opposed on the basis of oppositions of work versus entertainment, working class versus middle class, and male versus female. Such a structure establishes a thematic opposition between a pair of romantically involved lead performers.[6]

Often, additional oppositions embellish this dichotomy. Females frequently transform adolescent males into mature providers through marriage. Conversely, males control women's sexuality through prerogatives of wealth and power. Such a motif is implied by the portrayal of the man as an older, patriarchal figure and the woman as a younger, childlike character.[7] The film musical's portrayal of females as tamers of males and men as sexual controllers of women thus makes it an effective tool for naturalizing hegemonic sexual norms. The MTV music-video movie follows this pattern by recognizing the circumscription of men and women's roles on the basis of biological difference, lionizing wives and mothers while vilifying women who violate these nurturing functions by prioritizing career over family or opting for abortion rather than childbirth.

In contrast to the biracial buddy movie, which defines the male body as a site of physical sacrifice and redemption, the music-video movie constructs men's and women's bodies as sites of fashion accoutrement, exemplifying high concept's definition of characters on the basis of style. The classical Hollywood musical, as Altman observes, also defines the male and female leads on the basis of parallel traits, intricately interwoven into setting, iconography, music, and dance, as well as their personal styles of performance. Even the differences between Jeanette MacDonald and Maurice Chevalier's singing voices are representative of these parallel traits.[8]

In contrast, the music-video movie's definition of its male and female leads in foregrounded, self-conscious terms of style casts them as so-called types on the basis of cliché, superficial traits skimmed from television and movies. As Henry Jenkins observes, high-concept movies targeted a teenage audience raised on endless hours of television storytelling and the entire history of cinema on videocassette.[9] Directors of music-video movies often migrated to film from television advertising and programming.

Viewers of the music-video movie thus implicitly understand flourishes such as Ren McCormick's New Wave clothing and Walkman stereo as aspects of *Footloose*'s characterization of him as a fan of popular music and MTV. However, *Footloose* offers no further referents for Ren as a character on the basis of setting, music, or even his dance style, which draws upon gymnastics and aerobics. In this way, the music-video movie defines its male and female leads on the basis of superficial forms of shorthand iconography rather than opposing categories of intricately interrelated oppositions.

Long before the music-video movie, *Butch Cassidy and the Sundance Kid* incorporated the hit single "Raindrops Keep Fallin' On My Head" in an effort to create cross-marketing synergies. However, the Reagan-era music-video movie represented a much more calculated integration of marketing and advertising into movie aesthetics by drawing upon a style of television advertising popularized in the late 1970s. Adopted by music video directors with the dawn of MTV, this style of montage proliferated in music-video movies designed to be cross-marketed on the channel. However, as Wyatt observes, the music-video movie's visual excess is simultaneously indebted to the classical Hollywood musical's stylistic device of constructing a secondary utopian textual level in which extended spectacles allow characters to transcend their everyday lives through song and dance.[10]

THE MUSIC-VIDEO MOVIE

The filmed entertainment industry's focus on the music-video movie during the 1980s sprang from a confluence of changes within Hollywood. Warner Communications' cofounding of Warner Amex Cable with American Express in 1979 provides an early example of the trend of consolidation and concentration that shaped the music-video movie. The partnership resulted in Warner Amex's expansion into the sixth largest cable multi-system operator (MSO) in the United States in 1984, partially on the basis of the partners' success in developing MTV as a programming source. MTV was sold in 1985 to Viacom, owner of the programming services VH-1, Nickelodeon, and Lifetime, and of Viacom Cable Television, the fifteenth largest multi-system operator in the country in 1991 with 1.87 million subscribers.[11]

Founded by former radio programmer Robert Pittman, MTV's strategy of narrowcasting music videos to a traditionally hard-to-reach audience of white suburban teens made it an irresistible marketing outlet for record labels. The music channel achieved cost efficiency and tight diversification by striking upstream and downstream distribution agreements with record companies and multiple cable system operators. In the process, it limited its choice of musical artists to top-selling, mainstream acts with proven appeal to suburban teenage consumers. Artists with appeal to minority audiences were avoided because the primarily urban areas where they lived had not yet been wired for cable television. The channel's ability to provide advertisers with focused access to a suburban teenage television audience of moviegoers and record buyers also enabled moviemakers to more effectively target a youth market. MTV's ability to break new music on an exclusive basis made it an attractive source of presale opportunities and tie-in campaigns for movie producers, cable companies, record labels, and consumer goods advertisers anxious to connect with young consumers.

While federal deregulation of broadcast television nurtured cable TV's growth, FCC deregulation of the radio industry promoted further synergies between MTV and radio. The agency extended license terms to seven years and lifted prohibitions on a single entity owning radio and television stations in the same city. Deregulation of radio content requirements resulted in greater reliance on syndicated program packages of automated, prerecorded shows consisting of standardized music with brief breaks for station news, weather, and disc jockey patter.[12]

MTV's strategy of programming to appeal to white suburban teenagers promoted similar homogeneity in the channel's choice of music videos. As a virtual prohibition on black musical talent shaped its choice of videos over most of the 1980s, only black stars with crossover popularity, such as Michael Jackson, received any significant exposure. While record company executives still thought in terms of big hits with universal appeal, MTV based its content on VALS (values and lifestyle) typology and psychographics, creating programming that mirrored the leisure culture of its young, largely white audience. MTV's production mandate of designing advertisements to appeal to a youth target market also meant activating ideological assumptions about rock music and youth.[13] Simultaneously, MTV's adoption of market research as a basis for programming choices encouraged the channel's suppression of music videos that criticized its design as a vehicle for marketing rebellion as a lifestyle choice.

The channel's refusal to air Neil Young's "This Note's for You" video in 1988 lent credibility to left-wing criticisms that MTV suppressed the video because it overtly criticized the system of advertising imagery and the economic structure that supported the company. While MTV claimed that the video violated its standards policies, Young and his record label countered that MTV was afraid of offending the advertisers cited in the work.[14]

While the music-video movie was also essentially an advertisement, film musicals of the early 1970s were ambitious artistic commentaries. *Cabaret* (1972), *Nashville* (1975), and *All That Jazz* (1980) often self-consciously critiqued the musical's conventional celebration of the relationship between the production of music and the creation of community and its conservative equation of happiness with heterosexual romance and marriage.[15] Set in Berlin in 1931, *Cabaret* links the personal with the political by exploring a sexually freewheeling woman (Liza Minelli) and a gay man's (Michael York) attempt to structure their relationship on the basis of homosexuality and women's sexual liberation.

Nashville also confronts and disavows the musical's assumptions. Set in America's heartland, the film reveals the dissolution of folk tradition in a mass culture of product packaging and craven opportunism. *Nashville*'s credits are stylized to resemble cheap, garish advertisements, and an oversized billboard for Goo-Goo Clusters chocolate candy is conspicuously situated on a stage backdrop for the "Grand Ole Opry" television show.[16]

All That Jazz also confronts and disavows the musical's blithe assumptions. It questions the musical's easy slippage from reality into fantasy by suggesting that choreographer Joe Gideon's (Roy Scheider) attempt to retreat from his familial responsibilities behind a role or performance trivializes both his life and art.[17] The fetishization of the performer as a source of spectacle is also self-consciously explored in *All That Jazz*. As J. P. Telotte observes, the film is "less concerned with the creation of a show and the set of social relations it entails than with the individual's persistent desire for self-affirmation and completion through his own status as show, spectacle, or entertainment."[18]

All That Jazz's provocative deconstruction of the film musical in 1980 was an aberration amid Hollywood's all-encompassing focus on packaged, presold musical productions like *Saturday Night Fever* and *Grease*. *Saturday Night Fever*'s high-concept focus on the lifestyle trend of disco signaled a shift in the musical's mode of production towards capitalizing on sudden demographic shifts in popular taste. A product of agency packaging, the movie combined a focus on the culture of disco club dating, a television star (John Travolta), a hit screenwriter Norman Wexler (*Joe, Serpico*), and The Bee Gees, a popular group on Robert Stigwood's RSO (Robert Stigwood Organization) label.

The movie's promotion of the disco lifestyle illustrated how movies during the late 1970s became increasingly interwoven with processes of commodity production and consumption by priming consumer demand for an ever-expanding array of leisure goods such as soundtrack albums and fashionable clothing. Rejecting countercultural hedonism, *Saturday Night Fever* hinges its youthful hero's upwardly mobile aspirations on conformity to middle-class habits of expensive dress and self-discipline, anticipating an emerging culture of 1980s conservatism and conspicuous consumption. Revealing the film musical's increasingly symbiotic relationship to television, *Grease* relied on Travolta's popularity as a TV star while also modeling itself on TV situation comedies like *Happy Days* and *Laverne and Shirley*.

While *Saturday Night Fever* and *Grease* exemplified the growing interpenetration between television and movies on the basis of their promotion of music for consumption rather than production, the integration of music video's narrative and visual conventions into the American film musical resulted in a much greater compromise of the classical Hollywood musical's arrangement of plot, character, and music into an intricate form and seamless style. While motivated by an attempt to cross-market soundtrack albums and capitalize on lifestyle trends, Hollywood's embrace of music video's visual conventions was an attempt to more effectively market movies for a worldwide audience by transcending language barriers through a reliance on spectacle.

The American film musical once relied on an internal narrative logic, which constructed song and dance as integral means of telling a story about rites of romance and courtship.[19] Schatz suggests, for example, that *Easter Parade* (1948), which opens with Fred Astaire dancing down an avenue and singing greetings to passersby, integrates the star's dual roles as performer and romantic male lead.[20] The musical's convention of stars performing directly for the camera reified Astaire's status as a unique and talented individual because of the range of dramatic and performative demands required of the musical star.[21] Similarly, the male and female leads often alternate verses during singing duets that comment on the sexual duality that orders the plot's parallel focus on differences and similarities between men and women. George Gershwin's song "Bess You Is My Woman Now" illustrates how *Porgy and Bess* (1959) uses the interplay in melodic structure between the lines sung by the title characters to underscore the sexual duality between them.[22]

With the rise of MTV, the American film musical became a movie with music in it rather than a movie that says what it has to say in music, to paraphrase Michael Wood.[23] R. Serge Denisoff and William D. Romanowski note, for example, that songs were chosen for *Footloose* on the basis of interconglomerate arrangements that facilitated lower costs for music titles. Becky Shargo, music supervisor for *Footloose*, observed that CBS Records allowed Paramount to use a Quiet Riot song on an exclusive basis in the movie because the music company had a contract with Paramount to do *Footloose*'s soundtrack album.[24] Audiences heard Sammy Hagar's "The Girl Gets Around" while watching the movie, even though director Herbert Ross used Bob Seger's "Old Time Rock 'n' Roll" on the set during the actual filming of it.[25] In contrast to the classical Hollywood musical, the music-video movie's marketing-driven design resulted in the inclusion of songs with little or no direct relevance to its plot. Complex dance scenes were often executed through the use of a body double, compromising the classical Hollywood musical's dual construction of the performer as both star and romantic lead. *Flashdance* director Adrian Lyne hired dancer Maria Jahan to execute complex dance routines that couldn't be performed by star Jennifer Beals.

Hollywood's adoption of high-concept storytelling as a means of resituating a hit movie's plotline into a different generic context further compromised the musical's complex integration of story, song, and dance. The proliferation of *Rocky*'s theme of achieving moral redemption through physical perfection across *Fame, Staying Alive, Flashdance,* and *Footloose* provides one example of high concept's practice of targeting multiple audiences by mixing and matching genres.

Designed to be reiterated across a variety of contexts, *Fame, Staying Alive, Flashdance, Footloose,* and *Dirty Dancing* were also modeled on the basis of episodic television's recuperable story line and television and print advertising's definition of characters in terms of lifestyle.[26] In establishing marriage as the sole goal of romantic coupling, the music-video movie illustrates how high concept establishes sexual freedom as an immoral deviation from proper rites of middle-class familial reproduction.

PLOT: MALE MOBILITY, FEMALE DOMESTICITY

Hollywood's adoption of the musical as a loose generic template for the music-video movie was motivated by the fit between the goal of selling male and female lifestyle accessories to young moviegoers and the musical's focus on rites of courtship and leisure. As a genre of integration, the classical Hollywood musical conflates the formation of the couple with their transcendence of their gender and class differences. In this way, the musical juxtaposes the work ethic and its values with activities and qualities typically associated with entertainment.[27]

Leisure and work are characterized as class-based homologous oppositions because the Protestant ethic condones leisure only when it improves work efficiency.[28] Telotte suggests that working-class individualism and middle-class social restraint are addressed as the musical explores the conditions under which the individual's desire for expression can be integrated into a social structure that channels and represses spontaneity and impulse.[29] The musical complements this class-ordered dichotomy with a gender dichotomy that juxtaposes the freedom-loving, uninhibited male with a socially restrained, domesticating female counterpart. The principal characters' romantic coupling through actual or implied marriage celebrates the integration of such differences and signals narrative closure.

The high-concept music-video movie's incorporation of aspects of genres of integration and genres of order enables it to equate the formation of family and the eradication of others that threaten its self-sufficiency and harmony. In the Saturday Night Fever sequel Staying Alive, the incorporation of Rocky's plotline conflates the principal characters' achievement of romantic coupling with the elimination of a femme fatale vixen who threatens the couple's happiness. Urban Cowboy similarly resituates Saturday Night Fever's coming-of-age story in the context of a western. Like Tony Manero, Bud Davis (John Travolta) is a high school graduate seeking a sense of reprieve from his dead-end blue-collar job through Saturday nights on a nightclub dance floor with his dance partner and wife, Sissy (Debra Winger). Urban Cowboy also draws upon Rocky II in predicating the restoration of the couple after a trial separation on Bud's physical triumph over a romantic rival and prison convict (Scott Glenn), whom Sissy met while working outside the home. While Urban Cowboy's coming-of-age story line might have appealed to an adolescent audience, the western plot and country-and-western dance styles and country crossover music were demographic appeals to an older audience. Variety noted, "city slick teenagers in the audience may grow a bit bored with all the bull ridings, along with all the other trappings at Gilley's. Certainly, the dancing that goes on there is mainly a variation on the old two-step and while Travolta does it well, it's nothing to equal the flash of 'Fever' and 'Grease.'"[30]

Despite its somewhat modest opening, *Urban Cowboy* achieved greater box-office popularity over the course of its theatrical release. Its recovery was attributed to its music soundtrack, which proved popular among an eighteen-and-older audience on the basis of its use of 1970s Southern California rock stars like Joe Walsh and The Eagles to reinterpret and write country-and-western songs. The soundtrack generated triple platinum sales and a sequel album, demonstrating that the free publicity achieved through heavy radio promotion could offset the modest box-office opening of a movie.

The success of the rock-flavored country album revealed that America's fascination with disco music was waning. One reason for disco's declining popularity was MTV. Lisa Lewis is correct in observing that MTV's design as a visual arena for rock music was fundamentally at odds with the anti-commercial stance of rock's working-class discourse.[31] A system of address rooted in urban realism obscured the network's commercial intentions by frequently constructing its videos' social tableaus as street settings which celebrated male adolescent values. While this appeal to an adolescent male audience enabled white heavy metal artists such as Def Leppard to gain saturation airplay on MTV, the Bee Gees' association with rhythm and blues music and their falsetto style hampered the group's attempts to gain exposure on the channel.

Disco emerged from New York's black, Hispanic, and gay urban dance scenes in the early 1970s. The Reagan administration's overt opposition to the gay rights movement fostered a backlash against disco, which continued to be perceived as an aspect of gay and lesbian subculture despite its crossover popularity during the late 1970s. In courting the religious right, Reagan ignored gay and lesbian activists who exhorted him to address the proliferation of AIDS during the early 1980s. In the critical years of 1984–1985, according to Reagan's White House physician, Brigadier General John Hutton, the president thought of AIDS as though "it was the measles and it would go away."[32]

Staying Alive struggled to define Reagan-era screen masculinity during this ideological backlash against the gay and lesbian subculture of disco nightclubbing. Written and directed by Sylvester Stallone, *Staying Alive's* high-concept resituation of *Rocky's* theme of physical redemption in the context of a Broadway musical represented a poor fit between the sport success genre, which privileges the male body as a site of empowerment and physical prerogative, and the musical, which characterizes it as the passive, feminized object of a male gaze.[33] The masculine persona constructed for John Travolta by the *Rocky* story line's conflation of the title character's hypermasculine physique and his upward mobility was made problematic by the homophobic perception of disco by the early 1980s as a deviant lifestyle. Instead, as the 1980s progressed, *Rocky's* physical iconography was most successfully employed in action-adventure narratives, where the male body's exaggerated musculature complements the story's focus on a warrior's achievement of redemption through macho violence.[34]

Fame loosely weaves *Rocky*'s theme into a so-called let's put on a show musical, such as *Strike Up The Band* (1940), starring Mickey Rooney and Judy Garland, as it uses a series of episodic television vignettes to follow a group of students from their first auditions for a New York performing arts high school to graduation day. An opening series of audition scenes characterize the entertainment profession as a multiethnic, racially diverse meritocracy in which aspiring performers are admitted on the basis of talent and potential. The crosscutting that compares the performances of Ralph (Barry Miller), a brazen young Puerto Rican comedian who embellishes his performing experience before each audition, and Doris (Maureen Teefy), a withdrawn neurotic who freezes onstage, defines the pair as opposites whose eventual romantic coupling celebrates the formation of the students into a community.

Like *Rocky*, *Fame* equates Ralph's triumph over self-doubt with his successful wooing of Doris, who evolves under his tutelage from a shy young spinster into a beautiful woman. Their friendship with lonely, angst-ridden classmate Montgomery McNeal (Paul McCrane) completes the story's conformity to *Rocky*, substituting Doris and Montgomery for Adrian and Pauley. As in *Rocky*, the idle rich and immoral poor are juxtaposed with those who achieve upward mobility through meritocratic talent. Leroy (Gene Anthony Ray), for example, is a virtually illiterate black student cast as a brutal buck (he is stripped of a knife tucked in his waist band directly over his crotch upon his arrival for an audition) on the basis of his lust for a delicate white female student (Laura Dern) whose lack of talent and class privilege code her as a member of the idle rich. While Leroy graduates because of athletic talent, the young ballerina drops out.

Like *All That Jazz*, *Fame* focuses on the relationship between creative mentors and students and the process through which aspiring artists become consummate professionals. Unlike its predecessor, however, *Fame* avoids any self-conscious criticism of the musical's visual and narrative conventions. With a background in directing television advertisements, *Fame* director Alan Parker saw a movie about the various characters' trials and tribulations as an opportunity to celebrate America's redemptive myth of classlessness. "Their America is rather hopeful—an alternative to smashing up subway stations," the British Parker said of the characters in *Fame*. "These kids are very special. They have aspirations and dreams in a world where it is fashionable to be destructive—particularly coming from England, where this is the predominant feeling of most young people."[35] Certainly the song "Fame," with its soaring musical bridge during which singer Irene Cara proclaims "I'm gonna live forever," echoes this sense of optimism. However, a montage of New Yorkers dancing in the street to the song as it blares from a taxi cab bursts onto the screen immediately after Montgomery confesses his homosexuality to Doris, exemplifying the music video's role as an extractable passage that lacks any direct causal relationship to the events motivating the music-video movie's narrative.

Flashdance is a thinly disguised reprise of *Fame*, both in its reliance on the *Rocky* plotline and its inclusion of a catchy theme song ("What a Feeling") also recorded by Irene Cara. Like the students in *Fame*, the heroine of *Flashdance* is an aspiring dancer who achieves admission to a prestigious performing arts academy on the basis of talent rather than pedigree. Alex becomes a stand-in for Rocky, while her boss Nick substitutes for Rocky's father figure and trainer Mickey, and Alex's friend Jeanne serves as Pauley. Nick's role as a father figure results in a virtual inversion of *Saturday Night Fever*'s characterization of a middle-class woman as the agent of a working-class man's symbolic achievement of upward mobility through enlightenment. Instead, Nick becomes the facilitator of Alex's mobility, signified by her admission to a prestigious dance academy. In contrast, Alex's friend Jeanne fails in her aspiration to become a professional ice skater and lapses into a life of nightclub striptease and downward mobility.

Flashdance's design as a modular series of extractable music videos reveals high concept's marketplace-driven influence on the plot in other ways as well. Style rather than character motivation shapes Alex's story of class mobility as scenes of her doing an aerobic workout to the song "Maniac" and lifting weights with her friends to Joan Jett's "I Love Rock 'n' Roll" become truncated expressions of her tenacity and ambition. Simultaneously, the interlude establishes a secondary level of address that evokes the classical Hollywood musical's utopian song and dance sequence by celebrating the redemptive power of exercise in Alex's life.[36]

The high-concept strategy of appropriating prevailing cultural trends and packaging them for suburban teen consumption results in *Flashdance*'s contextualization of Alex's class mobility in terms of natural talents traceable to her urban, working-class lifestyle. While walking in downtown Pittsburgh, for example, she pauses to admire the breakdancing maneuvers of black and Hispanic teens performing for a small streetside audience. Her incorporation of the urban performers' moves into her successful audition for the dance academy becomes a further illustration of her status as a natural aristocrat who gains admission to the elite institution on the basis of imagination and ingenuity rather than background or privilege. While the classical Hollywood musical often structures relationships between leads on the basis of differing dance styles, *Flashdance*'s high-concept design as a modular series of music videos results in a definition of her as a natural aristocrat almost solely on the basis of a dance associated with urban working-class black and ethnic culture.

While *Flashdance* bases its high-concept premise on a manufactured dance trend that blandly appropriates black urban culture for white suburban adolescents, *Footloose* draws its inspiration from intertextual reference to teen exploitation movies of the 1950s. Inherent in the story about a rebellious high school outsider who squares off with religious right school authorities by planning a senior dance is a caricature of Reagan-era fundamentalism as an assault on clean-cut teenagers' right to have fun. Director Michael Cimino was originally hired to direct *Footloose*, but was dropped after he insisted on rewriting the script with a darker ending. "Cimino wanted to make a darker movie. We wanted to make an entertainment," coproducer Craig Zadan explained.[37] Producer Dan Melnick concurred. "People don't want to be confused," he noted.[38]

While *Footloose* recalls *East of Eden* (1955) and *Rebel Without a Cause* (1955), it also draws upon *Saturday Night Fever* and *Urban Cowboy* in its juxtaposition of repressive small-town tradition and big-city sophistication. The movie establishes this juxtaposition through its loose reiteration of *Rebel Without a Cause*'s story of a young misfit who moves to a new high school and bucks the system by upending adult authority through acts of juvenile delinquency while falling in love for the first time. *Footloose* is similarly about a young rebel's (Kevin Bacon) attempt to organize a school dance by overturning a town ban on dancing while also dealing with first love.

The opening of *Footloose* establishes a dichotomy between Ren's teenage rebellion and Lori's conformity by juxtaposing a music-video montage consisting of shots of anonymous feet dancing to the theme song with a conventional series of establishing shots that define Beaumont as a small town stuck in the 1950s. The frenetic movement of the dancing feet stands in stark contrast to the long, static shots of a small white church with a steeple, a tractor sitting in a plowed field, and a neatly trimmed front yard with a white picket fence.

The movie follows the high-concept practice of matching a soundtrack recording with a marketable concept drawn from contemporary popular culture trends by linking Kenny Loggins' FM-friendly dance anthem "Footloose" with the theme of adolescent rebellion against Reagan-era religious fundamentalism. In contrast to the classical Hollywood musical, the union of image and sound in *Footloose* creates bursts of excess that operate as stand-alone set pieces by working against the sequential advancement of the narrative. Modeled on television advertisements of the late 1970s that carefully combined lifestyle vignettes and mood music, these music-video montages conflate notions of adolescent rebellion, music, and community with carefully chosen soundtrack songs rather than directly commenting on the narrative.[39]

A comparison of two montages from the film illustrates how the incorporation of music-video techniques into the Reagan-era music-video movie uses the shorthand language of lifestyle imagery to contrast differences between Ren and Lori that become the basis for their eventual coupling. A montage carefully timed to Shalamar's "Dancing in the Sheets" intercuts shots of Lori and her friends conversing in the parking lot of a local drive-in hamburger restaurant with shots of a cook flipping a burger, a boy playing pinball, and a girl idly talking on the telephone. While the combination of music and imagery suggests that Lori is an integrated member of a small-town community of teens reminiscent of the 1950s, a subsequent montage during which Ren dances alone in a barn defines him as a loner alienated from his peers. Intercutting flashback vignettes of Ren's fights with local adults and peers, the montage equates the dancer's frenzied movements with adolescent frustration.

Simultaneously, *Footloose* undercuts this objectification of Ren in feminine terms by juxtaposing his masculine heroism with his peers' timid reticence. In an impassioned plea before the city council, Ren wins the city fathers over by quoting the Bible's definition of dance as a form of religious celebration, as his classmates look on encouragingly from the gallery. This construction of Ren as a self-assertive masculine rebel against repressive small-town tradition is complemented by the beating he gives a romantic rival who threatens Ariel outside the long-awaited dance. While the dance celebration signifies Ren and Ariel's unification as a couple, their coupling is dependent on Reverend Moore's relinquishment of hypocritical traits of middle-class propriety and prudery. Conversely, Ren's use of scripture to win over the reverend simultaneously evokes the motif of bonding between fathers and sons so prevalent in Reagan-era cinema.

Dirty Dancing also celebrates the formation of the middle-class family on the basis of intergenerational reconciliation between fathers and sons. Set in 1963, the era of John F. Kennedy's Camelot, the movie pairs Frances "Baby" Houseman (Jennifer Grey), an idealistic, middle-class girl, with Johnny Castle (Patrick Swayze), a working-class dancer, in a story about first love set in a toney Catskills resort. *Dirty Dancing*'s opening credits fulfill a standard narrative function of imparting key aspects of the movie's premise in concentrated and self-conscious form.[40] Shot in slow motion and grainy black-and-white, the credits feature Johnny and Baby dancing in sexually suggestive fashion while The Ronettes' 1963 hit "Be My Baby" plays over bubblegum-pink lettering. The use of black-and-white film stock and a well-known 1960s girl group hit imply that the setting is the precountercultural past, while the song lyrics foreshadow the couple's romantic coupling and the lettering suggests the theme of first love. In these ways, even though the carefully coordinated music and cutting create a spectacle of visual excess traceable to music-video techniques, the opening draws upon traits traditionally associated with the Hollywood movie credit sequence.

As Altman observes, the American film musical opens with a series of paired segments that foreshadow the principal couple's eventual romantic union.[41] *Dirty Dancing* immediately defines Johnny as brash and confident and Baby as shy and reserved by cutting between the handsome lead and his partner Penny (Cynthia Rhodes) performing a fiery rumba before an adoring crowd of onlookers and Baby stiffly practicing a waltz with a boyish looking partner on a crowded dance floor. A dance in the staff quarters soon draws Baby across a bridge leading from the guest accommodations, where her middle-class innocence again sharply contrasts with Johnny's working-class sensuousness as she watches him dirty dancing with Penny to the Contours' "Do You Love Me?" Tight framing and medium close-ups of staff members dancing groin-to-groin complement the sexually suggestive orange, red, and yellow lighting that glows behind Baby as she awkwardly winds her way through the crowd.

Johnny soon initiates Baby's maturation from adolescence to womanhood by grooming her to become his dance partner. Differences between his working-class earthiness and her middle-class restraint dissolve as Baby's emotional growth casts into relief the hypocrisy of the resort's affluent middle-class culture. Robby, a Harvard-bound waiter who vies with Johnny for Baby's affections, lends her a copy of Ayn Rand's *The Fountainhead*, a Cold War literary touchstone that champions rational economic self-interest over welfare altruism. Later, he impregnates Penny (who left a broken home at sixteen) and denies any involvement with her, provoking a subsequent beating from Johnny that symbolically counterbalances the feminizing objectification of him during dance sequences. When Penny nearly dies after a desperate alleyway abortion, Dr. Houseman successfully intervenes at the last minute and saves her.

While Dr. Houseman at first blames Johnny for Penny's pregnancy, he must face his own class prejudice upon learning the truth. Baby and Johnny's romantic coupling during a dance performance stems from Dr. Houseman's reconciliation with Johnny. Their romantic coupling as natural aristocrats and husband and wife also parallels the overthrow of a rich aristocracy represented by the elitist waiter who vied for Baby's attention and the redemption of an immoral libertine dancer who competed for Johnny. Johnny's integrity and obvious dance talent motivate his ascendance from working-class pauper to middle-class prince as Dr. Houseman blesses the romantic union by recognizing the handsome dancer as a future son-in-law.

SETTING: CLASS, CONSUMPTION, AND COMMUNITY

While the couple's romantic embrace signals their transcendence of class and gender differences, it simultaneously signals the bridging of internal differences between members of the community. The music-video movie thus draws upon the classical Hollywood musical's construction of a civilized setting, in which internal boundaries of gender and class difference must be bridged through the principal couple's romantic embrace, and the mediatory power of song and dance.

Urban Cowboy represents an attempt to resituate *Saturday Night Fever*'s focus on a Carter-era culture of minimal economic expectations in an emerging Reagan-era context of yuppie western chic. *Urban Cowboy*'s rural southwestern setting is a bleak, industrialized landscape of oil refineries, mobile homes, and tract housing reminiscent of the ethnic, working-class Brooklyn enclave that Tony Manero longs to escape from in *Saturday Night Fever.* While *Saturday Night Fever* focused on the lifestyle trend of disco, *Urban Cowboy* was inspired by an upscale country nightclub craze which briefly flourished in the early 1980s. Calling *Urban Cowboy* "perhaps the most symbolic precursor of the eighties yuppie film," William J. Palmer writes that the folk musical western "chronicles how the Old West of cowboys and bucking broncos has been replaced by a new yuppie West of designer-dressed cowboys riding mechanical bulls."[42]

While *Urban Cowboy*'s emphasis on fashion and lifestyle focused on twenty-something, yuppie chic, *Fame*'s shimmering, MTV-inspired spectacle of neon-lit signs and backlit dance scenarios was an attempt to capture teenagers by using the music video's male-preferred form of address. *Flashdance* also incorporates this male-preferred locale into its social tableaus. Its primary setting is a nighttime inner-city, working-class milieu of bars and streets which perfectly summarizes the male adolescent's quest for rebellion, sexual encounter, and peer activity, as well as the notion of public spaces being areas of male privilege. Director Adrian Lyne uses beer-sign-style neon lights and wet, reflective asphalt surfaces to glorify the ritualized male adolescent activities of stepping out and cruising in search of sexual fulfillment.

While this use of conventions of film noir clearly signifies the street as a domain of male adolescent privilege, it simultaneously demarcates it as off-limits for young women. In *Fame,* a pornographer accosts Coco (Irene Cara) as she sits alone in a Times Square coffee shop. In *Flashdance,* Johnny C., the owner of a strip club (and played by Lee Ving, front man of the early-1980s Los Angeles hard-core punk band Fear), repeatedly harasses Alex as she walks down the street.

The densely urban settings of *Fame* and *Flashdance* imply a link between street fashion and class identity grounded in *Rocky*-inspired, Darwinesque narratives of a natural aristocracy's survival in predatory urban conditions. In contrast to the packed sidewalks and fluorescent subway lights that typify life outside the performing arts academy in *Fame,* earthy hues of brown and yellow provide a backdrop for the performance scenes that take place within it, defining the space as a site of venerable artistic tradition where successive generations have launched their New York City stage careers. A distinction arises between privilege and talent when one of the taskmaster instructors informs an aspiring dancer that she simply lacks the talent and innate drive to matriculate the academy. "I don't want to be the best," the student moans. "Then you won't be," the teacher sternly replies. *Flashdance* similarly characterizes the elite dance academy to which Alex ultimately gains admission as a setting of achievement. A long shot that dwarfs Alex's form as she stands before the dance academy's massive stone entrance of arches and columns captures the sense of intimidation that grips her upon her first visit to the institution. Upon entering a reception area, she cautiously navigates a gauntlet of students practicing dance exercises with seasoned poise and discipline.

While *Fame* and *Flashdance* characterize the dance institute as a proving ground for a natural aristocracy of performing artists, *Dirty Dancing* defines a castle-like Catskills resort in similar terms. As the movie's primary setting, the resort echoes the class dichotomies established by the lead characters through its juxtaposition of the dancers' modest staff quarters and the guests' lavish, cabana-style quarters. Within this setting, Johnny Castle proves that he is a natural aristocrat by upholding a middle-class moral code of monogamy and familial loyalty. In doing so, he gains the approval of Baby's medical doctor father, whose professional standing and restrained manner code him as a king.

CHARACTERIZATION: "GOOD" WOMEN VERSUS "BAD" WOMEN

The music-video movie's high-concept focus on lifestyle also transformed the star into a lifestyle model whom the viewer could emulate through the purchase of lifestyle accessories like music and clothing. Stuart Ewen traces the emergence of the celebrity to America's turn-of-the-century urbanization and the parallel rise of a consumer culture. A corridor between anonymity and fame arose as middle-class urbanites discovered cabaret life, and performers who reached a wider audience became revered as objects of emulation and adulation.[43] As Douglas Kellner suggests, the television-mediated consumer society that has emerged since World War II further transformed the definition of individual identity into consumerist terms. Television's construction of the celebrity as a purchasable form of identity in turn gave rise to the music-video movie's construction of characters in terms of image, style, and fashion.[44]

The decision to cast two relative unknowns in the lead roles of *Fame*, *Flashdance*, *Footloose*, and *Dirty Dancing* in order to control costs led to an emphasis on fashion and style to flesh out the principal characters' opposing class and gender traits. *Fame* was indeed a virtual catalog of nostalgic clichés skimmed from Hollywood's history of stage musicals. The music-video movie's self-conscious use of style, as Andrew Britton suggests, results in highly political representations of race, class, and gender that persuade viewers of their cartoonish insignificance by posing as pure entertainment.[45] Unlike modernist, auteur-shaped early 1970s deconstructions of commercial film and television forms, music-video movies aped television's episodic structure and its relentless foregrounding of lifestyle and consumption. Critics suggested that director Alan Parker's background in television advertising led to *Fame*'s emphasis on superficial stylistic flourishes and trite, stereotypical characterizations. Comparing the film's visual style to a Coke commercial, Janet Maslin writes, "Whatever *'Fame'* is selling, it comes in the prettiest, shiniest package the movies have lately seen."[46]

The movie's foregrounding of its characters as types also compromises its dramatic depth. Bruno Martelli, a talented but self-absorbed pianist, has to learn to take direction from an old, crotchety music teacher. Lisa, whose classical training becomes an indicator of her privileged upbringing, must face the fact that her class background can't compensate for a lack of talent. Coco, a proud but starving artist of true ability, hides her disadvantaged background by having Bruno's father, a cab driver, drop her off in front of an upscale cooperative that she passes off as her sister's place. Doris's adoption of a black beret symbolizes her maturation from a neurotic with stage fright into a confident artist. Leroy, a muscular black dancer from Harlem, grabs his crotch and rear end during his audition and battles a tirelessly dedicated English teacher (Ann Meara) throughout his four years at the school. David Denby observed, "the filmmakers come close to racial stereotyping. . . . Gore and Parker celebrate Leroy's animal prowess, but they forget to make him a person."[47]

Flashdance's characterization of Alex as fascinated with fashion (she is listening to her Walkman and reading *French Vogue* when her boss and future husband first approaches her) similarly foregrounds her as a model, an object of a male gaze. The characterization of her as a sexual object becomes more explicit when a close-up of a hamburger patty sizzling on a grill follows a shot of an overhead bucket of water drenching her scantily-clad form as she performs her stage routine.

Dirty Dancing also defines its male and female leads in terms of fashion by resituating *Rebel Without a Cause*'s angst-ridden, tough guy loner and constrained middle-class girl within the generic context of a Fred Astaire and Ginger Rogers musical. While evoking *Flying Down to Rio* (1933) and other Astaire-Rogers musicals in which the happy-go-lucky commoner and the proper aristocrat with duties to her family fall in love in an exotic kingdom, *Dirty Dancing* simultaneously defines Johnny as a James Dean or Marlon Brando on the basis of his pompadour, leather jacket, black T-shirt, and jeans. Natalie Wood's prom queen look also shapes Baby's prim style of dress. The aptly titled *Fame* similarly foregrounds Ralph as a Freddie Prinze wannabe whose brief tailspin into depression is motivated by a vaguely defined desire to emulate the comedian's live fast, die young philosophy of excessive living. As Mark Crispin Miller observes, "celebrity is the story" in high-concept music-video movies.[48]

ICONOGRAPHY: GENDER, PERFORMANCE, AND MUSIC

The musical conveys its themes of courtship and entertainment iconographically by working out tensions between object and illusion, social reality and utopia.[49] While the plot structure resolves such tensions in a final show that unites different genders and classes, music and dance also provide means through which the characters transcend interpersonal conflicts. Men and women work out tensions between themselves during song and dance interludes in which they directly address the camera. Song and dance become an integral aspect of the musical's narrative during these sequences by interrelating the principal couples' dramatic personae with their talent as singers and dancers.

During these musical production numbers, men and women acknowledge their status as entertainers (and, by extension, entertainment's legitimacy as a form of work) by performing directly for the camera. Their overt acknowledgement of the camera transforms such sequences into performative vehicles during which the principal couple's multiple talents magnify their uniqueness as stars.[50] Similar moments occur in *Trading Places* and *Ferris Bueller's Day Off* when Billy Ray Valentine and Ferris engage in direct address theatrical asides to the audience, abstracting the line between their comedic star personas and their characters.

As Laura Mulvey argues in her essay, "Visual Pleasure and Narrative Cinema," the musical uses these performative interludes to construct the female form as the object of a male gaze.[51] The objectification of the female performer is a hallmark of film musical pioneer Busby Berkeley's movies, in which a tracking shot between the legs of a row of chorus girls counterbalances a similar shot of their faces. This technique balances the close-up, which personalizes a seemingly anonymous row of characters, with a voyeuristic shot which reduces each chorus girl to an interchangeable sex object.[52]

Steven Cohan argues that the musical complicates this distinction by feminizing both women and men's bodies as forms of erotic spectacle in show-stopping song and dance numbers. The characterization of the song-and-dance man as a feminized spectacle is problematic because erotic spectacle has traditionally been designated as feminine by Hollywood.[53] Cohan defines narcissism ("solo performances and special effects numbers"), exhibitionism ("challenge dance duets, or dances performed for a bystander, sometimes for purposes of seduction"), and masquerade ("dandyish costuming ... numerous plots of disguises, or mistaken identities") as techniques of objectification through which the musical feminizes the male.[54] In *Saturday Night Fever*, Tony Manero's narcissistic gaze upon himself in a mirror is coded as female, though a close-up of his bulging crotch simultaneously offers a blatantly overdetermined construction of masculinity.[55] By transforming men and women's bodies into spectacle, dance and music interludes disrupt the musical's advancement towards narrative containment and closure. The spectacle created by the construction of bodies as twirling forms of energy and motion that animate the space around them halts the narrative by exceeding its narrow focus on the resolution of parallel aspects of gender difference through courtship and marriage.[56]

While the action-adventure biracial buddy movie also fetishizes the male body as a form of spectacle, the context of physical torture and destruction in which it does so plays upon castration anxieties and fear of sexual difference. William Luhr writes that the proliferation of bodily armature signified by the hardbody motif of *Rocky, Lethal Weapon,* and *Die Hard* compensates for this fear of castration, as does the action-adventure hero's redemptive triumph over physical adversaries.[57] Conversely, Cohan argues in his study of the feminization of Fred Astaire that the musical's orchestration of the male body as a "site of joy" inverts this psychoanalytical construction of gender difference by displaying Astaire's body as "plentitude and not lack, presence and not absence."[58]

In *Saturday Night Fever*, Tony's solo dance similarly becomes an extension of the narrative's construction of him as the king of the 2001 disco, as the lit, mirror-balled dance floor transforms him from a minimum-wage high school graduate into a celebrity. It is through this foregrounding of lifestyle in the characterization of Tony that the movie also invited disco patrons to enter the fantasy themselves through their purchase of the soundtrack album. The construction of Ren's body as a site of fashion spectacle in *Footloose* and the animation of space around him in striking, high-concept terms during dance sequences provides another instance of the music-video movie's objectification of the male form. Reflecting the influence of high concept, physical space becomes in *Footloose* an extension of Ren's objectification in narcissistic terms as the banal interior of a barn becomes a stunningly glamorous backdrop of forward-jutting, contrasting shafts of light and darkness that cast the dancer's body in silhouette as it arcs gracefully through the air in low-angle, slow-motion shots.[59]

The classical Hollywood musical's recognition of its contrivance in this way frequently leads it to comment self-consciously on its technological artifice. In *Singin' in the Rain* (1952) for example, Gene Kelly's instant transformation of a bare soundstage into a quiet summer setting reveals the artifice behind classical Hollywood style's illusion of invisibility.[60] The music-video movie's foregrounding of its contrivance is carried out in highly superficial terms that gloss over rather than interrogate its construction of fantasy as reality. Rapid cutting, backlighting, minimal color schemes, and high-tech industrial settings result in the music-video movie's construction of fantasy in advertising-inspired terms, promising entry to such a world through the viewer's purchase of clothes and soundtrack albums.[61] Often, these ideals are associated during dance performance sequences with advertising-inspired images of bodily perfection. *Flashdance*'s logo, marketed across print ads, trailers, the soundtrack album cover, and television commercials promoting the film, consists of a shot of Alex being drenched by water during her floor show.

The association of the male and female leads with certain styles of music also contains the androgynous connotations inherent in the music-video movie's construction of men's bodies as the object of a male gaze. Reflecting the Reagan era's demonization of countercultural androgyny as a cause of economic and moral malaise during the 1970s, "disco sucks" became a homophobic catch phrase during the early 1980s amid the popularity of macho heavy metal and new wave music. For this reason, music-video movie soundtracks like *Footloose* embrace heavy metal and new wave and often use these styles during male dance performances to offset such a spectacle's potentially effeminate connotations.

NOTES

1. John Izod, *Hollywood and the Box Office, 1895–1986* (New York: Columbia University Press, 1988), 82.

2. Ibid., 103.

3. Rick Altman, *The American Film Musical* (Bloomington: Indiana University Press, 1989), 356.

4. Ibid., 355.

5. Ibid., 338.

6. Thomas Schatz, *Hollywood Genres: Formulas, Filmmaking, and the Studio System* (New York: Random House, 1981), 197.

7. Ibid.

8. Altman, *The American Film Musical*, 44.

9. Henry Jenkins, "Historical Poetics," *Approaches to Popular Film*, ed. Joanne Hollows and Mark Jancovich (New York: Manchester University Press, 1995), 116.

10. Justin Wyatt, *High Concept: Movies and Marketing in Hollywood* (Austin: University of Texas Press, 1994), 41.

11. Jack Banks, *Monopoly Television: MTV's Quest to Control the Music* (Boulder: Westview Press, 1996), 197.

12. Robert Britt Horwitz, *The Irony of Deregulatory Reform: The Deregulation of American Telecommunications* (New York: Oxford University Press, 1989), 261.

13. Lisa A. Lewis, *Gender Politics and MTV: Voicing the Difference* (Philadelphia: Temple University Press, 1990), 19.

14. Banks, *Monopoly Television*, 201.

15. J.P. Telotte, "All That Jazz: Expression on Its Own Terms," *Journal of Popular Film and Television* (fall 1993): 106.

16. Altman, *The American Film Musical*, 327.

17. Telotte, "All That Jazz," 107.

18. Ibid.

19. Schatz, *Hollywood Genres*, 192.

20. Ibid., 193.

21. Ibid., 191.

22. Altman, *The American Film Musical*, 40.

23. Michael Wood, *America in the Movies* (New York: Basic Books, 1975), 152.

24. R. Serge Denisoff and William D. Romanowski, *Risky Business: Rock in Film* (New Brunswick, N.J.: Transaction Publishers, 1991), 411.

25. Ibid., 401.

26. Wyatt, *High Concept*, 195.

27. Altman, *The American Film Musical*, 49.

28. Ibid., 337.

29. Telotte, "All That Jazz," 104.

30. J. Harwood, "Urban Cowboy," *Variety*, 4 June 1980, 22, quoted in Denisoff and Romanowski, *Risky Business*, 322.

31. Lewis, *Gender Politics and MTV*, 44.

32. Lou Cannon, *President Reagan: The Role of a Lifetime* (New York: Touchstone, 1991), 814.

33. Jeff Yanc, "'More Than a Woman': Music, Masculinity, and Male Spectacle in *Saturday Night Fever* and *Staying Alive*," *The Velvet Light Trap* 38 (1996), 48.

34. Ibid., 43.

35. Annette Insdorf, "Alan Parker: Finding 'Fame' on the Streets of New York," *New York Times*, 25 May 1980, sec. D15.

36. Wyatt, *High Concept*, 41.

37. "Inside Movies: The Business of Show Business," *Esquire*, February 1984, 94.

38. David Thomson, "Footloose and Fancy Free," *Cineaste* 13 (May–June 1984): 49.

39. Wyatt, *High Concept*, 40.

40. Ibid., 42.

41. Altman, *The American Film Musical*, 29.

42. William J. Palmer, *The Films of the Eighties: A Social History* (Carbondale: Southern Illinois University Press, 1993), 281.

43. Stuart Ewen, *All-Consuming Images: The Politics of Style in Contemporary Culture* (New York: Basic Books, 1988), 92.

44. Douglas Kellner, *Media Culture: Cultural Studies, Identity, and Politics Between the Modern and the Postmodern* (New York: Routledge, 1995), 234.

45. Andrew Britton, "Blissing Out: The Politics of Reaganite Cinema," *Movie* 31, no. 32 (winter 1986): 3–4.

46. Janet Maslin, "Film: 'Fame' Opens Bubbling with Life," *New York Times*, 16 May 1980, sec. C2.

47. David Denby, "Suffer Little Artists," *New York*, 19 May 1980, 64.

48. Mark Crispin Miller, "Advertising: End of Story," *Seeing Through Movies*, ed. Mark Crispin Miller (New York: Pantheon Books, 1990), 216.

49. Schatz, *Hollywood Genres*, 200.

50. Ibid., 189.

51. Laura Mulvey, "Visual Pleasure and Narrative Cinema," *Film Theory and Criticism: Introductory Readings*, 5th ed., ed. Leo Braudy and Marshall Cohen (New York: Oxford University Press, 1999), 837.

52. Altman, *The American Film Musical*, 223.

53. Steven Cohan, "'Feminizing' the Song-and-Dance Man: Fred Astaire and the Spectacle of Masculinity in the Hollywood Musical," *Screening the Male: Exploring Masculinity in Hollywood Cinema*, ed. Steven Cohan and Ina Rae Hark (New York: Routledge, 1993), 63.

54. Ibid., 48.

55. Yanc, "'More Than a Woman,'" 40.

56. Cohan, "'Feminizing' the Song-and-Dance Man," 55.

57. William Luhr, "Mutilating Mel: Martyrdom and Masculinity in *Braveheart*," *Mythologies of Violence in Postmodern Media*, ed. Christopher Sharrett (Detroit: Wayne State University Press, 1999), 234.

58. Cohan, "'Feminizing' the Song-and-Dance Man," 55.

59. Wyatt, *High Concept*, 41.

60. Schatz, *Hollywood Genres*, 194.

61. Wyatt, *High Concept*, 17.

Chapter 6

Class and the Yuppie Movie

The Reagan-era yuppie movie arose from changes in Hollywood's political economic structure under Reaganomics and deregulation. Hollywood's focus on marketing movies to cable-wired, suburban multiplex audiences resulted in the yuppie movie's focus on a narrow slice of class experience defined in terms of conspicuous consumption and lifestyle traits. Fueled by the rising cost of moviemaking, preproduction deals with consumer goods manufacturers, cable operators, and other tie-in companies resulted in the transformation of movies into commodities designed to stimulate demand for and consumption of leisure-culture merchandise. This shift in Hollywood's mode of production promoted a focus on movies that mirrored the lifestyles of the demographic group most likely to consume such merchandise: young, suburban, professional middle-class couples and their children.

The exploration of class identity in yuppie movies of the Reagan era is rooted in genres such as the screwball comedy and the coming-of-age movie. The screwball comedy arose during the 1930s and affirmed the myth of America as a classless society through its resolution of differences between characters of differing class backgrounds through marriage. *It Happened One Night* (1934), *My Man Godfrey* (1936), *Easy Living* (1937), and *The Lady Eve* (1941) are all about ambitious working-class characters who win the approval of father-figure patrons by proving their resourcefulness and self-sufficiency. In the process, these plucky heroes also redeem a stuffy, aristocratic order of snobbery and pretension. Often, marriage between the young protagonist and the father figure's daughter substantiates the hero's status as a member of a natural aristocracy.[1]

Incumbent in movies about mavericks who redeem the community is an affirmation of America's classlessness, since capitalism's inevitable distribution of wealth on the basis of birthright is redressed through its re-distribution of upward mobility on the basis of resourcefulness and merit. In *My Man Godfrey*, for example, a forgotten man (who turns out to be a renegade heir) successfully invests a decadent and virtually bankrupt family's money in the stock market, enabling him to open a nightclub on the former site of a municipal dump and put his hobo friends to work. In *Easy Living* and *The Lady Eve*, a socially inferior heroine, whose integrity and spirit define her as a natural aristocrat, assimilates into the upper class through marriage to a business tycoon's son.

The coming-of-age genre of the 1950s, exemplified by *Rebel Without a Cause* (1955), *East of Eden* (1955), *Giant* (1956), *Written on the Wind* (1956), *Peyton Place* (1957), *Tea and Sympathy* (1956), and *The Long Hot Summer* (1958), also explores the intergenerational tensions between fathers and sons and the process whereby the middle class reproduces itself. A crisis occurs in these melodramas when working-class fathers attempt to pass on to their sons traditions that are inassimilable into a white-collar world of Protestant suburbia, or when white-collar fathers find that their work as so-called paper pushers provides them with no masculine traditions of craftsmanship to pass on to their boys.

This crisis in masculine identity became irreconcilable in the 1960s as the coming-of-age movie *The Graduate* (1967) suggested that suburban af-fluence had so thoroughly corrupted the middle class's sense of inner self that parents had no moral traditions to pass on to their children. Raised in a Southern California suburban culture of forced and engineered commu-nity, the young male protagonist (Dustin Hoffman) in *The Graduate* finds himself alienated from his parents' affluent suburban world of material superficiality and moral hypocrisy after graduating cum laude from col-lege. In an act of Oedipal rebellion against inherited middle-class tradi-tion, he sleeps with the wife of his father's business partner and openly rejects his parents' suburban lifestyle. As Barbara Ehrenreich suggests, the student movement was also frequently constructed as an act of rebellion undertaken by postadolescents against surrogate father figures.[2]

During the mid-1970s, working-class heroes like Rocky became sym-bolic representatives of the middle-class anxieties about class mobility and masculinity engendered by this culture of permissiveness. In contrast to scathing liberal criticisms of working-class life in *Saturday Night Fever* (1977) and *Bloodbrothers* (1978), *Rocky* romanticized 1970s blue-collar life as a masculine culture of self-discipline and self-reliance that the middle class had allowed to slip from its grasp. While *Rocky* invoked President Carter's appeals to Americans to recover a lost sense of middle-class self-discipline and optimism, *Saturday Night Fever* played upon Carter's con-viction that America's middle class had lost its way in a post–Watergate, post–Vietnam era of spiritual malaise typified by its narcissistic focus on self-indulgent instant gratification.

Movies about political and corporate conspiracy such as *All the Presi-dent's Men* (1976) and *Network* (1976) mobilized a rightward-drifting middle class's anger over the Watergate scandal and its resentment of corporate America's indifference towards public safety and well-being. The war movies *Coming Home* (1978) and *The Deer Hunter* (1978) offer the working-class male as a screen upon which to project middle-class anxieties about loss of honor, national resolve, and self-discipline in the wake of the Vietnam War.[3] This crisis of confidence in the legitimacy of dominant institutions and the economy is also expressed in a cycle of horror films during the late 1960s and early 1970s that includes *Rosemary's Baby* (1968), *The Exorcist* (1973), and *The Omen* (1976). Ryan and Kellner note that *The Omen*, in which a devil-child uses corporate and military power to launch a takeover of the world, appeared a year after America's withdrawal from Vietnam and the public discrediting of national institutions like the Central Intelligence Agency.[4] Wood similarly observes that *The Omen*'s invocation of ancient prophesies of apocalypse suggests inevitable annihilation.[5]

THE YUPPIE MOVIE

The yuppie lifestyle of working hard, working out, and spending lavishly becomes in the 1980s a declaration that the middle class has lost none of its moral resolve in the wake of this countercultural confusion.[6] As a product of a culture of white-collar bureaucracy, the yuppie embodies the belief that the professions are a class fortress to which each generation gains access through education and self-discipline. This philosophy is rooted in Thomas Jefferson's conviction that America's lack of class barriers would inevitably give rise to a natural aristocracy of individuals whose success was the product of self-discipline and hard work rather than birthright. While inner-directed character served as the basis of the natural aristocrat's mobility in an agrarian society of self-sufficient farmers, conformity to outer-directed norms of consumption became, with the rise of a consumer society, the basis for the white-collar aspirant's achievement of membership in middle-class suburban society. As consumers began paying for goods and services they no longer made themselves, they turned to money as a source of status and exchange in a market economy. Physical possessions became an extension of oneself in a society where individuals declared their membership in a turn-of-the century middle class on the basis of dress and behavorial cues.

This preoccupation with outer-directed forms of conformity coalesced in the postwar era of the 1950s in the so-called organization man, a success icon criticized by sociologists C. Wright Mills and David Riesman as an overregimented team player. Condemnation of the white-collar workplace as a dehumanizing environment in which mobility requires the aspirant to be able to project the proper image at the right moment led to an alternative definition of personality as something to develop through one's immersion in a suburban leisure culture of domestic and affective ties between friends and family members. The construction of consumption as a form of self-fulfillment represented a commodification of Franklin and Jefferson's vision of individuals meeting in weekly support groups in a shared pursuit of intellectual self-improvement.

Hollywood absorbed, packaged, and explored this success philosophy across several interrelated yuppie movie subgenres: the Horatio Alger parody, the corporate-suburban narrative, the yuppies with children story, and yuppie horror. *Risky Business* (1983), *Ferris Bueller's Day Off* (1986), *The Secret of My Success* (1987), *Working Girl* (1988), and *Big* (1988) are adaptations of Horatio Alger's novels of the late-nineteenth-century. In Alger's self-help novels, a boy hero rises from poverty to middle-class respectability on the basis of a providential encounter with a wealthy patron who hires him. The hero's achievement of modest middle-class success through dint of hard work, deference, and frugality, during an era in which enormously wealthy robber barons attributed their success to competitive daring, led to another strain of self-help literature which champions a hero who succeeds on the basis of brash opportunism and the wily exploitation of others.[7] The heroes of *Risky Business*, *Ferris Bueller's Day Off*, *The Secret of My Success*, *Working Girl*, and *Big* similarly achieve mobility by manipulating interpersonal relations with others rather than through hard work and obedience, revealing these movies' indebtedness to the myth of the anti-Alger hero who succeeds on the basis of self-serving tactics rather than honesty and humility.

Like the Gilded Age robber baron, the yuppie embodies the notion that conspicuous consumption rather than moral merit is the yardstick of success. While the Alger parody champions its youthful protagonist as a success hero, it simultaneously implies that upward mobility hinges on class privilege and contacts. In *Risky Business*, for example, Joel Goodson's success in learning how to run a "business" results in his unearned admission to Princeton, while a teen prostitute who organizes and helps him run the operation after being forced into the streets by an abusive father remains mired in homelessness and poverty.[8]

The yuppie movie's focus on lifestyle and consumption habits reveals the influence of televisual style in its glamorization of the suburban home and corporate workplace as a showcase for consumer goods. The term yuppie was coined in 1983 to describe an emerging class of young professionals that cut across gender and race lines in its embrace of values of conspicuous consumption.[9] The yuppie plot thus typically focuses on the class politics of success in a gentrified urban or suburban setting. Given its primary focus on the white middle class, its principal characters are generally either college-bound adolescents or college-educated single or married adults. Its iconography includes lifestyle merchandise such as sports cars and consumer electronic goods, making it an apt vehicle for product plugs and capitalization on fleeting consumption trends.[10]

The seventy-hour workweek became within the yuppie code a means of purging oneself of the consumptive hedonism associated with conspicuous affluence. Working out became a means of purging one's body of the fattening effects of high-calorie food and sedentary desk work. Physical fitness, a visible emblem of high inner standards of self-discipline and abstinent purity, became a declaration of moral status that distinguished the yuppie from the idle rich and the slothful poor. For this reason, physical definition became a means of asserting boundaries between the middle class, the rich, and the poor.[11] The romanticization of the working class in *Rocky* as a vessel of traditional values and modest expectations thus evolves into a yuppie philosophy of earned class prerogative in *Rocky III*, in which the title character's relocation of his family from a modest urban row house to a gated suburban mansion becomes an index of his competitive superiority.

Incumbent in this motif of earned economic prerogative is the predication of familial stability on the nuclear unit's conformity to biologically defined gender roles and on its economic self-sufficiency. Conversely, the theme of competitively won mobility suggests that yuppie material affluence is no guarantee of happiness. As Alex P. Keaton on TV's *Family Ties*, for example, Michael J. Fox plays a bottom-line pragmatist whose self-serving material greed stands in sharp contrast to his parents' counterculture sensitivity and concern for others. Even as the series depicts Alex as soulless in relation to his spiritual, quasi-bohemian parents, it simultaneously implies that his shallowness will ultimately carry him to the top of the business world. Fox's role on the show became a template for the anti–Alger hero he plays in *The Secret of My Success*, in which he succeeds on the basis of self-serving intellect rather than earnestness and hard work.

Implicit in this self-consciously smug narrative is a cynical dismissal of the theme of achieving success by doing good deeds for others. The yuppie movie emphasizes the necessity of climbing to the top rung of the corporate ladder rather than balancing a middle-management position with a successful personal life. In these ways, the genre addressed the class preoccupations of a decade that conflated class distinction with material affluence and power.

PLOT: THE REPRODUCTION OF THE PROFESSIONAL MIDDLE CLASS

One strand of the yuppie narrative parodies the tales of Horatio Alger, Jr. in order to suggest in tongue-in-cheek fashion that the yuppie's lifestyle of conspicuous consumption is an earned prerogative achieved through competitive superiority in the workplace. In contrast to the typical boy hero of the Alger novel, who succeeds through dint of ambition, luck, and hard work, *Risky Business, The Secret of My Success, Ferris Bueller's Day Off, Big,* and *Working Girl* are about clever shape changers who matriculate the middle-class world of suburban high school life and corporate life through the adoption of playful disguises and manipulation of interpersonal relations.[12] The hero's resourceful reliance on these ruses reveals the shape changer narrative's indebtedness to the 1930s screwball comedy. A key plot device of the screwball comedy is the use of a character's mistaken identity (often based on class cues) to motivate a series of class and gender conflicts between the principal characters that are eventually resolved through the characters' integration into the community through marriage.

While conformity to the norm of heterosexual monogamy integrates the couple into marriage, a particular success philosophy, dependent upon both individual expression and conformity to group habits of behavior and work, orders the individual's admission into white-collar professional life. While this philosophy originated in Protestant theology, it became secularized with the rise of an industrial society, substituting the grace of middle-class material security for a sense of spiritual security rooted in divine salvation. In redefining success in material terms, the success ethic emphasized conformity to middle-class norms of behavior and dress, thus paving the way for the masses' integration into a society of white-collar corporate and suburban life in the postwar era.

Childraising manuals thus stress that the middle-class process of material and behavioral socialization begins at home. Parents should encourage their children to be expressive and innovative because these traits are valued in white-collar life. However, manuals also advise parents to inculcate habits of self-discipline and control within their children, since these habits are prerequisites for entry to the white-collar professions.[13] The Alger parody focuses on an ambitious young man who transforms his situation through personal initiative, reconciling conflicting impulses of independence and conformity in a way that confirms a middle-class success ethic based on these traits. While his success is a product of self-serving ambition rather than service to others, it is also attributable to his masterful ability to manipulate interpersonal relations with others. Ultimately, these traits win the approval of real fathers and paternalistic corporate executives, enabling the story to suggest that cleverness and an eye for opportunity, rather than class origin, are the keys to success.[14]

Intergenerational rivalries are thus healed in *Risky Business* when a high school senior gains his father's approval by gaining admission to Princeton. Having targeted Princeton as his first choice of colleges, Joel Goodson gains admission (signified by a visiting recruiter's praise) on the basis of the business savvy he displays in running a brothel out of his parents' home while they are on a weekend vacation. In doing so, Joel learns how ambition, exploitation of others, and free-market opportunity lead to success and reproduction of the professional middle class when he is crowned a natural aristocrat on the basis of admission to an Ivy League school.[15]

This theme was complemented during the Reagan era by the belief that forms of public community based on social activism and idealism were no longer relevant in the wake of New Deal liberal economic and social reforms, which had proven cost-inefficient and failed to achieve their goals. An emerging generation's internalization of this belief was evidenced by a trend of so-called premature pragmatism among adolescents during the 1980s. Ehrenreich observed in 1986 that since the 1970s there had been a noticeable decline in the number of college students enrolling in mind-enriching but modestly paid pursuits like history and math and a roughly parallel rise in the number studying business. Almost one-quarter of all college graduates were business majors in 1983, compared to about one-seventh in 1973. Those majoring in philosophy or literature shrank to less than 1 percent of college graduates.[16]

In *The Secret of My Success*, Brantley Foster (Michael J. Fox) is a recent college graduate whose resolve to make it on his own upon arriving in New York City alludes to the Alger myth's equation of success and self-sufficiency. However, he discovers upon arrival that his job has been eliminated in a corporate takeover. He finds upon applying elsewhere that personnel officers demand practical experience and display a negative attitude towards his educational credentials. Brantley, however, is adaptable. He invents work experience and falsifies it on his resume, but has no clever reply for a personnel officer who asks, "can you be a minority woman?"

Brantley ultimately invents a personality out of whole cloth in order to ascend the corporation's ladder after landing a job in its mailroom. He takes over control of the company by ousting its corrupt chairman, who has achieved his position through marriage to the deceased owner's daughter. The movie implies that Brantley's achievement of the position affirms his status as a natural aristocrat who has ascended the corporate ladder on the basis of competitive merit rather than birthright. [17]

Evoking the old tale of rags-to-riches, *Secret* celebrates its protagonist's rise to a position of earned wealth as a means of reestablishing boundaries around the deserving rich, making patent a differentiation between this elect group, the idle rich above, and the lazy poor below. As a morality tale, *Secret* dovetailed with the New Right's attack on the welfare state, which defined competitively won material success as an index of individual moral character. Conspicuous consumption became an emblem of membership in a yuppie natural aristocracy that touted appearances as a measurement of one's hard work and moral fiber.

Ferris Bueller's Day Off focuses upon a high school senior's (Matthew Broderick) manipulation of the public school system, a site of middle-class ideological reproduction that grooms the aspirant for college and white-collar life. The title character succeeds in playing hooky by feigning illness to his parents and persuading his best friend and girlfriend to join him. The ploy is particularly risky because it is Ferris's ninth sick day, and he will be held back a year if apprehended. However, Ferris frees himself from suspicion by accessing the school's computer and altering his attendance record while Rooney, the high school principal, watches helplessly on his office monitor. While the movie takes Ferris's careerist parents to task for their negligence, it also implies that Rooney's iron-fisted style of adolescent socialization is equally ineffective.[18]

Big also celebrates the achievement of upward mobility on the basis of a young boy's (Tom Hanks) successful manipulation of an adult world of repressive authority. The boy, Josh Baskin, goes to sleep one night after expressing a wish to an arcade game genie to be big and awakens to find his dream fulfilled. After landing a job as a toy company customer service agent, he adroitly ascends to vice-president by winning the approval of the company's president, who admires the boy's instinctive understanding of how to package leisure culture for child consumption.

Big illustrates the theme of paternal approval that substantiates Josh's confirmation as a natural aristocrat during an encounter between the boy and the company president, Mr. MacMillan (Robert Loggia), at the New York City toy store F.A.O. Schwarz. On a field trip to gather first-hand information about kids' toy buying habits, "the kind you can't get from a marketing report," MacMillan and Josh playfully bond while tapping out the two-part melody to "Heart and Soul" on a giant piano as they dance their way up and down its brightly colored keyboard. Josh's move into a spacious Manhattan loft confirms his arrival as a yuppie as he first furnishes it with expensive toys and later with handsome wood décor.

Working Girl offers an ostensibly feminist variation on the Alger parody. Reenacting the tale's opening emphasis on the hero's immigrant roots, Tess McGill (Melanie Griffith) treks each day on the Staten Island Ferry past the Statue of Liberty to work as a secretary in a Wall Street investment firm. Tess finds that Wall Street has little respect for her hard-won night school degree in marketing and her ambitious attempts to improve her diction with speech classes. Intelligent and hard working, Tess also discovers that her new boss, the patrician Katherine Parker (Sigourney Weaver), has hijacked her idea for a corporate merger. In retaliation, she moves into Katherine's corner office and assumes her identity while she's on vacation.

At a party, Tess makes contact with investment banker Jack Trainer (Harrison Ford), who in turn introduces her to wealthy industrialist Oren Trask (Philip Bosco), who adopts her plan for him to buy a group of radio stations, which the film juxtaposes with the medium of television in which Trask had originally planned to invest. *Working Girl* thus uses the contrast between a venerable, older medium and a more recent, evanescent one to champion Trask as a productive capitalist rather than a destructive one.[19] It also juxtaposes the Harvard-trained Katherine, a representative of the idle rich, with the self-made, working-class Tess, suggesting that the young Alger protégé's overthrow of her boss restores a culture of meritocratic mobility within the investment firm. As in the Alger hero's relationship with a paternal benefactor, Tess's relationship with Trainer results in her promotion to a middle-management position. As Traube observes, however, the final shot of her through the window of her new executive office, revealed to be a box in a hierarchy of similar boxes, represents the "sense of a threat contained."[20]

While it romanticizes the yuppie as a redeemer of class relations, the Alger parody criticizes the lack of moral depth beneath the hero's materially acquisitive lifestyle habits. Incumbent in the Alger parody's predication of success on the hero's cunning manipulation of both professional and personal relationships is a cynical assertion that the perfection of material possessions is a satisfying substitute for more complex interpersonal ties based on filial forms of affection between parents and children and friends and lovers. Shaping this contention is the nagging fear that affective ties between individuals and families have been eroded by a postwar culture that constructs individual identity in terms of lifestyles that are continually redefined in terms of evanescent fashion trends and must-have purchases.

While Hollywood constructed the youthful entrepreneur as a facile manipulator of a culture of workplace conformity, it also sought to denounce bureaucratic forms of organization as dehumanizingly cold and mechanical. However, Elizabeth Long suggests that the corporate-suburban success narrative differs in its definition of work from older success stories that sentimentalized home as a retreat from a workplace of immoral competitive individualism. Instead, work in the corporate-suburban tale is alienating because it is related less to a product than a process, making it very difficult to tell when the white-collar middle manager is doing it well.[21]

Critics of the yuppie hero argue that the outer-directed success ethic's emphasis on learning to self-consciously project a well-staged manner at the proper moment reveals how corporate life has transformed the inner-directed individual into an automaton. For this reason, other philosophers suggest that success rests on the ability to find in private consumption and family a therapeutic compensation for the limited opportunities for independence in corporate culture. This definition of success is traceable to rationalizations of the occupational and organizational structure that rapidly emerged after World War II. Aspirants working within this world of monopolization and conglomeration were encouraged by success philosophers of the day to set their sights on middle-management positions rather than the top.[22]

Incumbent in this corporate-suburban narrative is an equation of the private world of domestic and affective ties, held together by consumption, with the achievement of familial community. The genre defines success in terms of the good life, a balance of work and leisure in which work serves the purpose of providing comfort and happiness. In *Parenthood* (1989), for example, Gil's (Steve Martin) boss informs him that he lost a promotion to a company rival because he doesn't work hard enough. Behind the venetian blinds that line the boss's corner office, workers stare intently at projects on their desks as the superior informs Gil that his rival got the promotion because he spends evenings carousing with clients and procuring prostitutes for them. When Gil replies that he has to spend time with his son because the boy has special education needs that require him to see a psychiatrist, the boss stares back indifferently while furiously exercising on a treadmill. Gil resigns on the spot but gets his job back several weeks later with a raise and more time off.

The Breakfast Club condemns parents who place their own ambitions over their children by turning a Saturday high school detention session into a therapy session during which a group of students discover a shared sense of resentment toward their negligent parents. The opening credits reflect director John Hughes' background as a director of TV commercials by defining each student in the shorthand terms of lifestyle. Included in the montage are a front-page newspaper story on the wrestling team (the athlete, Emilio Estevez); a poster promoting the prom (the socialite, Molly Ringwald); a blackboard and a computer before a classroom (the nerd, Anthony Michael Hall); a series of ink blot tests on a guidance counselor's desk (the recluse, Ally Sheedy); and a hall locker with a "no trespassing" warning (the criminal, Judd Nelson).

In discovering a shared longing for community beneath class-imposed differences of money and style, the students learn to look beyond the boundaries of lifestyle that define each of them and their choice of friends. The symmetry of a long shot of the library's ground floor reading area captures the growth of trust between the students as they sit in a circle and confess their individual insecurities. A series of MTV video montages that celebrates the group's achievement of community simultaneously positions the movie soundtrack as a basis for achieving a meaningful sense of community with one's high school peers.

While *The Breakfast Club* celebrates the formation of a group of disillusioned teenagers into a surrogate family, *The Big Chill* (1983) figuratively celebrates their parents' transformation from disillusioned, self-absorbed yuppies into a family in the wake of their mutual college friend Alex's tragic suicide. While the film equates the friend's suicide with the death of countercultural optimism, Harold Cooper (Kevin Kline) becomes a redemptive Christ-like father figure for the group. He rejuvenates his houseguests with 1960s Motown and rock and roll classics, gives them running shoes so that they can shed their workplace anxieties, gives a panicky, thirty-something career woman a child, and redeems a disillusioned drug dealer into Alex's more healthy countercultural legacy. As the mediator of the group's passage from the 1960s to the 1980s, however, Harold also serves as a spokesman for neoconservative capitalist and family values, dispensing insider trading advice, echoing the belief that the family is under attack from black criminal scum, and chiding his friends for their bleeding heart liberalism.[23]

While the corporate-suburban narrative criticizes the Alger parody's conflation of happiness and conspicuous wealth, it simultaneously conceptualizes ideals of self-fulfillment and community in terms of one's consumption of packaged forms of leisure experience and shared lifestyle habits. Incumbent in the running shoes that Harold distributes to his weekend guests is a commodified version of health and spiritual balance, contingent upon one's conformity to an expensive lifestyle pattern typified by membership in a health club and the purchase of pricey exercise and fitness accessories.

Amplifying and cynically parodying this motif of the redeeming Christ-like capitalist, *Down and Out in Beverly Hills* (1986), a remake of Jean Renoir's *Boudu Saved From Drowning* (1932), suggests that material wealth frees the family from need while breeding an upwardly spiraling lifestyle of insatiable material expectations. A bum (Nick Nolte) who enters a Beverly Hills family's privileged existence one day counsels each of its members to find success through simple pleasures while simultaneously living off their considerable largesse. Intended by director Paul Mazursky to "poke fun at Beverly Hills, to make fun of my own life, so to speak," the movie suggests that beneath the family's comfortable lifestyle lie anorexia, bisexual confusion, and marital boredom.[24]

Wall Street (1987) also criticizes the unrestrained pursuit of material wealth as a threat to the welfare of the American economy and family. Like Reagan, Gordon Gekko (Michael Douglas) presumes that the financial interests of an elite class of investors should determine social and institutional policy. Under this logic, Gekko buys up companies on the basis of speculative wealth and sells them piecemeal at an enormous profit. Shortly after adopting Bud Fox (Charlie Sheen) as a protégé, Gekko focuses his interest on Blue Star Airlines, for which Bud's father, Carl (Martin Sheen), works as a mechanic. While Gekko's reckless entrepreneurship threatens the American economy, his cannibalism of Blue Star Airlines similarly threatens the American family. Carl is hospitalized by a heart attack after learning of Gekko's plan to carve up the airline and sell it in piecemeal fashion. *Wall Street* thus criticizes salesmanship and a paper economy based on speculative rather than tangible wealth as instances of Reagan's supply-side economics' devastating impact on public and private realms of class identity.

The class anxieties inherent in *Wall Street*'s construction of wealth as a threat to the family's stability also shape yuppie horror movies such as *Poltergeist* (1982), in which a real estate entrepreneur's material greed nearly rips the nuclear family apart.[25] The Freeling family lives in a subdivision owned by a company for which the father (Craig T. Nelson) has sold tens of millions of dollars of housing. Community within the subdivision is defined in terms of shared leisure-time habits of watching television and supplying children with expensive toys. Television is characterized as both a seducer, which lures the family into buying objects of play and entertainment, and a source of community that disintegrates in TV's absence.[26]

As a horror movie, *Poltergeist* explores the repressed anxieties produced by high-stress jobs and the fragility of a costly lifestyle that requires relentless commitment to one's work. As Barry Keith Grant observes, the yuppie's sense of self-esteem rested on professional success and the material affluence that signified this sense of earned class distinction. However, the yuppie's profligate spending habits were also a capitulation to hedonism. Neoconservative ideologues had since the 1960s argued that the middle class was in danger of succumbing to a softening consumer culture of affluence. Countercultural youth had first been labeled as evidence of the morally softening effects of 1950s middle-class affluence. During the Carter era of the 1970s, the middle class had scaled back its lifestyle habits during a culture of economic recession, rising fuel costs, and back-to-nature simplicity. During the 1980s, the yuppie creed of spending as much as one made also left the conspicuous consumer vulnerable to financial insolvency. For these reasons, lifestyles rather than lives are in peril in the yuppie horror movie.[27]

These fears achieve monstrous form in *Poltergeist* when the family's spacious, well-appointed home, built by father Steve Freeling's real estate company over a cemetery without his knowledge, literally rips asunder as the deceased awaken and arise one night beneath its foundation. The movie played upon the latent fears of downward mobility beneath the yuppie family's materially overextended, high-stress lifestyle. Freeling's act of removing the TV set from a motel room to which the family flees after the destruction of its home suggests that the family must guard against the seductive threat posed by a televisual lifestyle of conspicuous affluence.

The yuppies-with-children cycle of *Kramer vs. Kramer* (1979), *Mr. Mom* (1983), *Raising Arizona* (1987), *Three Men and a Baby* (1987), *Baby Boom* (1987), *She's Having a Baby* (1988), *Parenthood* (1989), *Look Who's Talking* (1989), and *Immediate Family* (1989) also explores the relationship between family and the bonds of consumption. While appealing to neoconservative anxieties over women abandoning their traditional roles of wife and mother, these movies also suggest that sensitive fathers who are actively engaged in childraising are the solution.[28]

Incumbent in this theme is a class-circumscribed equation of parental vigilance with appropriate middle-class norms of childraising. The permissive upbringing these parents enjoyed as children of the 1950s is blamed for their moral laxity in raising their own children. This contention builds on the arguments of neoconservatives who claimed that government-employed, New Class liberals who advocated social spending were spoiling women, minorities, criminals, and the poor, just as they spoiled their actual children and as they themselves had been spoiled. The neoconservative argument echoed the convictions of New Right moralists who condemned parents who spoiled their children through overindulgence and neglect. The liberal family of weak fathers who fail to exercise authority and selfish mothers who no longer find fulfillment in nurturing husbands and children serves as a primary cause of the breakdown of family values.[29] In this way, yuppies-with-children movies criticize the neglectful and permissive parents of *The Breakfast Club* and *Ferris Bueller's Day Off* who spoil their children with material goods or refuse to discipline them for their duplicitous and manipulative behaviors. The condemnation of these parents also characterizes the youthful heroes of the Alger parody as insufficiently self-disciplined and stuck in a state of irresponsible childhood.

Inherent in the formula's recurrent motif of abandonment is the question of who handles the task of childraising in a two-income household and the fear that no one will. The neoconservative view of men as breadwinners and indifferent nurturers was complemented by the conviction that women who left the home in ever-rising numbers were abandoning the family and hastening its breakdown. Anxiety over the authoritative father's inability to nurture was compounded by a fear of women's abandonment of the culture of motherhood.[30] Counterbalancing the anxiety in these movies is the suggestion that women and men share childraising duties as equals. Shared parenting is contingent upon the presence of hired help, a luxury available to a relatively narrow and privileged slice of middle-class families.

However, it is through an appeal to parental fears of child abandonment that yuppies-with-children movies code gender. Women who abandon their children or forfeit motherhood for career advancement either suffer from a barren womb syndrome or find that the pressure of juggling career and motherhood is too much.[31]

Yuppie executive J. C. Wyatt (Diane Keaton) finds in *Baby Boom* that the demands of juggling a career and single motherhood are overwhelming and relocates to the Vermont countryside. From one vantage point, the movie appeals to liberal middle-class feminists by suggesting that she can have it all when she marries a country doctor (Sam Shepard) and starts a gourmet baby food business in her kitchen. The movie's characterization of the doctor as caring and sensitive complements its construction of non-traditional parenting as the solution to childraising dilemmas in the era of the two-income household. However, the movie also appeals to a conservative, working-class reading of gender relations when J. C. ultimately sells the business to a large company and concentrates on childraising while the doctor continues working.

Similarly, *Mr. Mom* predicates familial stability on men and women's conformity to proper gender roles. Written by John Hughes and produced by television mogul Aaron Spelling, the movie explores the gender politics of a role switch that occurs when Jack (Michael Keaton) is laid off from his job as a car design engineer at a Detroit automobile plant. When Jack can't find a job, Helen (Terri Garr) goes to work at an advertising agency. While Jack at first fails miserably at housework and childcare, motivating a series of sitcom clichés, Helen finds that her new boss at work wants her to be his mistress. Jack is transformed into a bored and despondent "housewife" who must suffer Helen's degrading comments about his appearance. Finally, Jack gets his old job back when his company finds that its profits depend on long-term investment in product quality rather than short-term cost-cutting measures. Helen simultaneously discovers she is happier as a homemaker. Inherent in the comedy that arises from this role reversal is the assertion that familial stability depends on men and women's adoption of appropriate gender roles.

In *Kramer vs. Kramer*, Ivy League–educated wife and mother Joanna Kramer (Meryl Streep) decides after divorcing husband Ted (Dustin Hoffman) and suing him for custody of their seven-year-old son that the boy is better off living with his father. The movie defines Joanna from the outset as a frustrated housewife by opening with crosscut scenes that contrast her role as wife and mother with Ted's role as a breadwinner in the prime of his career. As Joanna tucks Billy (Justin Henry) into bed and packs a suitcase in anticipation of leaving her workaholic husband, Ted shares a laugh with his boss at the office while savoring the news that he's just helped the agency to win a key advertising client.

While Joanna's sudden departure initially turns the relationship between Ted and Billy upside down, father and son soon discover a middle ground based on mutual need. Ever the vigilant dad, Ted sits at the dining room table one night and ponders the pros and cons of fighting for custody of Billy as a backdrop of his son's elementary school artwork lines the wall behind him. Although Joanna wins custody of Billy because of the child's young age, she relinquishes it to Ted upon coming to pick her son up, realizing that he's already home. The movie closes with a shot of a relieved Ted smiling at his ex-wife as she boards the elevator to their former apartment to tell a tearful Billy the good news.

Three Men and a Baby resembles *Kramer vs. Kramer* in its construction of the motherless family as a self-sufficient unit in which fathers serve as breadwinners and nurturers in the absence of a woman who is unable to balance her career ambitions and childraising duties. The movie transforms the pressures of single parenthood into a festive fantasy in which three bachelors raise a baby whom one of them has conceived during a one-night stand with a struggling actress who abandons it on their doorstep as an infant. Intertwined with the comedy that arises from the men's delight in parenthood is a subplot about their efforts to shelter their home from drug dealers and police who have mistaken them for traffickers. Both storylines are resolved when the actress returns home to live platonically with the bachelors and help raise her child, suggesting that the restoration of boundaries between the family and the outside world is contingent upon the presence of two parents in the home.

Immediate Family juxtaposes a childless, thirty-something couple (Glenn Close, James Woods) with a postadolescent couple (Kevin Dillon, Mary Stuart Masterson) who give up their child to the older couple for adoption. Drawing upon the family melodrama, the film suggests that family is an antidote for a professional culture of deadline pressures and unfulfilling jobs. However, the movie also suggests that white-collar life makes possible a life of affluence that the working-class couple is unable to provide for the child.

Bad Influence (1990), *Pacific Heights* (1992), and *Single White Female* (1992) imply that beneath the yuppie trait of material acquisitiveness is a lurking fear of not being able to afford one's lifestyle. In *Pacific Heights,* the villain Carter Hayes (Michael Keaton) represents in monstrous fashion a young cohabitating couple's fear of not being able to afford their turn-of-the-century San Francisco Victorian home. Patty Parker (Melanie Griffith) and Drake Goodman (Matthew Modine) rent a portion of the house to the seemingly mild-mannered Hayes in order to subsidize the cost of their mortgage. Hayes, however, begins "renovating" his rented room late at night, haunting the couple's daily existence. Ultimately, they discover that Hayes is a yuppie con artist who has begun invading unsuspecting landlords' homes since his trust fund dried up.

In *Bad Influence,* Alex (Rob Lowe) similarly represents overworked yuppie Michael's (James Spader) repressed id, upsetting Michael's carefully learned sense of deference by goading him into asserting himself in situations where he normally wouldn't do so. Michael finally shoots Alex, who falls off a pier and disappears into the dark depths from which he emerged.[32] In Alfred Hitchcock's *Strangers on a Train* (1951), a similar plot unfolds when a tennis star (Farley Granger) meets a spoiled, mentally unstable young man from a wealthy background (Robert Walker) on a train ride. Walker buttonholes Granger, a tennis star anxious to rid himself of a clinging wife, and initiates a plan involving an exchange of murders between them. Walker murders Granger's wife, then threatens to incriminate the star if he doesn't follow through by murdering Walker's father. The murderous Walker is finally apprehended and killed by police, while Granger is free again.

SETTING: THE SUBURBAN HOME, HIGH SCHOOL, AND WORKPLACE

Yuppie movies are often set in the suburban home, high school, or workplace, evoking a class-specific set of associations about the nature of community in a world of great post–World War II geographic mobility. The suburb has symbolized the achievement of a common goal by like-minded people since its advent in the 1950s. This trait of like-mindedness springs from a shared professional middle-class success ethic that stresses group conformity to a particular lifestyle and form of behavior and individual matriculation of a system of meritocracy.

The Alger parody, the corporate-suburban narrative, the yuppies-with-children story, and yuppie horror construct the suburban home, high school, and workplace as both sites of middle-class ideological reproduction and sanctuaries from a success philosophy which stresses conformity at the expense of individualism. The yuppie movie characterizes the white-collar home and the workplace as sites in which this middle-class ideology is passed from one generation to the next. The young entrepreneur's assimilation of an Algeresque success philosophy in *Risky Business* parallels his restoration of his affluent parents' perfect Midwest suburban existence after its invasion by an avenging pimp.

A long tracking shot establishes in *Risky Business* a direct correlation between wealth and morality in the middle-class suburban family. Opening with Mr. Goodson (Nicholas Pryor) directly addressing the camera with a patronizing lecture to Joel about the rules of living under his roof, the scene ends with a track-in movement towards a crystal egg on top of the living room mantle. While the egg symbolizes the ideology of familial self-sufficiency and domestic harmony, it also implies that conspicuous consumption provides the basis for this solidarity. When Joel restores the egg to its rightful place, a crack in its otherwise flawless structure implies that the family is nonetheless still dysfunctional because of the parents' negligence and material superficiality.

Like *Risky Business, Ferris Bueller's Day Off* celebrates a high school senior's successful matriculation of the educational system through a work
ethic based on self-presentational style and appearances rather than hard
work or self-denial. In this way, school becomes a training ground for success in a corporate workplace where upward mobility is more often a
product of careful management of interpersonal relations than talent or
determination.

The corporate suburban movie often suggests that the predication of the
individual's upward mobility on his or her fulfillment of vague, impersonal workplace objectives denies the worker a sense of intrinsic satisfac-
tion. The suburb is often characterized as a symbolic place of respite from
the dehumanizing rhythms of this workplace bureaucracy. Denied a sense
of intrinsic fulfillment in work organized on the basis of vague impersonal
objectives, the suburbanite is encouraged by popular culture to seek satis-
faction in leisure culture and consumption.

Movies which characterize private bonds of family and emotional release as therapeutic compensation for the cold, impersonal corporate
world and the public school also proliferated alongside movies about how
to succeed in the technocratic workplace. *The Big Chill* takes place in a
sprawling southern mansion largely purchased with the small fortune
Harold has made merchandising the Running Dog line of sneakers. The
product's name is a coy Marxist reference to capitalism's dehumanization
of the individual. Ironically, the product itself springs from consumer culture's attempts to provide solutions for the very problems it creates in its
mechanization of daily life. Like the shoes which financed it, the country
estate is a metaphor for the recovery of individual identity through a consumptive version of the so-called strenuous life, an antidote to the inertia
engendered by working in a largely technocratic professional middle-
class order. Soothing pastel shades of mauve and beige form a backdrop
for the conversations that take place in the living room as the friends con-
template their collective past.

The Breakfast Club similarly suggests that the therapeutic culture of the
support group that revives the characters in *The Big Chill* is an antidote
for the dehumanizing environment of the public high school, in which
tracks of achievement follow corporate goals of efficiency and functional-
ity by funneling individuals into class-circumscribed job paths. A thirty-
something teacher who criticizes the working-class "loser" of the group
(Judd Nelson) as a useless delinquent amplifies the movie's suggestion
that school is a repressive authoritarian order that maintains the class
hierarchy by channeling working-class underachievers into minimum
wage, service industry labor. However, the young reprobate's integration into a group of peers from other class backgrounds simultaneously
suggests that the public school provides a sense of community which
counteracts the damage done at home by parents who have succumbed

to the workplace's dehumanizing influences. As do the premature pragmatist and yuppies-with-children cycles, the corporate-suburban cycle suggests that this sense of community is achieved through shared leisure-culture habits of musical taste and lifestyle. In *The Big Chill*, for example, college friends dance together in the kitchen to The Temptations' "Ain't Too Proud To Beg" as they prepare a sumptuous Saturday night dinner.

The yuppies-with-children cycle also characterizes the suburban home as a place of respite from the dehumanizing demands of the corporate workplace. J. C. Wyatt of *Baby Boom*, for example, achieves happiness by fleeing from a job in New York City to a country farm in Vermont, where she establishes a part-time business as a gourmet baby food entrepreneur. She is rewarded for choosing domesticity and childraising over a career in marketing, however, when a large company purchases her business for a huge sum and allows her to have it all.

If the self-employed yuppie mother working out of her country home represented a dream of having it all, the fear of losing it all was encoded into what Wood describes as the "terrible house" often found in the yuppie horror film.[33] Alongside the rise of a yuppie lifestyle of earned exclusivity was the popularization of the home office and the high-security suburban enclave whose incorporated status defined the ideal of community on the basis of demographic traits. The Bureau of Labor Statistics noted in 1985 that approximately 18 million Americans worked at home either full-time or as a supplement to their day jobs. By 1988, according to a survey conducted by New York's LINK Resources, the number of home workers had jumped to 25 million Americans.[34]

These developments represent the logical terminal point of a trend of so-called white flight from the cities to the suburbs, which began in the 1950s and had evolved by the 1980s into the phenomenon of incorporated suburbs with their own police departments, municipal services, and school systems. The yuppie horror film's terrible house serves as an embodiment of the monstrous fears of crime and financial insolvency beneath the placid surface of the suburban environment.[35] *The Money Pit* (1985), a remake of *Mr. Blandings Builds His Dream House* (1948), offers a comedic treatment of this theme on the basis of slapstick sight gags which arise when a yuppie couple discovers the hidden structural weaknesses in their fixer-upper dream home, releasing the tension within this nightmare through humor. The terrible house becomes a carnival funhouse of shaky staircases and faulty floors. Conversely, Michael arrives home in *Bad Influence* after confronting Alex about his con artistry only to find that the villain has stripped his overstuffed town home of its upscale furnishings and used it to murder a young woman, leaving the body in the bedroom in order to frame Michael.

CHARACTERIZATION: PARENTS AND CHILDREN

The yuppie movie's focus on the reproduction of the middle class necessarily explores the intergenerational aspects of this process. Dystopian tensions arise in both the workplace and the home in the premature pragmatist cycle between overdisciplinary, controlling fathers and self-indulgent, rebellious sons. While stern fathers embody an outmoded success philosophy of rising through hard work and frugality, their sons embody a Reagan-inspired philosophy of succeeding through careful manipulation of self-image and interpersonal relations with others.

The premature pragmatist cycle suggests that Oedipal rifts between fathers and sons arise in the home, the school, and the workplace on the basis of differing success philosophies. The condemnation of hard work as a means of upward mobility is explicit in *Ferris Bueller's Day Off*'s ridicule of Rooney, Ferris's high school principal. Tight lipped and humorless, Rooney personifies an outmoded and repressive system of authoritarian control. Juxtaposed with the stuffy principal is the skillfully manipulative Ferris, who matriculates the scholastic bureaucracy on the basis of his careful management of appearances and a breezy, blank superficiality.

Big contrasts Josh and a rival company vice-president (John Heard) on the basis of their differing approaches to market research. During a product development meeting, Josh's nemesis pitches a toy building that turns into a robot as his latest idea to a group of executives, backed by an impressive stack of research reports and diagrams that seemingly substantiate its marketplace potential. A boy stuck inside a man's body, Josh offers a devastating critique of the toy with a single offhanded question ("who wants to play with a building?") that juxtaposes work and play as competing strategies for reaching the top of the corporate hierarchy.

Invariably, the passage of authority from father to son parallels the restoration of a culture of meritocratic mobility in which material gain is an index of moral deservedness. Nonetheless, the predication of these sons' success on their careful management of self-image and interpersonal relations invests them with a certain blankness because their identities are thoroughly suffused with outer-directed consumption habits rather than inner-directed morality. In *Risky Business*, for example, Joel dons a pair of Wayfarer sunglasses after his father congratulates him on his admission to Princeton. As the camera moves in for a final closeup of Joel's expressionless face, the sunglasses deflect any deeper insight into the young man's identity. Viewers clearly identified with the image's mix of attitude and fashion as sales of Wayfarer shades skyrocketed in the months after *Risky Business*'s release.[36]

Tensions also arise in the corporate-suburban parable between workplace fathers who embody an ethos of self-denial and frugality and sons whose success depends on the rejection of such a philosophy for a fantasy of conspicuous consumption. In *The Secret of My Success* and *Mr. Mom*, for example, the aspiring male heroes succeed in the workplace by proposing expansions rather than cutbacks in production, echoing Reaganomics' contention that tax cuts would free capital for investment in new forms of production. Often, it is approving surrogate father figures who endorse such plans, suggesting a paternalistic, benign view of capitalism. In these ways, both narrative formulae suggest that corporate culture is actually a form of family, undercutting the tension between individualism and collectivism incumbent in white-collar culture's mobilization of individual will for impersonal collective goals.

Tensions between dystopia and utopia also arise in the yuppies-with-children cycle as fathers and mothers learn to conform to their proper roles as parents and couples. Mothers who go to work learn that they must choose between career and family, while fathers who adopt the role of caretaker must learn the responsibilities involved in raising kids. In *Parenthood*, an angry son protests his father's neglect of him by breaking into his dental office, taking a hammer, and smashing diplomas, dental molds, and a portrait of his dad with his new wife and son. As the boy scans the darkened office with a flashlight, the smashed objects serve as a quiet reminder of the father's narcissistic self-absorption and lack of concern for his first family. In *The Big Chill*, conversely, a track-in shot of Sarah Cooper's (Glenn Close) smiling face as she silently decides to allow her husband to father a child by her childless, thirty-something friend Meg (Mary Kay Place) idealizes her as a selfless maternal figure.

Parenthood also defines abortion as a threat to family solidarity. Gil and Karen Buckman (Mary Steenburgen) briefly consider aborting their fourth child after Gil quits his job. Within weeks, he returns to work, Karen bears a healthy baby girl, and three generations of the Buckman family squeeze in for a peek through the nursery window at their newest member in a tight shot that implies that the birth heals the rifts between them.

Evoking the Reagan administration's vilification of independent women as threats to the nuclear family's stability, yuppie movies vilify women who fail to conform to the roles of wife and mother as threats to the nuclear family. Appeals to such middle-class anxieties appear in horror and film noir–inspired sequences. In *Mr. Mom*, for example, a comedic film noir nightmare sequence arises in which Helen arrives home from work, finds Jack having an affair with a neighbor, and shoots him dead. *Fatal Attraction*, a film noir horror pastiche, characterizes its femme fatale, Alex Forrest (Glenn Close), as a Manhattan publishing company executive whose focus on career has provided her with an upscale lifestyle but no husband or child.

Popularized in part during the 1940s by a wartime backlash against women who worked outside the home, film noir roots the causes of domestic dysfunctionality in the threat posed by women who choose career over family. *Fatal Attraction* draws on this premise in demonizing Alex as a home wrecker who stalks the Gallagher family even though husband and father Dan (Michael Douglas) is responsible for initiating a weekend affair with her. As Alex's loneliness escalates into obsession, she becomes a monstrous embodiment of the threat to the family posed by women who fail to conform to the roles of wife and mother. Sitting alone in her stylish Manhattan apartment in a T-shirt that resembles a mental patient gown, she turns a table lamp on and off and listens to "Madame Butterfly," an opera about a suicidal lover, as light and darkness intermittently flash across her haunted face.

Other yuppie horror films characterize the villain as a monstrous embodiment of familial dysfunctionalities. In *Something Wild* (1986), for example, ex-convict Ray Sinclair (Ray Liotta) becomes the unrestrained embodiment of yuppie family man Charlie's (Jeff Daniels) longing for freedom from his responsibilities as breadwinner, husband, and father. Mixing *Bringing Up Baby* (1938) style comedy with film noir treachery and violence, Ray kidnaps his ex-wife Lulu (Melanie Griffith) and her new lover Charlie after the recently formed couple have bonded over a weekend of stealing liquor and having bondage sex. Lulu and Charlie escape to the latter's vacation retreat, only to find Ray suddenly bursting in through a patio plate-glass window. In a final scene, the two men struggle on the floor in a death embrace until Ray inadvertently lunges onto a knife held by Charlie. As in *Bad Influence*, Ray's death signals Charlie's banishment of his dangerous id.

Cape Fear (1991) similarly explores the dysfunctionalities beneath the well-adjusted exterior of a white, upper-middle-class suburban family. Among the family's dysfunctionalities are the husband lawyer's (Nick Nolte) flirtations with adultery, his wife's (Jessica Lange) neuroses, and the daughter's (Juliet Lewis) nascent interest in casual sex. A client (Robert DeNiro) whom the former district attorney allowed to go to jail by suppressing evidence that might have vindicated him becomes a monstrous embodiment of the moral hypocrisies incumbent in the husband's transgression of middle-class morality.

ICONOGRAPHY: FINANCIAL AND PHYSICAL FITNESS

An emphasis on outward appearances, both human and material, pervades yuppie movies. The ability to stage the proper mode of self-presentation at the appropriate moment in the premature pragmatist cycle finds metaphorical representation in the mirrored outer surfaces of the office towers in which such characters work. The mirrored surface also becomes a symbol of the blankness beneath such characters' own quest for self-sufficiency, rooted as it is in nothing more than a desire to attain the iconographic symbols of competitive triumph rather than an actual quest for self-improvement.

Wall Street comments at length on the premature pragmatist's fetishization of wealth as a foundation of individual identity and a vehicle for shaping popular perceptions of success. The pricey art and high-rise condominium that serve as outward symbols of Bud's class identity are juxtaposed with inner-directed notions of self based on his relationship with his family and his responsibility as a citizen of a nation-state founded on principals of honesty and fairness. The family is invariably the vessel through which such values pass from one generation to the next.

Also inherent in the focus on external surfaces is the characterization of the body as an index of morality. For men, physical fitness becomes a means of recovering a sense of moral stability. In *The Big Chill*, Harold's passion for fitness serves as a foundation for his role as Christ-like capitalist and moral redeemer of his family of friends. Fitness became within the yuppie lifestyle a symbolic means of expiating oneself of the polluting effects of an indulgent lifestyle of conspicuous consumption associated with idle wealth and of reclaiming a sense of control over one's life in a work world in which stress became a byproduct of an overmechanized white-collar professional world.

For women, a healthy body became a natural extension of a success philosophy that equated fulfillment with childbearing, as feminists who decided not to have kids or neglected their maternal responsibilities were demonized as unstable, morally impure threats to the family. In this way, Hollywood's representations of class and fitness habits drew upon tropes of exclusivity and privatization in their reestablishment of symbolic boundaries between the morally fit middle class and the morally unfit idle elite and immoral poor below. As Sarah Harwood observes, illness was morally deviant during a decade in which health and fitness were associated with moral virtue.[37]

The characterization of the body in these ways reflects Reagan-era culture's mediation of themes of class identity. The Religious Right suggested that women's bodies were vessels of family values threatened by liberal New Class initiatives such as legal abortion and Planned Parenthood. Neoconservative free-market economists also claimed that men needed the responsibility of family to achieve their full earning potential, while women needed to be homemakers in order to ensure the inculcation of proper middle-class values in their children.

NOTES

1. Thomas Schatz, *Hollywood Genres: Formulas, Filmmaking, and the Studio System* (New York: Random House, 1981), 154.

2. Barbara Ehrenreich, *Fear of Falling: The Inner Life of the Middle Class* (New York: Pantheon, 1989), 70.

3. Peter Biskind and Barbara Ehrenreich, "Machismo and Hollywood's Working Class," *American Media and Mass Culture: Left Perspectives,* ed. Donald Lazere (Berkeley: University of California Press, 1987), 204.

4. Michael Ryan and Douglas Kellner, *Camera Politica: The Politics and Ideology of Contemporary Hollywood Film* (Bloomington: Indiana University Press, 1988), 171.

5. Robin Wood, *Hollywood from Vietnam to Reagan* (New York: Columbia University Press, 1986), 88.

6. Ehrenreich, *Fear of Falling,* 231.

7. John Cawelti, *Apostles of the Self-Made Man* (Chicago: University of Chicago Press, 1965), 66.

8. Justin Wyatt, *High Concept: Movies and Marketing in Hollywood* (Austin: University of Texas Press, 1994), 197.

9. Barry Keith Grant, "Rich and Strange: The Yuppie Horror Film," *Contemporary Hollywood Cinema,* ed. Steve Neale and Murray Smith (New York: Routledge, 1998), 281.

10. Ibid.

11. Ehrenreich, *Fear of Falling,* 236.

12. Elizabeth G. Traube, *Dreaming Identities: Class, Gender, and Generation in 1980s Hollywood Movies* (Boulder: Westview Press, 1992), 102.

13. Ehrenreich, *Fear of Falling,* 84.

14. Traube, *Dreaming Identities,* 94.

15. Wyatt, *High Concept,* 197.

16. Barbara Ehrenreich, *The Worst Years of Our Lives: Irreverent Notes from a Decade of Greed* (New York: HarperPerennial, 1991), 32.

17. Traube, *Dreaming Identities,* 94.

18. Ibid., 80.

19. Ibid., 112.

20. Ibid., 113.

21. Elizabeth Long, *The American Dream and the Popular Novel* (Boston: Routledge and Kegan Paul, 1985), 85.

22. Ibid., 89.

23. Ryan and Kellner, *Camera Politica,* 277.

24. Julie Richard, "Down and Out in Beverly Hills: 'A Different View of the Rich,'" *Box Office,* 12 February 1986, 12, quoted in R. Serge Denisoff and William D. Romanowski, *Risky Business: Rock in Film* (New Brunswick, N.J.: Transaction Publishers, 1991), 532.

25. Douglas Kellner, *Media Culture: Cultural Studies, Identity, and Politics Between the Modern and the Postmodern* (New York: Routledge, 1995), 129 .

26. Ibid.

27. Grant, "Rich and Strange," 286.

28. Traube, *Dreaming Identities,* 126.

29. Ibid., 130.

30. Ibid., 124.

31. Susan Faludi, *Backlash: The Undeclared War Against American Women* (New York: Crown Publishers, 1991), 116.

32. Grant, "Rich and Strange," 285.

33. Wood, *Hollywood from Vietnam to Reagan*, 90.

34. Laura Bergheim, "Pluggies," *Culture in an Age of Money: The Legacy of the 1980s in America* ed. Nicolaus Mills (Chicago: Elephant Paperbacks, 1990), 86.

35. Grant, "Rich and Strange," 282.

36. Dave Karger, "Undie Film Movement," *Entertainment Weekly*, 30 July 1999, 84.

37. Sarah Harwood, *Family Fictions: Representations of the Family in 1980s Hollywood Cinema* (New York: St. Martin's Press, 1997), 67.

Chapter 7

The Legacy of the Reagan Era

The multinational corporation's Hollywoodization of world cinema, its colonization of foreign economies, and its westernization of other cultures reflect a larger trend in industry toward reducing the globe to a huge system of capitalist production and consumption. A valid concern about Hollywood's treatment of changes in global economic and cultural relations arises from the filmed entertainment industry's penchant for reducing issues of economic mobility and disenfranchisement to entertaining terms.

These trends have intensified since Reagan's two terms in office as successive waves of company mergers and acquisitions have crested. Tino Balio writes that several factors promoted this trend, including economic growth in Western Europe, the Pacific Rim, and Latin America, the end of the Cold War, the commercialization of state broadcasting systems, and the development of new distribution technologies.[1] The FCC's suspension of the fin-syn rules in 1996 led to greater horizontal concentration within the media industry. The centralization of financial resources created by multiple waves of mergers enabled conglomerates such as News Corporation and Disney to avail themselves of new opportunities abroad in formerly Communist countries and industrializing nations. The companies seized these opportunities by using a strong base of domestic operations to expand abroad. Their strategy focused on expanding horizontally to tap emerging markets worldwide, expanding vertically to form alliances with independent production companies to enlarge their rosters, and partnering with foreign investors to secure new sources of financing.[2]

These companies pursued horizontal expansion on the basis of their construction of overseas multiplexes, their purchase of recently privatized communications networks, and their use of satellite communication to supply programming for these distribution infrastructures. These deals demonstrate how an international capitalist class's expanding software and hardware alliances are eclipsing nation-state relations as an influence on economic and cultural relations. When the European Union decided not to remove trade barriers and tariffs on movies and television programs in 1992, for example, Time Warner, Turner, Disney, Viacom, and NBC responded by forming partnerships with European television producers, broadcast stations, cable and satellite networks, and telecommunications services. Rather than continuing to view European markets as programming outlets, Time Warner invested in satellite broadcasting in Scandinavia, FM radio in England, and pay-TV in Germany and Hungary.[3] Ownership in these media promises to provide the communications giant with substantial influence over these countries' media cultures.

The proliferation of home video in Western Europe also promoted Hollywood's horizontal expansion abroad. VCR sales in Western Europe soared from 500,000 in 1978 to 40 million, or nearly one-third of all households, in 1988. By 1990, the major Hollywood studios dominated video sales in Western Europe, which had reached nearly $4.5 billion. What fueled video sales in Europe and the United States were hits. While international theatrical rentals abroad achieved parity with domestic receipts at home in 1990, the overseas market surpassed the domestic market in film rentals in 1994.[4]

The Reagan administration played a pivotal role in setting the stage for Hollywood's overseas expansion through its aggressive redirection of federal spending into defense programs. Expenditure on defense skyrocketed 160 percent over the administration's tenure, ending the Cold War in 1989 by propelling the Soviet Union into economic chaos and, ultimately, disintegration. While Reagan claimed credit for the Soviet Union's downfall, internal dissension within Communism's member nations was also responsible for the breakup of the USSR.[5]

The expansion of a worldwide market for Hollywood movies resulted in the further proliferation of Reagan era–inspired stories about the Protestant success ethic and the redemption of race, gender, and class relations over the 1990s. Sequels based on some of the most popular franchises of the Reagan era continued to dominate the box-office totals in the wake of the president's retirement from office. In 1989, for example, *Variety*'s annual list of box-office champs included *Indiana Jones and the Temple of Doom* (#2; $179 million), *Lethal Weapon 2* (#3; $147 million), *Back to the Future, Part II* (#6; $118 million), and *The Karate Kid III* (#29; $39 million). The overwhelming commercial success of Time Warner's *Batman* (1989; $251 million) in the wake of the giant conglomerate's formation also revealed the ongoing viability of the Reagan era's blockbuster filmmaking strategy.

Other films typical of the Reagan era also dominated box-office rankings in subsequent years. They included *Back to the Future III* (1990; $87 million), *Die Hard 2* (1990; $117 million), *Three Men and a Little Lady* (1990; $71 million), *Home Alone* (1990; $285 million), *Look Who's Talking, Too* (1990; $47 million), *The Last Boy Scout* (1991; $59 million), *Home Alone 2* (1992; $173 million), *Lethal Weapon 3* (1992; $144 million), *Look Who's Talking Now* (1993; $10 million), *Beverly Hills Cop III* (1994; $42 million), *Die Hard with a Vengeance* (1995; $100 million), *Men in Black* (1997; $250 million), *Lethal Weapon 4* (1998; $130 million), and reissues of *Star Wars* (1997; $461 million), *The Empire Strikes Back* (1997; $290 million), and *Return of the Jedi* (1997; $309 million).

Hollywood's agenda of maximizing shareability between movies and television intensified its focus on casting television stars in A-list and blockbuster movies. Damon Wayans (*In Living Color*), Kirstie Alley (*Cheers*), Ted Danson (*Cheers*), Bruce Willis (*Moonlighting*), and Will Smith (*The Fresh Prince of Bel-Aire*) were among the most visible stars to make the transition from television to the movies on the basis of their presold popularity with TV audiences. The use of television as a springboard for popularizing black stars with crossover audiences also perpetuated Hollywood's practice of casting a narrow range of African Americans as minstrels and sidekicks whose loyalty to their white buddies assimilates them into a dominant white culture. Hollywood's design of movies for televisual shareability further compromised the breadth of the movies' representation of race, gender, and class mobility.

Reagan-era themes continued to dominate the movie landscape after the president's departure from office in 1989 because they appealed to a culture of economic and moral conservatism. A focus on Reagan-era success tropes proved effective in appealing to overseas audiences because of their incorporation of readily recognizable genres and themes drawn from Hollywood's formulaic history.

The themes of the Reagan presidency shaped subsequent presidential administrations. George Bush maintained the two-prong platform of strong national defense and neoconservative family values that Reagan had so effectively used to mobilize public support. Bush campaigned on the basis of his experience as vice-president, former head of the CIA, and former U.S. ambassador, while his vice-presidential running mate Dan Quayle defended the nuclear family and the need for a two-parent household. In the wake of the Soviet Union's demise, however, defense expenditure was eclipsed as a priority by concerns about balancing the looming national debt, stemming the flow of illegal drugs and immigrants into the U.S., and stabilizing the American economy in the face of mounting Japanese and European competition.

Inherent in these themes was a warning about the need to protect national borders from drug cartels, illegal aliens, and international terrorists that had replaced the Soviet Union as threats to American moral and economic stability. Cautionary tales about the threats to the American family posed by divorce, single-parent families, and two-income households with latchkey kids rivaled concerns about international threats to American well-being. Presidential candidate Ross Perot revealed his indebtedness to Reagan in 1992 when he focused on the necessity of further dismantling big government in order to balance the budget and played upon his status as a Washington outsider. After bursting into the national spotlight in 1979 when he funded a successful operation to rescue two of his employees from an Iranian prison, Perot dropped out of the 1992 presidential election only to reenlist and finish a strong third on the basis of strong public support.

Candidate Pat Buchanan similarly focused on the need to strengthen borders between the U.S. and other nations by warning of the drain on public programs posed by the influx of immigrants from Mexico and other Third World countries into the United States. These candidates' campaigns were also made possible by a growing resentment of government that stemmed from the public's perception of the U.S. government and corporations as legislative bedfellows.

Promoting himself as a Washington outsider from the populist South, Bill Clinton campaigned on a platform of purging government of corruption by embracing John F. Kennedy's ideals of public service and accountability to the people. However, the continued popularity of Reagan's agenda of downsizing government, balancing the budget (even as he dramatically increased it), cutting taxes, and deregulating industry forced the Clinton presidency to curtail its John F. Kennedy–inspired liberalism by scaling back its costly health care initiatives and further cutting taxes for the wealthy. In a 1996 cover story, the *New York Times Magazine* wrote that President Reagan had so successfully championed small government that President Clinton "must now pay it lip service" in order to avoid being associated with New Deal liberalism.[6]

Hollywood retained its focus on the Reagan-era theme of maintaining and protecting boundaries between races, genders, and classes while also shifting its definition of the forces that threaten interracial harmony, the nuclear family structure, and class mobility. While *Die Hard* defined the crusading white male vigilante as a protector of the nuclear family from foreign terrorists, Hollywood intensified its focus on family values as the 1990s unfolded, characterizing workaholic fathers, unwed mothers, domestic and international terrorists, and immigrants as the key threats to the family's safety, moral stability and economic self-sufficiency.

Hollywood's ongoing production of Reagan-era movies and their commercial popularity both in the United States and abroad suggest that the movie formulas that prevailed over the Reagan era have enduring appeal both as franchises for the major studios and as consumable cultural commodities for an expanding global audience. The trend also suggests that blockbusters made for a global audience will continue to reduce issues of race, class, and gender mobility to entertaining terms which condone capitalism's global colonization of domestic and foreign labor markets.

RACE

In the wake of the Soviet Union's demise, the biracial buddy movie's themes of interracial harmony, police camaraderie, and the formation of family continued to resonate with voters as the Bush administration identified South American drug cartels and Third World terrorist nations with access to nuclear weapons as ongoing threats to American political sovereignty, workplace safety, and familial security. Hollywood grafted these themes onto the biracial buddy genre because the form's focus on action-adventure spectacle, interracial bonding and violence, and paramilitary adventure proved tailor-made for them. The genre continued to be very popular over the 1990s and included *Die Hard 2, The Last Boy Scout, Lethal Weapon 3, Beverly Hills Cop III, Independence Day, Die Hard with a Vengeance, Men in Black,* and *Lethal Weapon 4.*

While Hollywood continued to construct male buddies as surrogate families, it balanced this subtext with a more overt emphasis on their formation or recovery of stable lives as family men through acts of redemptive violence. *Lethal Weapon 2,* for example, predicates Martin Riggs and Roger Murtaugh's overthrow of a South African drug cartel on their recovery of Murtaugh's kidnapped daughter from the crime syndicate. *The Last Boy Scout* combines *Lethal Weapon*'s formula of two mismatched black and white buddies with a virtual reprise of *Die Hard*'s characterization of Bruce Willis as an honest working-class cop who mends a failing relationship with his wife and family by defending them from conspiratorial political elites, white-collar businessmen, and street-level thugs. *The Last Boy Scout* capitalizes on the presold appeal of *In Living Color* television star Damon Wayans by casting the African-American comedian alongside Willis in a role in which, according to *Sight and Sound*, he "gracefully accepts his secondary Robin ranking."[7]

An ex-football player, banned from the league for gambling, whose wife was tragically run over by a pickup truck, Wayans is a recovering substance abuser who achieves redemption by helping Willis clean up his former team by ridding it of drugs and betting. In tracking down the killer of a stripper-girlfriend (Halle Berry) whom Wayans turned to in the wake of his wife's death, the pair discovers that the white corporate world of professional sports franchise ownership is rife with corruption. Berry was killed, it turns out, because she threatened to reveal that the team manager was forcing his players to use drugs so they could play well enough to beat the point spread and that the owner was bribing a U.S. senator in order to sway a vote on legalizing gambling.

As in *Die Hard,* Willis is held hostage by the criminals and escapes only through a black sidekick's able assistance. In the climactic finale, a shootout occurs in the Los Angeles Coliseum during a football game and foils the owner's plan of framing Willis for the assassination of the senator, who has turned uncooperative. Willis' success in saving the senator, whose immoral conduct had previously prompted Willis to resign his post as a Secret Service agent, parallels his redemption in the eyes of his family, with whom he reunites after turning the case over to the police.

Die Hard is thinly reprised in *Passenger 57* (1992), described by the *Village Voice* as a "*Die Hard* meets *Die Harder* proposition."[8] Wesley Snipes is cast as antiterrorist expert John Cutter. Shortly after being hired by Atlantic Airlines as head of security, Cutter happens to board the same flight as Charles Rane (Bruce Payne), an English terrorist highly reminiscent of the corrupt villain Hans in *Die Hard.* Rane, who is being transported to Los Angeles by the FBI (which is apparently unconcerned about passenger safety) in handcuffs, is accompanied by evil accomplices who have some-how boarded the plane disguised as airline employees and other ground crew personnel. Rane's accomplices lull the guards and hijack the plane. Cutter retreats with a stewardess into the plane's hold, where they release enough fuel to force the airplane to land at a small Louisiana airstrip.

Rane manages to escape by creating a diversion by releasing half of the hostages and is pursued by Cutter through a fairground. New threats to the hostages still aboard the plane emerge after an accomplice-at-large alerts his fellow thugs that the FBI has captured Rane, forcing the police to allow Rane to reboard the plane. Cutter, too, manages to reboard the plane by jumping from a car onto its landing gear as it takes off. Rane is killed after a struggle with Cutter when he falls through an open door. The plane returns to the airport and Cutter and the stewardess walk off to the fair to-gether.

Like Martin Riggs of *Lethal Weapon,* Cutter is recovering from his wife's untimely death and finds salvation in rescuing innocent people held hostage by international terrorists. Like Riggs and John McClane of *Die Hard,* the black Cutter is hampered in his heroic efforts by the political an-tics and stupidity of those who should be helping him (in this case, white, racist Louisiana lawmen). Alluding to the moviemakers' television back-grounds, the *Los Angeles Times* wrote that "'Passenger 57' plays like a cookie-cutter 'Movie of the Week' dead set against anything that so much as hints at originality!"[9]

A virtual rehash of *Lethal Weapon* and *Lethal Weapon 2, Lethal Weapon 3* is one running joke about Murtaugh's attempts to survive his last week on the job before retirement. Halting periodically to adjust a girdle, Mur-taugh helps Riggs chase down a former Los Angeles Police Department officer turned gunrunner responsible for plundering weapons from a po-lice evidence warehouse. While the dealer is a threat to the all-male police family's values of law and order, his introduction of a young friend of Murtaugh's son to drugs also constructs him as a menace to the black, middle-class nuclear family. Forced to shoot the boy after a gun battle erupts in the middle of a drug deal, Murtaugh (like Al Powell of *Die Hard*) must recover a fractured sense of masculinity in order to successfully help Riggs apprehend and eradicate the gunrunner.

While *Lethal Weapon 3* reprises *Die Hard*, *Beverly Hills Cop 3* reiterates Axel Foley's role as a Detroit cop who purges respectable society of international criminal conspirators who operate invisibly within it. Acting as a one-man police force, Foley ferrets out a counterfeiting ring whose leader doubles as the head of security at a Los Angeles theme park and uses its facilities as a base for its manufacturing operations. A virtual carbon copy of *Beverly Hills Cop* and *Beverly Hills Cop 2*, *Beverly Hills Cop 3* equates Foley's apprehension of the ring with the restoration of the park as a family-safe environment. "I wonder what time the park opens?" Foley queries a fellow officer in the final scene after vanquishing the leader in a lengthy gun battle that showcases the modern theme park as a virtual extension of the Hollywood blockbuster.

The Distinguished Gentleman (1992) draws heavily on *Trading Places* (1983) by casting Eddie Murphy as a black con man who redeems himself and the political system by purging Congress of corrupt white powerbrokers. Incumbent in the movie's inversion of *Mr. Smith Goes to Washington's* (1939) sunny story of a freshman senator who redeems Capitol Hill by overturning a corrupt order of political elites is a Reagan-inspired commentary on the necessity of downsizing big government. In *Smith*, a naive and idealistic small-town Boy Scout troop leader (Jimmy Stewart) is elected to succeed a U.S. senator who has died in office. Upon his arrival, his jaded secretary (Jean Arthur) tells him that the election was rigged by political bosses who expect him to mindlessly follow their bidding. During a twenty-three-hour filibuster, Smith succeeds in gaining passage of a law, which will provide the Boy Scouts with a camp in the freshman senator's home district. In the process, his unsinkable idealism also wins over his cynical assistant and they fall in love.

While *Smith* pays homage to the founding fathers' vision of a city on a hill, *The Distinguished Gentleman* plays on an early 1990s backlash against Congressional politics by implying that Murphy's racially stereotypical background as a phone sex con artist provides him with the perfect credentials for scamming his way onto a powerful committee. The movie simultaneously implies that the crooked politicians who facilitate his election to the Power and Industry Committee think that his skin color will allow him to be easily manipulated. "Consistently anti-incumbent, mocking Bush as well as the Congress, *The Distinguished Gentleman* has a backbeat of populist Perot-mania," the *Village Voice* observed.[10] While Murphy at first revels in the corruption that prompted him to run for office under the tutelage of Congressman Dick Dodge (Lane Smith), he experiences a change of heart upon falling in love with a congressman's niece and devotes his energies to reforming the system. Like that of *Beverly Hills Cop*, *The Distinguished Gentleman*'s loosely structured plotline is a pretext for allowing Murphy numerous opportunities to reprise his stand-up comedy routine of jokes and impersonations in a largely white cultural setting in which conspicuous wealth conceals pervasive corruption among the rich and powerful. While praising director Jonathan Lynn for investing the movie with "wit and edge," the *New York Times* simultaneously contended that its setting "reflects a mostly integrated world, much like the one that television sitcoms see all around them ... "[11]

The Distinguished Gentleman's heavy reliance on *Trading Places* was paralleled by *The Power of One*'s (1991) resituation of the *Rocky* story in 1940s South Africa. Directed by *Rocky*'s John Avildsen, *The Power of One* chronicles the attempts of a blond, blue-eyed boy named PK to fight racial injustice. Introduced as a small child, PK first encounters racism when he visits his German grandfather at a British prison where he has been incarcerated for the duration of WWII and witnesses the brutality inflicted on black prisoners. While visiting, PK is befriended by Geel Piet (Morgan Freeman), a black inmate described by the *New York Times* as having "a disconcertingly servile manner" because he calls the boy "Little Boss."[12] The movie's South African natives are similarly characterized as superstitious innocents after being led to believe by Piet that PK is a messiah who possesses magical powers.

Reprising *Rocky III*, *The Power of One* celebrates the interracial bonds that form between Piet and PK as the selfless black man teaches the boy to box and transforms him into a champion. PK's triumph over a vicious Nazi cements himself, his grandfather, Piet, and the pampered daughter of a rich landowner into a family that symbolizes the ideal of a colorblind, classless society. The plotline's reliance on hoary episodic television clichés was recognized by *Variety*'s observation that "'The Power of One' might have been better realized as a miniseries."[13]

The theme of black and white buddies teaming up to overthrow fascist threats to the ideal of racial colorblindness is also used in *Independence Day*, which casts music and television star Will Smith alongside a white costar (Jeff Goldblum) in a largely white cultural context. Smith plays brash young Top Gun recruit Steven Hiller, assigned by the military to destroy hostile aliens who have encircled the Earth and threatened to annihilate it. According to *Cineaste*, "the success of both character and actor serve as a living testament to the end of racism and the superfluity of Affirmative Action."[14] Together, Smith and Jewish computer genius David Levinson (Goldblum, reprising his role from *Jurassic Park*) defeat the alien armada by disarming the invaders' defense system with a computer virus.

Before they do, though, the aliens' terroristic threat to American values of racial colorblindness, familial stability, and economic autonomy is made manifest by their spectacular destruction of the White House and the Statue of Liberty as the weak-willed U.S. president (Bill Pullman) equivocates over how to handle the crisis. The potential cost of the president's indecision is made explicit by his daughter's hovering presence in the background. The First Lady is also constructed as a negligent mother who has compromised her parental responsibilities by being absent in California on a business trip when news of the alien attack reaches the White House.

The role of masculine vigilance in protecting U.S. borders from the threat posed by "illegal aliens" is conflated with the preservation of the American family. Before going off to war, Hiller weds a girlfriend who is also the mother of his child, giving his boy a father. Levinson is also defined as a dutiful son and husband who dotes over his ailing father and still wears his wedding band three years after a painful divorce, while a traumatized war veteran (Randy Quaid) redeems himself in the eyes of his children by sacrificing his life in order to thwart the alien menace. *The Village Voice* mused that "*Independence Day* is an unabashed booster of patriarchs, paterfamilias, and presidents."[15]

While the biracial buddy movie celebrated men as defenders of a private sphere of women and children, it also continued to uphold the restoration of boundaries between races and ethnicities. In *Men in Black*, a New York City policeman (Will Smith) joins a secret government agency, MIB, which monitors the whereabouts of interplanetary alien refugees seeking sanctuary in the United States. Like Eddie Murphy in *48 Hrs.*, *Trading Places*, and *Beverly Hills Cop*, the brash young Smith makes light of bureaucracy, laughing at the brainwashed marines who surround him at a recruitment session for saying they are there simply because MIB is "looking for the best of the best."

Smith nonetheless upholds the agency's commitment to patrolling U.S. borders that are threatened by corrupt interplanetary aliens. Inherent in this premise is a focus on the threat posed to national borders by hostile others who prove inassimilable into white, middle-class society. In this way, *Men in Black* reprises a principal theme of *Independence Day* through its characterization of the space aliens as illegal immigrants whose otherness is implied by the grotesque insect forms beneath the human forms they invade and inhabit.

GENDER

The Reagan-era theme of the need for responsible parenting in an age of two-income families was reiterated over the late 1980s and 1990s, albeit in a slightly altered form that implied that parental vigilance was more necessary than ever during a decade in which single-parent families had eclipsed the nuclear family as a demographic trend. The threat of nuclear family fragmentation became a focus of national debate in the early 1990s as divorce, test tube babies, single mothers, and negligent parents were targeted as imminent dangers to the middle class's ability to successfully reproduce a success ideology based on responsible parenting. Vice President Dan Quayle, for example, assailed television character Murphy Brown (Candice Bergen) for bearing a child out of wedlock and opting to raise it as a single parent.

Echoing *Raising Arizona* in a print ad that featured a baby in sunglasses imposed over block lettering, *Look Who's Talking* (1989) reshaped the comedy into a story about the need for single parents to find mates for the sake of their kids. In *Look Who's Talking*, thirty-five-ish accountant Mollie (Kirstie Alley) gives birth to a baby who was conceived during a one-night stand with Albert (George Segal), a client who is also the married father of two teenage daughters. The unwed mother's anger toward the man who fathered her baby but has yet to meet him spills out in blind rage as she tells the infant, "you have no idea how hard it is to love someone so much who looks like someone you hate." Mollie's resentment of Albert's childish outlook and workaholic self-absorption reaches a crescendo when she defiles his expensive new desk.

The young mother's rage is simultaneously channeled into an effort to find a suitable father for her baby. While she goes out on a series of uninspiring dates, a cab driver named James (John Travolta) who helped her to the hospital delivery room assumes baby-sitting duties. In turn, Mollie allows James to use her address in order to get his grandfather Vincent into a nursing home. Echoing the yuppies-with-children cycle's contention that childraising is a two-parent task, James readily immerses himself in the job and ultimately marries Mollie and fathers a second child with her. However, the working-class James's loyalty to his family is juxtaposed with the upper-middle-class Albert's devotion to his job, suggesting that the material affluence championed by the yuppies-with-children cycle is no guarantee of familial happiness.

Three Men and a Little Lady (1990), the sequel to *Three Men and a Baby*, similarly contends that the unwed parents of a five-year-old who have lived together since the child's birth owe it to her to marry and provide her with a proper home. After living platonically with the father of her baby (Tom Selleck) and his two bachelor pals Michael (Steve Guttenberg) and Jack (Ted Danson), English actress Sylvia Bennington relocates to England to marry a wealthy British theatrical director after distressing over the fact that her young daughter needs a more stable home because she is picking up adult words.

After a hollow attempt to recapture their carefree past with a party, the bachelor trio travels to England for Sylvia's wedding. The movie's adherence to screwball comedy formula becomes evident when Sylvia (coded as upper class on the basis of her British lineage) realizes during the ceremony that she is marrying the director because of his privileged background rather than her love for him. Described by the *New York Post* as a banal and predictable "She's Marrying the Wrong Man scenario," *Three Men and a Little Lady* builds to a climax when Jack, disguised as a vicar, performs the wedding with the hope it will not be binding. Peter arrives after the wedding, confesses his love for Sylvia, and ultimately marries her in a subsequent, legal ceremony.[16]

CLASS

Reagan-era Hollywood's focus on parental vigilance and yuppie angst also pervaded movies of the 1990s as forty-something white-collar professionals shifted their attention from the workplace to their families. In movies of the 1980s, the yuppie lifestyle of conspicuous consumption serves as a declaration of self-made class status that the young professional has earned through relentless devotion to a seventy-hour workweek. In movies of the 1990s, however, the yuppie philosophy of working relentlessly in order to afford an affluent lifestyle poses an eminent threat to the middle-class family's stability.

Drawing from the biracial buddy movie, yuppie angst movies of the 1990s frequently contextualize friendship in terms of the sentimental bonds that develop between men of different races when a black costar selflessly redeems the white lead's sense of moral obligation to others. The middle-class family's moral sanctity is juxtaposed with the immorality of jaded aristocrats and street criminals who value money over responsibility to others.

In *Grand Canyon* (1991), for example, a tow-truck driver named Simon (Danny Glover) rescues a white immigration lawyer (Kevin Kline) from a Los Angeles gang when the yuppie's BMW breaks down. Described by the *Village Voice* as a "dark-skinned angel," Glover's concern for his daughter at college and his single-parent sister and her children awakens Kline to the need to recover a sense of obligation to the less fortunate which he has lost sight of over the years in becoming wealthy from his law practice.[17] In a virtual reprise of his role as the Christ-like capitalist in *The Big Chill*, Kline achieves redemption from the tainting effects of wealth by adopting a homeless Hispanic baby his wife finds in a grove of trees while jogging, fixing Simon up with a single woman from his workplace (Alfre Woodard), and helping Simon's sister relocate herself and her son to a safer neighborhood. Incumbent in the film, however, is a redefinition of the community in racially diverse terms that critiques the class and race barriers erected by white flight and yuppie self-absorption.

Regarding Henry (1991) also draws on the biracial buddy movie in its celebration of lawyer Henry Turner's (Harrison Ford) achievement of a childlike sense of moral redemption through his friendship with a black physical therapist who nurses him back to health after a devastating brain injury. The story opens with Turner summing up a huge case that he will later win at the expense of an old man who has sued a hospital for malpractice. At home, he also yells at his daughter for spilling orange juice only to offer a cursory apology which evokes one of his summation speeches. One night he goes out for a pack of cigarettes and is shot in the head by a mugger.

The *Village Voice* wrote that Bradley (Bill Nunn), a huge, gentle physiotherapist rather than a doctor, plays a "male mammy (feeding, changing, etc.)," whose nurturing support helps Henry develop a rapport with a black butler, a Latin housekeeper and other people of color whom he had previously ignored both around his own house and at his colleagues' parties.[18] Bradley's role as a calming, wisdom-imparting mentor in Henry's life also draws heavily on the stereotype of black men as earthy and in touch with mystical spirituality.

Finally, Henry recovers a sense of family as he and his wife retrieve their daughter from an exclusive boarding home to which they had earlier sent her in order to concentrate on their own lives. Calling the story "a shallow soap opera," the *New York Times* observed that the movie "never abandons its narrow class assumptions" about the universal affordability of an expensive rehabilitation hospital or the ease with which an average family could negotiate the loss of its single breadwinner's income.[19]

Home Alone (1990) offers an extension of the yuppies-with-children cycle by playing upon the idea that parents too caught up in their own pursuit of material gratification can easily overlook their responsibilities to their kids. Rushing to whisk the family off to Paris for a lavish Christmas vacation, two suburban Chicago parents (John Heard and Catherine O'Hara) discover midway through their flight that they left behind their eight-year-old son Kevin (McCauley Culkin), the youngest of their large brood. While the father and the children remain in Paris, the mother frantically attempts to crisscross her way back to the home in order to ensure the child's safety. Beneath this comically inflected premise is a deep-seated anxiety about the safety of latchkey children left unattended by two working parents. Portraying family crisis professionals and the police as both inept and indifferent, the movie plays upon neoconservative assertions that bureaucracy is incapable of substituting for parental vigilance in the home. Parental negligence results in the boy's lapse into sloven laziness and bad eating habits as he gorges himself on pizza and allows the house to lapse into disrepair.

However, the movie also constructs the unattended child as a remarkably self-sufficient loner who ably protects the family home from bumbling criminals who repeatedly attempt to break into it on Christmas Eve. Slapstick comedy diffuses the potentially horrific implications of the situation as the boy arranges a series of booby-traps to foil the intruders. Portrayed as emotionally distant from a family that blames him for its squabbles and berates him for his perceived irresponsibility, the boy seeks solace in a Christmas Eve church service and befriends a surrogate grandfather figure who shares his sense of alienation from his immediate family. While the entire family is suddenly reunited in their home on Christmas morning, incumbent in this aspect of the story is an extension of the yuppie movie's contention that a consumer society's emphasis on lifestyle has compromised parents' focus on their children and their kids' ability to establish meaningful and lasting emotional bonds with others.

Home Alone 2 (1992) recycles this plotline as Kevin mistakenly boards a plane to New York City as his family boards another bound for Miami on their annual Christmas vacation. Entrusted with the vacation fund and his parents' credit card, Kevin checks into the Plaza Hotel while the rest of the family is forced to stay in a sleazy Miami motel. Amplifying the theme of Kevin's spiteful self-sufficiency in the absence of his family, the boy advances from conning his way past a grocery store clerk to booking himself a luxury hotel suite and a white stretch limousine. This idealization of America as a land of material ease and affluence is complemented by *Home Alone 2*'s incorporation of a product plug for the Plaza Hotel's 800 number for reservations and a walk-on appearance by Donald Trump. The *New York Times* also ran a photograph of McCauley Culkin somewhere in the newspaper and challenged readers to find it, fill in a coupon, and send it in for a chance to win a weekend for four at the Plaza Hotel or a gift certificate to Bloomingdale's department store. A staple of tabloid newspaper practices, the contest was a first for the prestigious publication.[20]

Noting that *Home Alone* producer John Hughes also guided the production of *Dutch* (1991), the *New York Post* observed "'Dutch' is like 'Home Alone' except without the earning potential."[21] Like *Home Alone*, *Dutch* explores how parental negligence threatens parents' ability to instill middle-class values of self-discipline and behavioral conformity in their children. It also mimics *Home Alone* in its characterization of acts of both child abuse and displaced aggression towards other adults as slapstick comedy rather than as disturbing instances of the familial dysfunctionality it criticizes.

Dutch (Ed O'Neill) is an unabashedly blue-collar man in love with the divorced mother (JoBeth Williams) of a spoiled thirteen-year-old boy named Doyle (Ethan Randall). The premise borrows heavily from the studio-era screwball comedy *It Happened One Night* (1934), in which a spoiled heiress and a working-class newspaper reporter discover a mutual respect for each other as they travel together cross-country. Initially divided by their gender and class differences, the pair is united into a couple by the time they arrive at their destination. *Dutch* similarly uses a journey from the boy's private boarding school to Chicago for Thanksgiving dinner as a motif for celebrating the shared decency beneath the superficial and fleeting class differences that initially divide the surrogate father and son pair. Ultimately, the boy's arrogance is revealed to be a cry for attention, created by an absent, workaholic father's devotion to his girlfriend and his job.

While *Dutch* draws heavily from *It Happened One Night*, *Doc Hollywood* (1991) is modeled on *Mr. Smith Goes to Washington*. In *Doc Hollywood*, Michael J. Fox plays a Washington, D.C. intern who crosses paths with a variety of Bible Belt eccentrics in Grange ("the squash capital of the South") while stranded and awaiting the repair of his car on a cross-country trip to a job interview in Beverly Hills. While small-town Southern culture is at first caricatured in *Doc Hollywood* as hopelessly stuck in a 1950s culture of innocence, Fox falls in love with a local girl and discovers that beneath their big-city versus small-town class tensions lies a shared respect for traditional ideals of community and individual integrity. Revealing the ongoing overlap between movies and television, *Doc Hollywood* was modeled on the hit television show *Northern Exposure.* In *Northern Exposure,* a recent medical school graduate relocates to a small town in Alaska after its citizens agree to pay off his school loans in exchange for his willingness to serve as the local doctor for a period of time.

Like *Doc Hollywood*, *Forrest Gump* (1994) romanticizes the Old South as a bastion of traditional values and a holdout against the cultural shockwaves caused by the civil rights movement, the Vietnam War, Watergate, and the AIDS crisis. Similar to *Regarding Henry*, *Forrest Gump* champions an adult with learning disabilities (Tom Hanks) as a Christ-like redeemer of family values who single-handedly raises his son in the wake of his sexually promiscuous mother's death from AIDS. Like *Doc Hollywood*, *Gump* suggests that simple faith in Reagan-era ideologies of moral conservatism and free-market individualism is the key to redeeming America from its countercultural past.

Gump's characterization of Tom Hanks as a redeemer of the American family was paralleled by *Jerry Maguire*'s (1996) celebration of Tom Cruise as the patriarchal savior of a single mother and her son. Like other movies of the 1990s, *Jerry Maguire* relies heavily on generic formula in its use of Billy Wilder's *The Apartment* (1960) as the basis for its plotline. A thoughtful rumination on the white-collar culture of the 1950s, *The Apartment* tells the story of a lonely, vulnerable insurance clerk (Jack Lemmon) who attempts to negotiate his way up the corporate ladder by lending his apartment to senior executives for extramarital affairs. Lemmon reconsiders the morality of his commitment to his job after watching his boss use his apartment to woo a shy young elevator operator (Shirley MacLaine) with whom the young clerk has fallen in love. Renouncing the rat race, Lemmon upbraids his boss for his infidelity, renounces his ambition, and pledges his love to the young woman.

Jerry Maguire exemplifies the yuppies-with-children cycle in its suggestion that devotion to white-collar corporate life compromises parents' responsibilities to their children. The movie adopts this motif by celebrating the title character's redemption of the greedy world of sports management after renouncing it for its exploitation of its clientele of professional athletes. Maguire is a blindly ambitious agent who one day circulates a mission statement arguing that the company should focus more attention on a fewer number of clients. A week later, he is fired. While Maguire pleads with his colleagues and clients to help him form a new company, only Arizona Cardinal Rod Tidwell (Cuba Gooding, Jr.) and Dorothy Boyd (Rene Zellwegger), a single mother in the accounts department, agree to follow him.

Jerry soon marries Dorothy, but they split up when the agent goes on the road to follow Rod through the football season. At a crucial game, broadcast on national TV, Rod makes the winning touchdown and survives a crippling tackle. An overnight sensation, he professes his indebtedness to Jerry and is re-signed to the Cardinals for $11.2 million. Realizing that money means nothing without Dorothy, Jerry bursts in on a divorce support group and reconciles with her.

The movie carefully avoids high-concept formula by acknowledging the paralyzing fear of failure beneath the shallow and brashly self-confident exteriors of previous Cruise characters like Joel Goodman of *Risky Business* and Maverick of *Top Gun*. Maguire's relationship with Tidwell also transcends the simple motif of black loyalty to a white friend by defining the football player as a keen judge of character who sticks by the agent because of his willingness to represent Tidwell fairly. Like other tales about yuppie angst, however, *Jerry Maguire* suggests that money is no substitute for the emotional bonds provided by a spouse and children.

CONCLUSION

The pervasiveness of Reagan-era themes in Hollywood movies over the 1990s suggests that the changes which took place in the filmed entertainment industry during the 1980s had an ongoing influence on the construction of success. The filmed entertainment industry's profitability continues to be buoyed by franchises such as the *Lethal Weapon* series and white male stars such as Mel Gibson.

The major studios' ongoing domination of the video industry provides an example of why Hollywood remains committed to a strategy of maximizing economies of scale by relying on blockbuster movies and saturation booking strategies. Blockbuster releases serve as tent-pole movies capable of generating the profits necessary to finance smaller in-house and pickup productions designed to appeal to niche audiences as well as broader crossover markets. For this reason, the trends in Hollywood production, distribution, and exhibition, which coalesced under the nurturing influence of the Reagan administration's philosophy of success, will continue to grow for the foreseeable future.

NOTES

1. Tino Balio, "'A Major Presence in All of the World's Important Markets': The Globalization of Hollywood in the 1990s," *Contemporary Hollywood Cinema*, ed. Steve Neale and Murray Smith (New York: Routledge, 1998), 69.

2. Ibid., 58.

3. Ibid., 64.

4. Ibid., 60.

5. Garry Wills, "It's His Party," *New York Times Magazine*, 11 August 1996, 33.

6. Ibid., 31–32.

7. Phillip Strick, "The Last Boy Scout," *Sight & Sound*, March 1992, 49.

8. Lisa Kennedy, "Passenger 57," *Village Voice*, 17 November 1992, 102.

9. Kenneth Turan, "Passenger 57," *Los Angeles Times*, 6 November 1992, Calendar section, p. 1.

10. J. Hoberman, "The Distinguished Gentleman," *Village Voice*, 15 December 1992, 65.

11. Vincent Canby, "The Distinguished Gentleman," *New York Times*, 4 December 1992, sec. C1.

12. Janet Maslin, "The Power of One," *New York Times*, 27 March 1992, sec. C20.

13. Amy Dawes, "The Power of One," *Variety*, 23 March 1992, 106.

14. Patt Dowell, "Independence Day," *Cineaste* 22, no. 3 (1996): 39.

15. Georgia Brown, "Independence Day," *Village Voice*, 9 July 1996, 41.

16. Jami Bernard, "Three Men and a Little Lady," *New York Post*, 21 November 1990, 71.

17. Georgia Brown, "Grand Canyon," *Village Voice*, 31 December 1991, 52.

18. ———. "Regarding Henry," *Village Voice*, 23 July 1991, 58.

19. Caryn James, "Class Not Dismissed: Screenplays with an Attitude," *New York Times*, 11 August 1991, sec. 2, p. 18.

20. Douglas Gomery, "Home Alone II," *Magill's Cinema Annual, 1993* (Englewood Cliffs, N.J.: Salem Press, 1993), 162.

21. ———. "Dutch," *Village Voice*, 23 July 1991, 58.

Appendix: Top 10 Movies of 1970–2002

1970

1. *Airport*
2. *Mash*
3. *Patton*
4. *Bob & Carol & Ted & Alice*
5. *Woodstock*
6. *Hello Dolly!*
7. *Cactus Flower*
8. *Catch-22*
9. *On Her Majesty's Secret Service*
10. *The Reivers*

Source: "Big Rental Films of 1970," *Variety,* 6 January 1971: 11.

1971

1. *Love Story*
2. *Little Big Man*
3. *Summer of '42*
4. *Ryan's Daughter*
5. *The Owl and the Pussycat*
6. *The Aristocats*
7. *Carnal Knowledge*
8. *Willard*

9. *The Andromeda Strain*
10. *Big Jake*

Source: "Big Rental Films of 1971," *Variety,* 5 January 1972: 9.

1972

1. *The Godfather*
2. *Fiddler on the Roof*
3. *Diamonds are Forever*
4. *What's Up Doc*
5. *Dirty Harry*
6. *Last Picture Show*
7. *Clockwork Orange*
8. *Cabaret*
9. *The Hospital*
10. *Everything You Always Wanted to Know About Sex*

Source: "Big Rental Films of 1972," *Variety,* 3 January 1973: 7.

1973

1. *The Poseidon Adventure*
2. *Deliverance*
3. *The Getaway*
4. *Live and Let Die*
5. *Paper Moon*
6. *Last Tango in Paris*
7. *Sound of Music*
8. *Jesus Christ Superstar*
9. *The World's Greatest Athlete*
10. *American Graffiti*

Source: "Big Rental Films of 1973," *Variety,* 9 January 1974: 19.

1974

1. *The Sting*
2. *The Exorcist*
3. *Papillon*
4. *Magnum Force*
5. *Herbie Rides Again*
6. *Blazing Saddles*
7. *Trial of Billy Jack*

8. *The Great Gatsby*
9. *Serpico*
10. *Butch Cassidy and the Sundance Kid*

Source: "Big Film Rentals of 1974," *Variety,* 8 January 1975: 34.

1975

1. *Jaws*
2. *Towering Inferno*
3. *Benji*
4. *Young Frankenstein*
5. *The Godfather II*
6. *Shampoo*
7. *Funny Lady*
8. *Murder on the Orient Express*
9. *Return of the Pink Panther*
10. *Tommy*

Source: "Big Rental Films of 1975," *Variety,* 7 January 1976: 18.

1976

1. *One Flew Over the Cuckoo's Nest*
2. *All the President's Men*
3. *The Omen*
4. *The Bad News Bears*
5. *Silent Movie*
6. *Midway*
7. *Dog Day Afternoon*
8. *Murder By Death*
9. *Jaws*
10. *Blazing Saddles*

Source: "Big Rental Films of 1976," *Variety,* 5 January 1977: 14.

1977

1. *Star Wars*
2. *Rocky*
3. *Smokey and the Bandit*
4. *A Star Is Born*
5. *King Kong*
6. *The Deep*

7. *Silver Streak*
8. *The Enforcer*
9. *Close Encounters of the Third Kind*
10. *In Search of Noah's Ark*

Source: "Big Rental Films of 1977," *Variety,* 4 January 1978: 21.

1978

1. *Grease*
2. *Close Encounters of the Third Kind*
3. *National Lampoon's Animal House*
4. *Jaws 2*
5. *Heaven Can Wait*
6. *The Goodbye Girl*
7. *Star Wars*
8. *Hooper*
9. *Foul Play*
10. *Revenge of the Pink Panther*

Source: "Big Rental Films of 1978," *Variety,* 3 January 1979: 17.

1979

1. *Superman*
2. *Every Which Way But Loose*
3. *Rocky II*
4. *Alien*
5. *The Amityville Horror*
6. *Star Trek*
7. *Moonraker*
8. *The Muppet Movie*
9. *California Suite*
10. *The Deer Hunter*

Source: "Big Rental Films of 1979," *Variety,* 9 January 1980: 21.

1980

1. *The Empire Strikes Back*
2. *Kramer vs. Kramer*
3. *The Jerk*
4. *Airplane*
5. *Smokey and the Bandit*

6. *Coal Miner's Daughter*
7. *Private Benjamin*
8. *Blues Brothers*
9. *The Electric Horseman*
10. *The Shining*

Source: "Big Rental Films of 1980," *Variety,* 14 January 1981: 29.

1981

1. *Raiders of the Lost Ark*
2. *Superman II*
3. *Stir Crazy*
4. *9 to 5*
5. *Stripes*
6. *Any Which Way You Can*
7. *Arthur*
8. *The Cannonball Run*
9. *Four Seasons*
10. *For Your Eyes Only*

Source: "Big Rental Films of 1981," *Variety,* 13 January 1982: 15.

1982

1. *E.T. The Extra-Terrestrial*
2. *Rocky III*
3. *On Golden Pond*
4. *Porky's*
5. *An Officer and a Gentleman*
6. *The Best Little Whorehouse in Texas*
7. *Star Trek II: The Wrath of Khan*
8. *Poltergeist*
9. *Annie*
10. *Chariots of Fire*

Source: "Big Rental Films of 1982," *Variety,* 12 January 1983: 13.

1983

1. *Return of the Jedi*
2. *Tootsie*
3. *Trading Places*
4. *WarGames*

  5. *Superman III*
  6. *Flashdance*
  7. *Staying Alive*
  8. *Octopussy*
  9. *Mr. Mom*
 10. *48 Hrs.*

Source: "Big Rental Films of 1983," *Variety,* 11 January 1984: 13.

1984

  1. *Ghostbusters*
  2. *Indiana Jones and the Temple of Doom*
  3. *Gremlins*
  4. *Beverly Hills Cop*
  5. *Terms of Endearment*
  6. *The Karate Kid*
  7. *Star Trek III: The Search for Spock*
  8. *Police Academy*
  9. *Romancing the Stone*
 10. *Sudden Impact*

Source: "Big Rental Films of 1984," *Variety,* 16 January 1985: 16.

1985

  1. *Back to the Future*
  2. *Rambo: First Blood Part II*
  3. *Beverly Hills Cop*
  4. *Cocoon*
  5. *The Goonies*
  6. *Witness*
  7. *Police Academy 2—Their First Assignment*
  8. *National Lampoon's European Vacation*
  9. *A View to a Kill*
 10. *Fletch*

Source: "Big Rental Films of 1985," *Variety,* 8 January 1986: 22.

1986

  1. *Top Gun*
  2. *The Karate Kid II*
  3. *Crocodile Dundee*

4. *Star Trek IV: The Voyage Home*
5. *Aliens*
6. *The Color Purple*
7. *Back To School*
8. *The Golden Child*
9. *Ruthless People*
10. *Out of Africa*

Source: "Big Rental Films of 1986," *Variety,* 14 January 1987: 25.

1987

1. *Beverly Hills Cop II*
2. *Platoon*
3. *Fatal Attraction*
4. *Three Men and A Baby*
5. *The Untouchables*
6. *The Witches of Eastwick*
7. *Predator*
8. *Dragnet*
9. *The Secret of My Success*
10. *Lethal Weapon*

Source: "Big Rental Films of 1987," *Variety,* 20 January 1988: 19.

1988

1. *Who Framed Roger Rabbit*
2. *Coming to America*
3. *Good Morning, Vietnam*
4. *Crocodile Dundee*
5. *Big*
6. *Three Men and a Baby*
7. *Die Hard*
8. *Cocktail*
9. *Moonstruck*
10. *Beetlejuice*

Source: "Big Rental Films of 1988," *Variety,* 11–17 January 1989: 16.

1989

1. *Batman*
2. *Indiana Jones and the Last Crusade*

3. *Lethal Weapon 2*
4. *Honey, I Shrunk the Kids*
5. *Rain Man*
6. *Back to the Future, Part II*
7. *Ghostbusters II*
8. *Look Who's Talking*
9. *Parenthood*
10. *Dead Poets Society*

Source: "Big Rental Films of 1989," *Variety*, 24 January 1990: 24.

1990

1. *Home Alone*
2. *Ghost*
3. *Dances with Wolves*
4. *Pretty Woman*
5. *Teenage Mutant Ninja Turtles*
6. *Hunt for Red October*
7. *Total Recall*
8. *Die Hard 2*
9. *Dick Tracy*
10. *Kindergarden Cop*

Source: www.worldwideboxoffice.com

1991

1. *Terminator 2*
2. *Robin Hood: Prince of Thieves*
3. *City Slickers*
4. *Home Alone*
5. *The Silence of the Lambs*
6. *The Addams Family*
7. *Dances with Wolves*
8. *Sleeping With the Enemy*
9. *The Naked Gun 2 1/2*
10. *Teenage Mutant Ninja Turtles II*

Source: "Top Rental Films for 1991," *Variety*, 6 January 1992: 82.

1992

1. *Home Alone 2: Lost in New York*
2. *Batman Returns*

3. *Lethal Weapon 3*
4. *Sister Act*
5. *Aladdin*
6. *Wayne's World*
7. *A League of Their Own*
8. *Basic Instinct*
9. *The Bodyguard*
10. *A Few Good Men*

Source: "Top Rental Films for 1992," *Variety,* 11 January 1993: 22.

1993

1. *Jurassic Park*
2. *The Fugitive*
3. *The Firm*
4. *Sleepless in Seattle*
5. *Aladdin*
6. *Mrs. Doubtfire*
7. *Indecent Proposal*
8. *In the Line of Fire*
9. *Cliffhanger*
10. *A Few Good Men*

Source: "1993 Film Grosses," *Variety,* 24–30 January 1994: 14.

1994

1. *The Lion King*
2. *Forrest Gump*
3. *True Lies*
4. *The Santa Clause*
5. *The Flintstones*
6. *Clear and Present Danger*
7. *Speed*
8. *The Mask*
9. *Mrs. Doubtfire*
10. *Maverick*

Source: "The Lowdown on '94's Record Box Office Heights," *Variety,* 3 January-5 February 1995: 17.

1995

1. *Batman Forever*
2. *Apollo 13*

3. *Toy Story*
4. *Pocahontas*
5. *Ace Ventura: When Nature Calls*
6. *Casper*
7. *Die Hard with a Vengeance*
8. *Goldeneye*
9. *Crimson Tide*
10. *Waterworld*

Source: "B.O. Performance of Films in 1995," *Variety*, 8–14 January 1996: 38.

1996

1. *Independence Day*
2. *Twister*
3. *Mission: Impossible*
4. *The Rock*
5. *The Nutty Professor*
6. *Ransom*
7. *The Birdcage*
8. *101 Dalmations*
9. *A Time to Kill*
10. *Phenomenon*

Source: "Studios Cheer Boffo B.O. Year," *Variety*, 6–12 January 1997: 16.

1997

1. *Men in Black*
2. *The Lost World: Jurassic Park*
3. *Liar Liar*
4. *Air Force One*
5. *Star Wars*
6. *My Best Friend's Wedding*
7. *Titanic*
8. *Face/Off*
9. *Batman & Robin*
10. *George of the Jungle*

Source: "Top 250 of 1997," *Variety*, 26 January–1 February 1998: 17.

1998

1. *Titanic*
2. *Armageddon*
3. *Saving Private Ryan*

4. *There's Something about Mary*

5. *The Waterboy*

6. *Dr. Doolittle*

7. *Deep Impact*

8. *Godzilla*

9. *Rush Hour*

10. *Good Will Hunting*

Source: "The Top 250 of 1998," *Variety,* 11–17 January 1999: 33.

1999

1. *Star Wars: Episode I—The Phantom Menace*

2. *The Sixth Sense*

3. *Toy Story 2*

4. *Austin Powers: The Spy Who Shagged Me*

5. *The Matrix*

6. *Tarzan*

7. *Big Daddy*

8. *The Mummy*

9. *The Runaway Bride*

10. *Blair Witch Project*

Source: "The Top 250 of 1999," *Variety,* 10–16 January 2000: 20.

2000

1. *Dr. Seuss' How the Grinch Stole Christmas*

2. *Mission Impossible 2*

3. *Gladiator*

4. *The Perfect Storm*

5. *Meet the Parents*

6. *X-Men*

7. *Scary Movie*

8. *What Lies Beneath*

9. *Dinosaur*

10. *Erin Brockovich*

Source: "The Top 250 of 2000," *Variety,* 8–14 January 2001: 20.

2001

1. *Harry Potter and the Sorcerer's Stone*

2. *Shrek*

3. *Monsters, Inc.*

4. *Rush Hour 2*

5. *The Mummy Returns*

6. *Pearl Harbor*

7. *Jurassic Park III*

8. *Planet of the Apes*

9. *Lord of the Rings: The Fellowship of the Ring*

10. *Hannibal*

Source: "Top Grossing Pics of 2001," *Variety,* 7–13 January 2002: 38.

2002

1. *Spider Man*

2. *Harry Potter: The Chamber of Secrets*

3. *Star Wars: Episode II—Attack of the Clones*

4. *Lord of the Rings: The Fellowship of the Ring*

5. *Lord of the Rings: The Two Towers*

6. *Men in Black 2*

7. *Signs*

8. *Ice Age*

9. *Minority Report*

10. *Die Another Day*

Source: "Top 125 Worldwide," *Variety,* 13–19 January 2003: 32.

Bibliography

PRIMARY REFERENCES

"Big Rental Films of 1970." *Variety,* 6 January 1971, 11.
"Big Rental Films of 1971." *Variety,* 5 January 1972, 9.
"Big Rental Films of 1972." *Variety,* 3 January 1973, 7.
"Big Rental Films of 1973." *Variety,* 9 January 1974, 19
"Big Rental Films of 1974." *Variety,* 8 January 1975, 34.
"Big Rental Films of 1975." *Variety,* 7 January 1976, 18.
"Big Rental Films of 1977." *Variety,* 4 January 1978, 21.
"Big Rental Films of 1978." *Variety,* 3 January 1979, 17.
"Big Rental Films of 1979." *Variety,* 9 January 1980, 21.
"Big Rental Films of 1980." *Variety,* 14 January 1981, 29.
"Big Rental Films of 1981." *Variety,* 13 January 1982, 15.
"Big Rental Films of 1982." *Variety,* 12 January 1983, 13.
"Big Rental Films of 1983." *Variety,* 11 January 1984, 13.
"Big Rental Films of 1984." *Variety,* 11 January 1985, 13.
"Big Rental Films of 1985." *Variety,* 8 January 1986, 22.
"Big Rental Films of 1986." *Variety,* 14 January 1987, 25.
"Big Rental Films of 1987." *Variety,* 20 January 1988, 19.
"Big Rental Films of 1988." *Variety,* 11–17 January 1989, 16.
"Big Rental Films of 1989." *Variety,* 24 January 1990, 24.
"Top Rental Films for 1991." *Variety,* 6 January 1992, 82.
"Top Rental Films for 1992." *Variety,* 6 January 1993, 82.
"1993 Film Grosses." *Variety,* 24–30 January 1994, 14.
"The Lowdown on '94's Record Box Office Heights." *Variety,* 30 January–5 February 1995, 17.
"B.O. Performance of Films in 1995." *Variety,* 8–14 January 1996, 38.
"Studios Cheer Boffo B.O. Year." *Variety,* 6–12 January 1997, 16.
"Top 250 of 1997." *Variety,* 26 January–1 February 1998, 17.
"The Top 250 of 1998." *Variety,* 11–17 January 1999, 33.

"The Top 250 of 1999." *Variety*, 10–16 January 2000, 20.
"The Top 250 of 2000." *Variety*, 8–14 January 2001, 20.
"Top Grossing Pics of 2001." *Variety*, 7–13 January 2002, 38.
"Top 125 Worldwide." *Variety*, 13–19 January 2003, 32.
www.variety.com, 15 July 2002..
www.worldwideboxoffice.com, 15 July 2002.

SECONDARY REFERENCES

Allen, Jeanne Thomas. "The Decay of the Motion Picture Patents Company." In *The American Film Industry*, edited by Tino Balio, 119–134. Madison: University of Wisconsin Press, 1976.
Altman, Rick. *The American Film Musical.* Bloomington: Indiana University Press, 1989.
Ames, Christopher. "Restoring the Black Man's Lethal Weapon." *Journal of Popular Film and Television* 3, no. 20 (fall 1992): 52–60.
Ansen, David. "A Revival of Black Movies?" *Newsweek*, 7 January 1985, 50–51.
———. "An Officer and a Comedian." *Newsweek*, 3 December 1984, 81–82.
Attanasio, Paul. "Box Office Breakthroughs: Moving Beyond Race in American Film." *The Washington Post*, 31 March 1985, sec. G1.
Austin, Bruce A. "Home Video: The Second-Run 'Theater' of the 1990s." In *Hollywood in the Age of Television*, edited by Tino Balio, 319–350. Boston: Unwin Hyman, 1990.
Bagdikian, Ben. "The Lords of the Global Village." *The Nation*, 12 June 1989, 805–820.
Balio, Tino. "Introduction to Part I," *Hollywood in the Age of Television*, edited by Tino Balio, 3–40. Boston: Unwin Hyman, 1990.
———. "Introduction to Part II," *Hollywood in the Age of Television*, edited by Tino Balio, 259–296. Boston: Unwin Hyman, 1990.
———. "'A Major Presence in All of the World's Important Markets': The Globalization of Hollywood in the 1990s." In *Contemporary Hollywood Cinema*, edited by Steve Neale and Murray Smith, 58–73. New York: Routledge, 1998.
Banks, Jack. *Monopoly Television: MTV's Quest to Control the Music.* Boulder: Westview Press, 1996.
Barnouw, Erik. *Tube of Plenty: The Evolution of American Television.* 2nd ed. New York: Oxford University Press, 1990.
Bartlett, Donald L., and James B. Steele. *America: What Went Wrong?* Kansas City: Andrews and McMeel, 1992.
Belton, John. *American Cinema/American Culture.* New York: McGraw-Hill, 1994.
Bergheim, Laura. "Pluggies." In *Culture in an Age of Money: The Legacy of the 1980s in America*, edited by Nicholaus Mills, 83–94. Chicago: Elephant Paperbacks, 1990.
Bernard, Jami. "Three Men and a Little Lady." *New York Post*, 21 November 1990, 71.
Bettig, Ronald V. *Copyrighting Culture: The Political Economy of Intellectual Property.* Boulder: Westview Press, 1996.

————. "Who Owns Prime Time? Industrial and Institutional Conflict over Television Programming and Broadcast Rights." In *Framing Friction: Media and Social Conflict*, edited by Mary S. Mander, 125–160. Urbana: University of Illinois Press, 1999.

Bierbaum, Tom. "Year of Growth for Homevid: Eyed $10-Bil in Retail Biz." *Variety*, 11–17 January 1989, 89.

Biskind, Peter. "Blockbuster: The Last Crusade." In *Seeing Through Movies*, edited by Mark Crispin Miller, 112–149. New York: Pantheon, 1990.

————. *Easy Riders, Raging Bulls: How the Sex-Drugs-and-Rock 'n' Roll Generation Saved Hollywood*. New York: Simon & Schuster, 1998.

Biskind, Peter, and Barbara Ehrenreich. "Machismo and Hollywood's Working Class." In *American Media and Mass Culture: Left Perspectives*, edited by Donald Lazere, 201–215. Berkeley: University of California Press, 1987.

Bohlcke, Diane, and Sandra Harper. "The Interplay Between Media Rhetoric and Administration Rhetoric: An Examination of the Image of the American Criminal Justice System." In *Visions of Rhetoric: History, Theory and Criticism*, edited by Charles W. Kneupper, 248–260. Arlington, Tex.: Rhetoric Society of America, 1987.

Britton, Andrew. "Blissing Out: The Politics of Reaganite Cinema." *Movie* 31, no. 32 (winter 1986): 3–4.

Brown, Georgia. "Independence Day." *Village Voice*, 9 July 1996, 41.

————. "Grand Canyon." *Village Voice*, 31 December 1991, 52.

————. "Regarding Henry." *Village Voice*, 23 July 1991, 58.

Brown, Jeffrey A. "Bullets, Buddies, and Bad Guys: The 'Action Cop' Genre." *Journal of Popular Film and Television* 21, no. 2 (summer 1993): 79–87.

Burns, Rex. *Success in America: The Yeoman Dream and the Industrial Revolution*. Amherst: University of Massachusetts Press, 1976.

Business Wire, Inc. "Paramount Pictures Television Group Will Promote Pay-Per-View and Videocassette Sales Simultaneously." 24 February 1987.

Canby, Vincent. "The Distinguished Gentleman." *New York Times*, 4 December 1992, sec. C1.

Cannon, Lou. *President Reagan: The Role of a Lifetime*. New York: Touchstone, 1991.

Caputi, Jane, and Helene Vann, "Questions of Race and Place: Comparative Racism in *Imitation of Life* (1934) and *Places in the Heart* (1984)," *Cineaste* 15, no. 4 (1987): 19.

Cawelti, John G. *Apostles of the Self-Made Man*. Chicago: University of Chicago Press, 1965.

————. "*Chinatown* and Generic Transformation in Recent American Films." In *Film Genre Reader*, edited by Barry Keith Grant, 183–201. Austin: University of Texas Press, 1986.

Cohan, Steven. "'Feminizing' the Song-and-Dance Man: Fred Astaire and the Spectacle of Masculinity in the Hollywood Musical." In *Screening the Male: Exploring Masculinities in Hollywood Cinema*, edited by Steven Cohan and Ina Rae Hark, 46–69. New York: Routledge, 1993.

Dawes, Amy. "The Power of One." *Variety*, 23 March 1992, 106.

Denby, David. "Suffer Little Artists." *New York*, 19 May 1980, 64.

Denisoff, R. Serge, and William Romanowski. *Risky Business: Rock in Film*. New Brunswick, N.J.: Transaction Publishers, 1991.

Diawara, Manthia. "Black Spectatorship: Problems of Identification and Resistance." In *Black American Cinema*, edited by Manthia Diawara, 211–220. New York: Routledge, 1993.

Dowell, Pat. "Independence Day." *Cineaste* 22, no. 3 (1996): 39.

Edsall, Thomas Byrne. *The New Politics of Inequality*. New York: W.W. Norton, 1984.

Ehrenreich, Barbara. *Fear of Falling: The Inner Life of the Middle Class*. New York: Pantheon, 1989.

———. *The Worst Years of Our Lives: Irreverent Notes from a Decade of Greed*. New York: HarperPerennial, 1991.

Ewen, Stuart. *All-Consuming Images: The Politics of Style in Contemporary Culture*. New York: Basic Books, 1988.

Faludi, Susan. *Backlash: The Undeclared War Against American Women*. New York: Crown Publishers, 1991.

Fiske, John. *Television Culture*. New York: Routledge, 1987.

Gallagher, Mark. "I Married Rambo: Spectacle and Melodrama in the Hollywood Action Film." In *Mythologies of Violence in Postmodern Media*, edited by Christopher Sharrett, 199–226. Detroit: Wayne State University Press, 1999.

Garner, Jack. "The Screening Room." Gannett News Service, 10 May 1989.

Gelman, Eric et al. "The Video Revolution." *Newsweek*, 6 August 1984, 50.

Gilder, George. *Wealth and Poverty*. San Francisco: Institute for Contemporary Studies, 1993.

Goldin, Milton. "Ronald Reagan and the Commercialization of Giving." *Journal of American Culture* (fall 1990): 31–36.

Gomery, Douglas. "Vertical Integration, Horizontal Regulation: The Growth of Rupert Murdoch's US Media Empire." *Screen* 27, no. 3–4 (May–August 1986): 78–86.

———. "The Reagan Record." *Screen* (winter/spring 1989): 92–99.

———. "Home Alone II." *Magill's Cinema Annual, 1993*, 162. Englewood Cliffs, N.J.: Salem Press, 1993.

———. "Dutch." *Village Voice*, 23 July 1991, 58.

Grant, Barry Keith. "Rich and Strange: The Yuppie Horror Film." In *Contemporary Hollywood Cinema*, edited by Steve Neale and Murray Smith, 280–293. New York: Routledge, 1998.

Grover, Ronald. "Paramount's Hot Streak is Untouchable—For Now." *Business Week*, 14 September 1987, 153.

Guback, Thomas. "Hollywood's International Market." In *The American Film Industry*, edited by Tino Balio, 387–409. Madison: University of Wisconsin Press, 1976.

———. "Patterns of Ownership and Control in the Motion Picture Industry." *Journal of Film and Video* (winter 1986): 7–22.

———. "Government Financial Support to the Film Industry in the United States." In *Current Research in Film: Audiences, Economics, and Law*, Vol. 3, edited by Bruce A. Austin, 88–104. Norwood, N.J.: Ablex Publishing Corporation, 1987.

———. "The Evolution of the Motion Picture Theater Business in the 1980s." *Journal of Communication* 37, no. 2 (spring 1987): 60–77.

Guerrero, Ed. *Framing Blackness: The African American Image in Film*. Philadelphia: Temple University Press, 1993.

Guterson, David. "Enclosed. Encyclopedic. Endured." *Harper's*, August 1993, 49–56.

Hall, Stuart. "The Whites of Their Eyes: Racist Ideologies and the Media." In *Silver Linings*, edited by George Bridges and Rosalind Hunt, 28–52. London: Lawrence and Wishart, 1981.

Harmetz, Aljean. "Hollywood Battles Killer Budgets." *New York Times*, 31 May 1987, sec. 3, 1.

———. "Now Showing: Survival of the Fittest." *New York Times*, 22 October 1989, sec. H1.

———. "Figuring Out the Fates of 'Cop II' and 'Ishtar.'" *New York Times*, 4 June 1987, sec. C1.

Harvey, David. *The Condition of Postmodernity*. Cambridge: Basil Blackwell, 1989.

Harwood, Sarah. *Family Fictions: Representations of the Family in 1980s Hollywood Cinema*. New York: St. Martin's Press, 1997.

Hillier, Jim. *The New Hollywood*. New York: Continuum, 1994.

Hilmes, Michelle. "Pay Television: Breaking the Broadcast Bottleneck." In *Hollywood in the Age of Television*, edited by Tino Balio, 297–318. Boston: Unwin Hyman, 1990.

Hoberman, J. "Ten Years that Shook the World." *American Film*, June 1985, 384–59.

———. "The Distinguished Gentleman." *Village Voice*, 15 December 1992, 65.

Holden, Stephen. "Sweet Sweetback's World Revisited." *New York Times*, 2 July 1995, sec. H9.

Horwitz, Robert Britt. *The Irony of Regulatory Reform: The Deregulation of American Telecommunications*. New York: Oxford University Press, 1989.

Hunt, Dennis. "'Top Gun': Pepsi Ad Fires First Shot," *Los Angeles Times*, 23 January 1987, sec. 6, 1.

Insdorf, Annette. "Alan Parker: Finding 'Fame' on the Streets of New York." *New York Times*, 25 May 1980, sec. D15.

"Inside Movies: The Business of Show Business." *Esquire*, February 1984, 94.

Izod, John. *Hollywood and the Box Office, 1895–1986*. New York: Columbia University Press, 1988.

James, Caryn. "Class Not Dismissed: Screenplays with an Attitude." *New York Times*, 11 August 1991, sec. 2, 18.

Jefferson, Thomas. *The Portable Thomas Jefferson*. Edited by Merrill D. Peterson. New York: Penguin Books, 1975.

Jeffords, Susan. *Hardbodies: Hollywood Masculinity in the Reagan Era*. New Brunswick, N.J.: Rutgers University Press, 1994.

Jenkins, Henry. "Historical Poetics." In *Approaches to Popular Film*, edited by Joanne Hollows and Mark Jancovich, 99–122. New York: Manchester University Press, 1995.

Jhally, Sut. "The Political Economy of Culture." In *Cultural Politics in Contemporary America*, edited by Ian Angus and Sut Jhally, 65–81. New York: Routledge, 1989.

Karger, Dave. "Undie Film Movement." *Entertainment Weekly*, 30 July 1999, 84.

Kart, Larry. "Eddie Murphy: Comedy's Supernova Sends Humor into a Different Orbit." *Chicago Tribune*, 7 April 1985, sec. C8.

Kellner, Douglas. *Media Culture: Cultural Studies, Identity, and Politics Between the Modern and the Postmodern*. New York: Routledge, 1995.

Kennedy, Lisa. "Passenger 57." *Village Voice,* 17 November 1992, 102.

Kowinski, William Severini. "The Malling of the Movies." *American Film,* September 1983, 52–56.

Landro, Laura. "Sequels and Stars Help Top Movie Studios Avoid Major Risks." *Wall Street Journal,* 6 June 1989, sec. A1.

LeSueur, Stephen C., and Dean Rheberger. "*Rocky IV, Rambo II,* and the Place of the Individual in Modern American Society." *Journal of American Culture,* (summer 1988): 25–34.

Lewis, Jon. "Money Matters: Hollywood in the Corporate Era." In *The New American Cinema,* edited by Jon Lewis, 87–121. Durham: Duke University Press, 1998.

Lewis, Lisa A. *Gender Politics and MTV: Voicing the Difference.* Philadelphia: Temple University Press, 1990.

Lipsius, Frank, and Christopher Lorenz. "Small Unit Style for Making Big Films." *The Financial Times Limited,* 2 January 1985, 22.

Long, Elizabeth. *The American Dream and the Popular Novel.* Boston: Routledge and Kegan Paul, 1985.

Lubow, Arthur. "Blacks in Hollywood: Where Have They All Gone?" *People,* 17 May 1982, 30.

Luhr, William. "Mutilating Mel: Martyrdom and Masculinity in *Braveheart.*" In *Mythologies of Violence in Postmodern Media,* edited by Christopher Sharrett, 227–246. Detroit: Wayne State University Press, 1999.

Magnet, Myron. *The Dream and the Nightmare: The Sixties' Legacy to the Underclass.* New York: William Morrow and Company, 1993.

Mandese, Joe. "Hollywood's Top Gun." *Media & Marketing Decisions,* March 1988, 109.

Marchetti, Gina. "Action-Adventure as Ideology." In *Cultural Politics in Contemporary America,* edited by Ian Angus and Sut Jhally, 182–197. New York: Routledge, 1989.

Maslin, Janet. "Film: 'Fame' Opens Bubbling with Life." *The New York Times,* 16 May 1980, sec. C2.

———. "Film: 'Footloose,' Story of Dancing on the Farm." *New York Times,* 17 February 1984, sec. C12.

———. "The Power of One." *New York Times,* 27 March 1992, sec. C20.

Miller, James A. "From Sweetback to Celie: Blacks on Film into the 80s." In *The Year Left 2: Toward a Rainbow Socialism,* edited by Mike Davis et al., 139–159. London: Verso, 1987.

Miller, Mark Crispin. "Advertising: End of Story." In *Seeing Through Movies,* edited by Mark Crispin Miller, 186–246. New York: Pantheon, 1990.

———. "Prime Time: Deride and Conquer." In *Watching Television,* edited by Todd Gitlin, 183–228. New York: Pantheon, 1986.

Moldea, Dan E. *Dark Victory: Ronald Reagan, MCA, and the Mob.* New York: Viking Penguin, 1986.

Mulvey, Laura. "Visual Pleasure and Narrative Cinema." In *Film Theory and Criticism: Introductory Readings,* 5th ed., edited by Leo Braudy and Marshall Cohen, 833–844. New York: Oxford University Press, 1999.

Nadel, Alan. *Flatlining on the Field of Dreams: Cultural Narratives in the Films of President Reagan's America.* New Brunswick, N.J.: Rutgers University Press, 1997.

Nasar, Sylvia. "Fed Gives Evidence of 80s Gains by Richest." *New York Times*, 22 April 1992, sec. A1.

Nicholson, Tom, David T. Friendly, and Peter McAlevey. "Hollywood's Socko Summer." *Newsweek*, 28 June 1982, 63.

Palmer, William J. *The Films of the Eighties: A Social History.* Carbondale: Southern Illinois University Press, 1993.

"Paramount's Program for Success: Program for Many Media." *Broadcasting*, 16 January 1984, 90.

Pfeil, Fred. "From Pillar to Postmodern: Race, Class, and Gender in the Male Rampage Film." In *The New American Cinema*, edited by Jon Lewis, 146–186. Durham: Duke University Press, 1998.

Pond, Steve. "$100 Million Mania: 9 Films in 9 Figures." *Washington Post*, 4 January 1991, sec. D6.

Prindle, David F. *The Politics of Glamour: Ideology and Democracy in the Screen Actors Guild.* Madison: University of Wisconsin Press, 1988.

———. *Risky Business: The Political Economy of Hollywood.* Boulder: Westview Press, 1993.

PR Newswire Association. "Blockbuster Sequel 'Lethal Weapon 2' Crashes into Home Video Feb. 8 at $24.98 Suggested List Price." 13 November 1989.

Ray, Robert B. *A Certain Tendency of the Hollywood Cinema, 1930–1980.* Princeton, N.J.: Princeton University Press, 1985.

Reagan, Ronald. *An American Life.* New York: Simon & Schuster, 1990.

"Rebel With a Cause." *Broadcasting*, 19 May 1980, 35.

Ryan, Michael, and Douglas Kellner. *Camera Politica: The Politics and Ideology of Contemporary Hollywood Film.* Bloomington: Indiana University Press, 1988.

Schatz, Thomas. "The New Hollywood." In *Film Theory Goes to the Movies*, edited by Jim Collins, Hilary Radner, and Ava Preacher Collins, 8–36. New York: Routledge, 1993.

———. *Hollywood Genres: Formulas, Filmmaking and the Studio System.* New York: Random House, 1981.

Schickel, Richard. "Bone Crack." *Time*, 23 March 1987, 86.

"Sharp Contrasts with Carter's Economics." *Business Week*, 31 March 1980, 94.

Sharrett, Christopher. "Afterword: Sacrificial Violence and Postmodern Ideology." In *Mythologies Of Violence in Postmodern Media*, edited by Christopher Sharrett, 413–434. Detroit: Wayne State University Press, 1999.

Slotkin, Richard. *Regeneration through Violence.* Middletown, Conn.: Wesleyan University Press, 1973.

Smith, Henry Nash. *Virgin Land: The American West as Symbol and Myth.* Cambridge: Harvard University Press, 1950.

Southwestern Newswire, "Paramount Pictures' Motion Picture Division Sets New High for February Box Office Totals, Grosses $13 Million." 23 February 1984.

Stallone, Sylvester. *The Official Rocky Scrapbook.* New York: Grosset & Dunlap, 1977.

Stanfill, Francesca. "Living Well is Still the Best Revenge." *New York Times Magazine*, 21 December 1980, 20.

Stenger, Josh. "Consuming the Planet: Planet Hollywood, Stars, and the Global Consumer Culture." *The Velvet Light Trap* 40 (fall 1997): 42–55.

Straayer, Chris. "Redressing the 'Natural': The Temporary Transvestite Film." In *Film Genre Reader II*, edited by Barry Keith Grant, 402–427. Austin: University of Texas Press, 1995.

Strick, Phillip. "The Last Boy Scout." *Sight & Sound*, March 1992, 49.

Telotte, J.P. "All That Jazz: Expression on Its Own Terms." *Journal of Popular Film and Television* (fall 1993): 104–113.

Thompson, Kristin. *Exporting Entertainment*. London: British Film Institute, 1985.

Thomson, David. "Footloose and Fancy Free." *Cineaste*, May–June 1984, 49–55.

Traube, Elizabeth G. *Dreaming Identities: Class, Gender, and Generation in 1980s Hollywood Movies*. Boulder: Westview Press, 1992.

Turan, Kenneth. "Passenger 57." *Los Angeles Times*, 6 November 1992, Calendar section, 1.

Tusher, Will. "Nation's Screen Tally Reached a New High in '90." *Variety*, 28 January 1991, 3.

U.S. Congress, Congressional Budget Office. *Measuring the Distribution of Income Gains*, CBO Staff Memorandum. Washington, D.C.: Congressional Budget Office, March 1992, 3.

Vaughn, Steven. *Ronald Reagan in Hollywood: Movies and Politics*. New York: Cambridge University Press, 1994.

Von Damm, Helene. *Sincerely Ronald Reagan*. Ottawa, Illinois: Green Hill Publishers, 1976.

Wasko, Janet. *Hollywood in the Information Age*. Austin: University of Texas Press, 1994.

Weinraub, Bernard. "On the Set with Sylvester Stallone: All Right Already, No More Mr. Funny Guy." *New York Times*, 9 June 1993, sec. C1.

Wiese, Michael. *Film & Video Marketing*. Ann Arbor, Michigan: Braun-Brumfield, 1989.

Wilburn, Deborah A. *Eddie Murphy: Entertainer*. New York: Chelsea House Publishers, 1993.

Williams, Tony. "Woo's Most Dangerous Game: Hard Target and Neoconservative Violence." In *Mythologies of Violence in Postmodern Media*, edited by Christopher Sharrett, 397–412. Detroit: Wayne State University Press, 1999.

Wills, Garry. *Reagan's America: Innocents at Home*. Garden City, N.Y.: Doubleday, 1987.

———. "It's His Party." *New York Times Magazine*, 11 August 1996, 30.

Wilson, William Julius. *The Truly Disadvantaged: The Inner City, the Underclass, and Public Policy*. Chicago: University of Chicago Press, 1987.

Wood, Michael. *America in the Movies*. New York: Basic Books, 1975.

Wood, Robin. "Ideology, Genre, Auteur." In *Film Genre Reader*, edited by Barry Keith Grant, 59–73. Austin: University of Texas Press, 1986.

———. *Hollywood from Vietnam to Reagan*. New York: Columbia University Press, 1986.

Wyatt, Justin. "Marketing/Distribution Innovations." In *The New American Cinema*, edited by Jon Lewis, 64–86. Durham: Duke University Press, 1998.

———. *High Concept: Movies and Marketing in Hollywood*. Austin: University of Texas Press, 1995.

Yanc, Jeff. "'More Than a Woman': Music, Masculinity, and Male Spectacle in *Saturday Night Fever* and *Staying Alive*." *The Velvet Light Trap* 38 (fall 1996): 40–50.

Index

About the Author

CHRIS JORDAN is Assistant Professor of Communication at the Pennsylvania State University. He has published articles in journals including *The Journal of Popular Film and Television* and collections including *The St. James Encyclopedia of Popular Culture* and *The Encyclopedia of Documentary Film.*